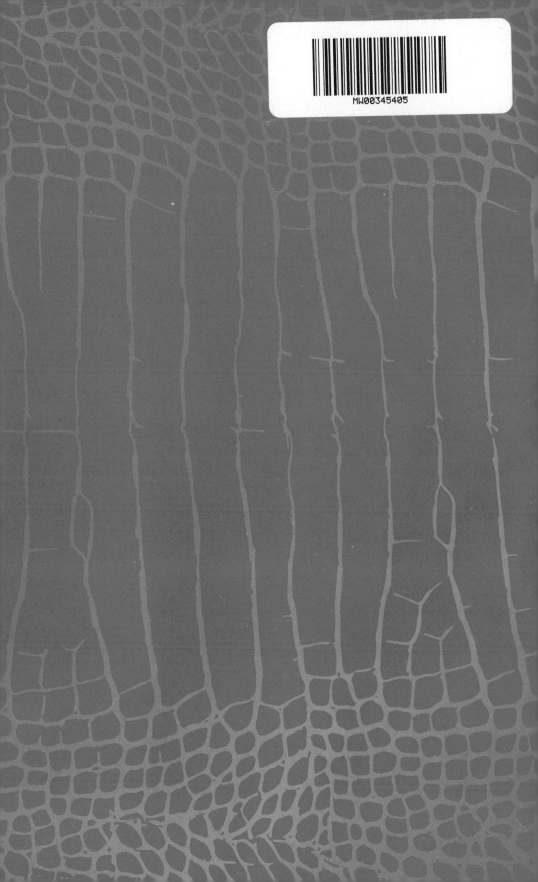

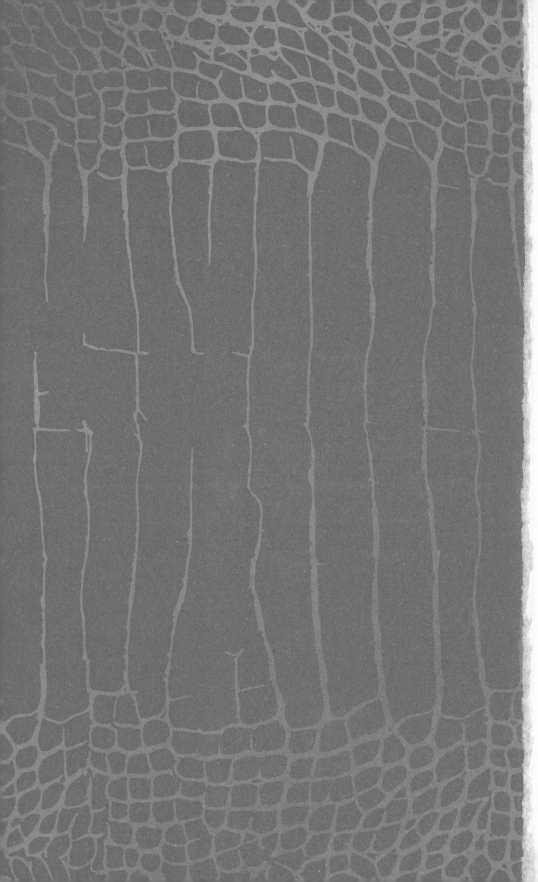

The Tap-Dancing Knife Thrower

The Tap-Dancing Knife Thrower

PAUL HOGAN

with Dean Murphy

HarperCollins*Publishers*

We gratefully acknowledge the permission granted by copyright holders to reproduce the copyright material in this book. All reasonable attempts have been made to contact the copyright holders; the publisher would be interested to hear from anyone not acknowledged here, or acknowledged incorrectly.

HarperCollins*Publishers*
Australia • Brazil • Canada • France • Germany • Holland • Hungary
India • Italy • Japan • Mexico • New Zealand • Poland • Spain • Sweden
Switzerland • United Kingdom • United States of America

First published in Australia in 2020
by HarperCollins*Publishers* Australia Pty Limited
Level 13, 201 Elizabeth Street, Sydney NSW 2000
ABN 36 009 913 517
harpercollins.com.au

Copyright © Paul Hogan and Signature Tom Pty Ltd 2020

The right of Paul Hogan and Dean Murphy to be identified as the authors of this work has been asserted by them in accordance with the *Copyright Amendment (Moral Rights) Act 2000*.

A catalogue record for this book is available from the National Library of Australia.

ISBN 978 1 4607 5929 5 (hardback)
ISBN 978 1 4607 1299 3 (ebook)
ISBN 978 1 4607 8724 3 (audiobook)

Cover and internal design by Lisa Reidy
Front cover image: Publicity still for *The Paul Hogan Show*, starring Paul Hogan and John Cornell
Back cover image by Everett Collection Inc/Alamy Stock Photo
Internal layout by Jude Rowe
All photos are from the collection of Paul Hogan unless otherwise noted
Photo on page vii: Paul Hogan having a drink in a pub in Paddington, Sydney, 1972,
by John Carnemolla/Corbis via Getty Images
Photo on page 369: Paul Hogan on the Sydney Harbour Bridge, c. 1974
Printed and bound in Australia by McPherson's Printing Group
The papers used by HarperCollins in the manufacture of this book are a natural, recyclable product made from wood grown in sustainable plantation forests. The fibre source and manufacturing processes meet recognised international environmental standards, and carry certification.

For providing my ancestors with free passage to Australia,
I dedicate this book to the wonderful judges
of the Old Bailey.

Contents

The Tap-Dancing Knife Thrower

The Wombat Wins

It all started in a little box at the top of the arch of the Sydney Harbour Bridge. The little box was known as a crane cabin, and that's where I'd sit on my break with my workmates, having our morning smoko.

It was 1971 and I'd been a rigger on the 'Coat Hanger' for a decade or so. I was thirty-one years old and had worked in dozens of jobs, but this was the one I'd stuck with. It was in the great outdoors, with one of the best views in the world, and with good blokes all around me.

This was a Monday. We were dragging on our cigarettes and talking about the weekend's television, though there wasn't much to choose from. There was *Skippy* and *The Mary Tyler Moore Show* and *I Love Lucy* repeats all in black and white, but the most popular show was Australia's own *New Faces*. It was the godfather of *Australia's Got Talent*, *Australian Idol*, *X Factor*, *Y Factor*, *The Voice*, *The Voice for Kids* and *The Voice for Old Age Pensioners*. It was the original. However, as nice an idea as it may have been, the trouble they had in 1971 was that Australia didn't have much talent.

Maybe for that reason, the show had rapidly deteriorated into a competition between celebrity judges. They'd have a panel of them, passing judgement on the amateurs. It was mostly a contest between them to see who could be the funniest or the snarkiest, or the most sarcastic. And that was supposed to be the entertainment.

I said to the blokes, 'I think that's too cruel. It's like watching the Christians being fed to the lions. Just once, it'd be nice if one of the Christians jumped up, you know, and bit the nuts off a lion.'

'You could do that, Hoges,' my mate Athol said. 'You're a sarcastic bastard.'

'Yeah, I'd like to do that,' I said. 'I'd like to go up there and, on behalf of the amateurs, give all the celebrities a bit of a serve.'

Another mate, Archie, wished me luck. 'You'd never get on the show. My niece has been accepted – she can sing a bit – but she won't be on until July of next year. It's like a two-year waiting list.'

Two years? I couldn't be bothered waiting that long. I'd lose interest. But then I thought, *They're not really looking for talent, they're looking for galahs who think they've got talent. You know, so they can tear them apart. I can do that.*

Now, to get on the show in those days, you sent in a letter. And for the young ones reading this, that's when you get a pen and a piece of paper … actually, your parents can tell you about it. So anyway, I wrote this letter, and I remember pretty clearly how it went.

Dear Sirs,

I am a former shearer from Lightning Ridge, and a former trapeze artist. I am currently working on the Sydney Harbour Bridge, but there's an extraordinary talent I wish to share with you and your viewers: I am Australia's leading tap-dancing knife thrower. Looking forward to your eager response and the opportunity to share my gift with all of Australia.

That'll get them, I thought. And you know about that waiting list of two years? Two weeks later a letter arrived. 'Congratulations Mr Hogan, you'll be appearing live next Sunday.'

It had worked! But, umm, now what?

Well, first off, I needed some knives. Big dangerous-looking knives. So I went to see my mate Ruffy, the boss carpenter, and got him to knock me up some big dummy knives. And by the way, in that lovely, subtle Australian way, we called him Ruffy because he had a rough head. There was another guy on the Bridge who used to wear a really bad toupee. So naturally we all called him Wiggy. He still thought we didn't know. On a really windy day, he'd put this elastic band over it and under his chin, and you'd see him walking up the arch, and it'd be folded back over on itself and at times floating an inch above his head. At night when he got changed, he'd go down to his locker where he kept his hat and he'd put his head in the locker and reappear with the hat on. And the toupee was ginger and his own hair was brown. Completely undetectable.

Anyway, once I had my knives, I was thinking, *Tap-dancing knife thrower. What does a tap-dancer wear? What sort of outfit?* Couldn't think, so I decided, *They're already guessing I'm a nut, they know I work on the Bridge, I'll go in my work clothes.* Well in those days, in the summer, the building worker's uniform was the same all over Australia: hobnail boots, footy socks, a pair of stubbies, which are now called hot pants I believe, and a shirt with the sleeves torn out.

So I fronted up to Channel 9 in Willoughby, just past the northern end of the Bridge, and they were keeping us contestants in a big holding room, behind the stage. There I was with my props, standing apart from the other contestants. Their choice, not mine. Suddenly I realised I was freaking them out with the knives. So I had a bit of a scout around, and I found a nice clean rubbish bin. Yeah, that'd do it. Now they wouldn't be scared. With the knives safely in there, I sort of looked like a professional entertainer. Or a lost garbo. With the first obstacle cleared, I was feeling pretty cocky. Then the stage manager came up. 'Mr Hogan,' he said, 'you're next. Time to rehearse.'

'What?'

'You've got to rehearse.'

I didn't even have an act. I was only going out there to get into those celebrities and tear them a new one, you know? But I didn't want to give that away. And I couldn't tap-dance or throw knives with any great accuracy.

'I can't rehearse,' I said.

'What do you mean you can't?'

'No, sir, it's too dangerous,' I said. 'You know, dancing and throwing knives at the same time. It could get really nasty, so it's probably better if I just do it once.'

The stage manager rolled his eyes and walked away. He came back two minutes later with Desmond Tester, the producer of

New Faces. Desmond was a real Pommy bloke. He'd been in show business his whole life, had seen everything. 'Mr Hogan,' he said, 'I believe you're having a problem with … well, I've been told you don't want to rehearse?'

'No, it's pretty dangerous stuff that I'm doing. I won't kill anybody, but I should only do it once.'

He nodded slowly. 'All right,' he said. 'I see on your application you're also a former shearer and a trapeze artist? Did you do both of those at the same time too?'

'Only once!' I said.

Desmond looked at me for about five seconds. 'Let him go on,' he said to the stage manager. 'I've got to see this.'

So I'd got away with it.

The show was now going live to air and I was standing in the wings waiting my turn. As one of the other acts finished I heard Terry Dear, the announcer, say: 'Ladies and gentlemen, stay tuned. After the commercial break we've got some really exciting acts, including a tap-dancing knife thrower. I'm really looking forward to seeing that one myself.'

With that, the harsh reality suddenly crashed in. The sensible part of my brain, the bit in the front, said, *What the hell are you doing? You're no entertainer. You can't go out there. You'll make a complete idiot of yourself. You'll embarrass your family, your friends and yourself. Nitwit. What are you thinking?*

The answer was, I wasn't thinking. Looking around, I noticed a door in the corner that led outside. And I thought, *Yeah, that's what I'll do. I'll just sort of gradually sidle my way towards the door and, when no one is looking, I'll get out and run away. It's the smart thing to do.* But then I heard from the back part of my brain, the part that comes out with all the dopey ideas you've ever had in your life, the part of the brain I call the Wombat. *Hang on a minute,* the Wombat said. *You told all your mates you were going to go and tear these judges a new one on behalf of the poor contestants. Now you're going to run off like a coward?*

I couldn't work out whether to listen to the voice of reason or the voice of the Wombat. But at that point fate intervened. I was working my way back towards the door and the act on before me was a young teenage girl, twelve or thirteen, who was an improvisational jazz dancer. And the poor kid wasn't very good at it. She wasn't the fittest dancer I'd ever seen either.

So of course these celebrity judges were merciless. You know, 'Who did the choreography? Nuns?' Ha, ha, ha. 'And when you're doing more dance lessons, and God knows you need them, it wouldn't hurt to also look at a diet.' That sort of thing.

I was almost at the door, about to bolt, when the poor kid came off the stage and ran right past me. Her little lip was trembling, and her eyes were welling up with tears. And then it hit me: *Why am I running away? This is exactly why I'm here. Idiot! I mean, when I come off the stage, someone might be crying. But it won't be me.*

Yes, it was time for the tap-dancing knife thrower from Lightning Ridge!

1

Not So Ridgy-Didge

Looking back, I now realise that the unusual path my life has taken is partly thanks to John Wayne. That's because when I was a little kid he and his seemingly countless movies were my inspiration: *Fort Apache, Rio Grande, Red River, The Sands of Iwo Jima*. Every boy wanted to be The Duke. He was tall, he was fearless and he was always the hero.

This complex first surfaced, as far as I can remember, when I was about ten. A friend of mine, Warren, came over to me in the school yard crying and bleeding at the mouth. 'What's the matter?' I said. 'What happened?'

'Big Tony thumped me.'

'Why?'

'I bumped into him and he punched me in the face.'

What would John Wayne do in a situation like this? I asked myself. There was only one answer.

'I'll handle this,' I said to Warren. And off I went to front Big Tony. In the best John Wayne fashion, I walked right up to him and stood there, legs apart, hands on hips, and snarled, 'Hey, Boofhead, you just thumped my friend.'

Big Tony laughed. 'Yeah, he was asking for it. What are you going to do about it?'

I looked straight into his big, goofy eyes. 'How'd you like to try that on someone your own size?'

Now, that was my first mistake. No, actually, my first mistake was standing there with my hands on my hips. The second mistake was saying, 'Try that on someone your own size,' because like a fox terrier taking on an Alsatian, I realised too late that I wasn't anywhere near his size and he was called Big Tony for a reason. I was more the bog-standard size of my friend Warren. Big Tony also did this calculation and immediately thumped me. Dropped me like a bag of shit.

I should have learnt the lesson. I wasn't John Wayne. I wasn't The Duke. I wasn't half his size. I was also a bit of a know-all and a troublemaker. A stirrer. I liked to get a reaction, which is another reason I'd later front up to Channel 9 as a tap-dancing knife thrower from Lightning Ridge. Simply to see what would happen.

As for that 'Lightning Ridge' bit, somewhere I still have a beautiful belt buckle made out of black and fire opal with a crocodile on it. It was sent to me by the mayor to thank me for putting their little outback town on the map. Years later some people in Lightning Ridge were still telling tourists,

'Oh yeah, he used to live here and, yep, that was his house over there.'

For that reason, I never went around telling people that I *didn't* actually come from Lightning Ridge. I couldn't shoot it down, I felt I owed them that. However, sometimes I'd say I was *conceived* in Lightning Ridge.

The truth's a bit less interesting. I was a dead-set Westie, as we call it, and proudly so. As in, I was born in Parramatta, in the heart of Sydney's Western Suburbs. I grew up next door in Granville and lived in the Blue Mountains, Chullora, Bankstown and Greenacre. If it was out west, at some point I lived there.

World War II had started just a month before I arrived in 1939. So, like everyone else, we had a bomb shelter in our tiny backyard. Well, when I say 'bomb shelter', it was more just a big hole in the ground with tin over the top of it. I'm not sure what happened when it rained … I vaguely remember our tiny weatherboard house, or bungalow, had black curtains over all the windows in case of air raids. Mum and Dad would sombrely sit around the radio trying to hear the scratchy news reports. Luckily, I was too little to fully understand what all this meant.

In 1942 Japan bombed Darwin then followed up by sending submarines into Sydney Harbour. There'd often be sirens going and I remember how we'd have to run and turn off all the lights and lower the black curtains. Mum would try to turn it into some kind of game. What I don't remember now though is whether this worked and was exciting or scary for a little kid.

As the full force of Japan's invasion fleet was thundering on its way from Japan to invade Australia, it just happened to run into the US Navy in the Coral Sea. Luckily for us, the Yanks

23 Victoria Street, Granville, one of my childhood homes.

didn't just blow them off course, they blew them out of the water. I think that was one of the first times Australia sat up and took notice of the United States because, as a former British Colony, we were so focused on the Mother Country and all that it represented. I was only five or six when the war ended, but I remember thinking those Yanks were all right. They stood up to the bullies.

• • •

My father, Jack, was in the army but didn't have to fight overseas during World War II. He mysteriously had a big toe on one foot missing, so he wasn't frontline material. He spent most of the war in Cowra, where the Japanese prisoners of war were kept.

Dad stayed with the army after the war, but was no longer in uniform as he had become the chief purchasing officer for army canteens. We saw a lot more of him then, but Dad and I never had a great, warm relationship. He certainly wasn't a bad guy, just typical of fathers of the time, particularly straight after the war. Many men then seemed to stand by the old adage 'Kids are to be seen but not heard.'

Still, he came from a large, entertaining brood. He had eight brothers and sisters, so the Hogan picnics were something of a big event. There were lots of people and games, and plenty of clowning about, and my father would sing. He fancied himself as a good singer. He wasn't. 'Ivory Tower' was his show-stopping number – 'Come down, come down from your ivory tower' – and he'd sing it very sincerely. People would certainly stop whatever they were doing to see who was making all the racket. It may have been terrible, but it was certainly memorable.

Jack and Flo Hogan (aka Mum and Dad) stepping out.

My mum, Florence, was old-fashioned, a very self-contained, steady woman. She had a lot of friends and never seemed to worry about anything. Looking at old photos of her, snapped when I was a kid, I'm struck by how glamorous and stylish she was. She was also unflappable and tough and, like all mums, expert at cutting you down to size. I remember one day I was strutting out of the house feeling a million bucks and Mum sang out, 'I hope you're wearing clean underpants. You might get run over by a truck.'

What sort of logic is that? If you get run over by a truck, your underpants are going to change colour anyway. And what did Mum think went on at the hospital? That a doctor would come along and say, 'Oh, this poor kid has a broken leg, I can fix that … Oh no, hold it, he's got dirty underpants on. Get him out of here, I'm not gonna touch him!'

Maybe she thought it was going to be in the paper: 'Kid Wearing Dirty Underpants Hit by Truck.'

I think this was pretty typical, as we were just a regular family for the area – but it was a different era. You left school at fourteen or fifteen and worked for a living. You never travelled anywhere unless there was a war on. Going on holidays meant visiting your cousins across town.

There were three of us Hogan kids: my older sister, Wendy, who was two years older than me, and, later, my younger brother, Pat, two years younger. Right through my childhood we lived in that tiny weatherboard bungalow in Granville. It was a short walk from my first school, St Oliver Plunkett Primary School.

We Hogan siblings liked each other, but we didn't really knock around together. We sort of did our own things. I think we all got that gene from my mother. We were very self-

My sister, Wendy, and me.
I'm the one on the right.

Hat. Warm jacket. No pants. Life as a kid.

sufficient and there was never a neediness. We obviously saw each other at home, but in those times home was just a place you went to sleep. By day we kids were always out and about.

• • •

According To Hoges ...

Gang Wars

I remember how important it was when I was about seven or eight to be a member of a gang. All the gangs in our neighbourhood were usually formed at school, so the names sort of reflected the schools we went to. There was the Burns Road Murderers, the Hackett Street Assassins, and our gang, which didn't seem to get much respect from the others, The Little Soldiers of St Oliver Plunkett.

Generally, the main rivalry between the gangs revolved around sport, primarily 'street cricket'. There were no parks where I lived, so fifteen feet of black tar was our SCG. This was fun, but we usually wound up with scores like 'Ronnie Smith out for thirty-seven runs, clean bowled by a Ford utility'. So we moved on to new games we made up. One of my favourites: stealing hubcaps. That was really exciting, especially in our street because cars didn't stop there.

Friday afternoon we'd have the gang wars. We were only little kids, seven or eight, so that usually meant we would go down to the storm water canal and we'd stand on one side and the other gang would stand on the other side and we'd shout insults across the divide. Really tough and cutting lines like:

'What are youse looking at?'

'Drop dead and rot.'

This used to go on for half an hour, and we usually won those gang wars because the toughest kid in our gang – well, actually, any gang – Janice Foster, she used to come out with some really brilliant sort of cutting lines that stopped them in their tracks. Things like, 'Back off, hairy legs.' And the most brilliant one she ever came out with, 'Sit on that, you dirty rat.' We'd never heard anything so funny.

We had all sorts of kids in our gang. One boy, I remember, Piggy Ghana, was so rich that he didn't even have to take his lunch wrap and paper bag home every day. I remember one really hot day he bought two bottles of lemonade. He drank one in front of us and the other one he slowly poured over his feet to cool them off. We killed him.

I was never the class clown, contrary to what you might imagine. My sense of humour didn't really come from my father, or my mother, and I didn't really share it with my brother or sister either for that matter. What fascinated me was other people. I found them endlessly entertaining. I was just amused by the world.

Brother Pat, sister Wendy and little eight-year-old me.

Not by school, though. I had no real interest in it. I had no ambition to speak of. This seemed to work fine when I first started at the Marist Brothers high school in Parramatta, but then my sister Wendy complicated things. She got something like the second highest marks in the state in the Intermediate Certificate, the one you took if you were still at school at fifteen. Suddenly, a lot more was expected of me too. And then, just when I convinced everyone that Wendy was the only clever one in the family, the worst thing happened: they brought in IQ tests.

Everyone had to do one and it turned out I was in the top three or four students in the whole school. I looked at the other two or three, who were boring gooses. *I don't wanna be with this lot*, I thought. I enjoyed playtime and sports, and not much else, and this revelation wasn't going to interrupt that. So when, a week later, they pulled a group of us out of class to do more IQ tests, I was like, *I'm not going to think about this, I'll just put down the first thing that comes into my head and get it over and done with.* But the first thing to come into my head was obviously, and unfortunately, the right thing. My stupid score went up! This made life terrible, because the teachers turned on me. 'Why aren't you top of the class in this? And why aren't you top in that?'

'Cos I don't like it,' I said. The only thing I liked was physics. Not history, maths or anything else. Just physics because, well, that's what the world's about, what we're all about. But now I was constantly under pressure to live up to something more. I wasn't really clever, though. All I was good at was doing bloody IQ tests!

• • •

According to Hoges ...

Saturday at the Pictures

One of the Great Australian Traditions when I was a kid was Saturday arvo at the pictures. It's died out a bit today and that's a great pity cos the pictures used to be the place where most kids had their first date. And for me it was very special because that was the place where I had my first fair-dinkum passionate kiss.

Dorothy was her name and she looked like a movie star – well, she looked like Popeye's girl, Olive Oyl. Anyway, the hard part always was getting your arm around the girl. It was very embarrassing for kids of that age. The most common technique and the one I used was the old yawn: you'd stretch out and do your best to then casually drape your arm over her shoulder.

Step Number 2 was to go for the kiss. The trick was to wait for something romantic to happen on the screen. Well, I was lucky. The picture Dorothy and I were at was called *Tarzan up the Amazon* or something like that. And Tarzan had been knocked unconscious and Cheetah was trying to bring him around by licking his face. And I thought, *Now that's romance, here we go.* I pouted me lips, shut my eyes tight and suddenly *whoomph*, she swooped on me.

Well, I suddenly understood why Popeye knocked around with Olive Oyl. Dorothy kissed with her mouth wide open. Hot and wet. It was like someone had stuck one of those bathroom plungers on my face. And being a young kid, on my first encounter, I freaked out! Thought all my birthdays had come at once. I thought, *I've got one of those nymphomaniacs on my hands here. I wonder if the police know about her.*

And, I can tell you, I didn't have to put my hand in my pocket to know my Violet Crumble bar had melted.

2

The Awkward Years

It was the 1950s, so I was one of the first 'teenagers'. Before
then, the expression was never heard. You were a boy, and
then you were an embarrassment because you were going
through puberty, and then you were a young man.

Elvis and rock 'n' roll came along and also a hot young
movie star called James Dean. Before Jimmy Dean, all the
movie stars were grown-ups: Cary Grant, Kirk Douglas, James
Stewart and that lot. So thanks to Elvis and James and also to
Marlon Brando in *The Wild One*, we became the first teenagers.

We were the pioneers. We wrote the book on how to
do it. We'd stand around looking troubled like Jimmy Dean
or rocking away with The King. But while we might have

Did I mention I was a bit of a poser? Left to right, 'Elvis', 'Lezza', 'Fats', Rani and me, aka 'Rocky', with our pride and joy, Lezza's car, circa 1956.

looked like we knew what we were doing, we didn't have a clue. One example: girls! Boy, were we so, so naïve about girls. After all, there wasn't any sex education at school. The nearest we fourteen-year-olds got to it was a hygiene lesson once a month from the local priest. He'd say, 'Keep your body clean. If you have impure thoughts, take a long, cold shower.' Well, that didn't work; I was the soggiest kid in high school.

This was the pre-permissive era, so it was before there were any pictures of topless girls in the newspapers. About the only place you could get a good look at a girl back then was in the New Guinea section of *National Geographic*. I spent so much time studying *National Geographic* Mum and Dad thought I wanted to be an archaeologist or anthropologist.

Due to this lack of information, at fifteen we were scared of girls, though we never let on. I remember cruising down the street in my mate Lezza's car, sticking my head out the window and saying very suavely to a girl, 'G'day, how about a bit?'

She looked me straight in the eye and said, 'A bit of what?'

I suddenly looked stupid and said, 'Umm, I don't know.' And I didn't. I was so embarrassed we just drove off.

A little later, when my mate Les had his licence (or perhaps just the keys to his dad's car), we were cruising along and saw a couple of older women. You know, eighteen-year-olds. We pulled up alongside them.

'G'day, you want to come for a ride?'

'Yeah,' they said, and hopped in the back. Les and I panicked and jumped straight out. We stood, frozen, staring at these two exotic women in the back of our car. We didn't know what to do.

• • •

I left the Marist Brothers high school in Parramatta the moment I turned fifteen because as everyone knows, when you're fifteen, there's nothing more they can teach you. I got a job straight away, as an apprentice moulder in an iron foundry.

You wouldn't see many fifteen-year-olds doing a job like that these days. They're too smart. Being a moulder was like working in hell. Not only was it HOT, it was filthy and dirty, and a bloody hard slog. Worse still, when you were the kid, the apprentice, like me, you did a lot of the hard yakka for the more senior men. You'd shovel black sand in the morning, then pour metal in the afternoon. At times you'd be standing in front of what was basically molten lava with a long steel rod, pushing the slag back in. All I got out of it was muscles and a face full of blackheads. But I was a sharp kid, and it only took me about two years to look around and go, 'Well, this sucks.' Then I left, vowing never to work indoors again.

The next job I had might have been the best job I ever had. I was a swimming pool attendant and lifeguard at Granville Olympic pool. Schools used to come down to the pool on their sports day, including my old school. Once, apparently, a teacher who'd taught me pointed me out to some of the kids. 'He was at our school,' the teacher said. 'Used to get 100 out of 100 in physics tests. Could have been a physicist or something. But instead of that, look at him now – nothing but a swimming pool attendant.'

Some of those kids told me years later that seeing me there was the first time they thought seriously about leaving school too. There I was, seventeen years old, sitting up on the springboard in my cossies, sunbaking, checking out the high-school girls and generally having a good life. I was being paid to do that, and only occasionally did I have to jump in the water and pull some kid out. And then, of course, everyone cheered and thought I was a hero.

Yeah, bugger physics, they were thinking. *That's the life I want! He's basically got his own private pool, flirts with girls, and gets an adult wage.*

There were only about three swimming pools in all of Sydney that had Olympic diving towers and Granville was one of them. And because I was a local I'd started diving there well before I worked there. I got pretty good at it too and started diving competitively. Made it to state level and became part of what was called the Australian Junior Diving Troupe.

However, there was another kid in the troupe named Mickey Baker. Mickey was my age and he was just a natural. When he entered the water it was like you'd dropped a nail in the pool. There was no splash. He was like the Chinese girls in the Olympics – they go into the water and there's nothing but a ripple. Mickey was so naturally graceful.

I can never be as good as him, I thought, so I stopped competitive diving. When you see someone else the same age who is so much better, it can turn you off. And it did.

Maybe the other thing about diving that turned me off is that you can't try harder. You just do your dive, whatever it happens to be, as best you can. And if someone else is better, they win. It's not like a race where you push harder to get past someone, or ignore the pain of hitting 'the wall' to beat them. You can't. In competition diving, you're just diving against yourself all the time, and I lost interest in that.

Diving was one passion. Motorbikes was another, thanks mainly to Marlon Brando. I was mad about them. I'd got my first one when I was sixteen and on learner plates. Of course, being sixteen I didn't want anyone to see the L plates, so I'd always accidentally-deliberately forget to put them on. The bike was a Triumph Tiger 100, with the 100 signalling it was good for 100 miles an hour. If I'd found a stretch of road long enough, I would have probably checked that out.

Then I moved onto a Thunderbird, the very machine that Marlon Brando had ridden in *The Wild One*. I hooned it up, of course – that was compulsory – to make it more like the one in the film. Cropped the mufflers to make them sound better, lowered everything that was lowerable, stuff like that. Everyone wanted to be Marlon Brando in the 1950s and I was no different. I even had a leather jacket that had a big phoenix on the back. It was the coolest thing I'd ever seen, but it might as well have been a bloody big target for the police to aim at.

Sadly, I had to get rid of my bike. It was the police's idea, really. They suggested I didn't ride it. Ever again. They first made this observation when they spotted me trying to do a handstand on the handlebars while tearing down the middle of the road. They were right behind me, which I obviously didn't know. Otherwise I'd have at least stopped and put my L plates on. They made me wheel the bike home and tell my parents. It was only a couple of miles, but humiliating. Yeah, I was a galah.

There were other transgressions, then a long period without any motorised transport. I ended up getting a car years later, in my twenties. But after having two-wheelers I found them so boring. Yet I never went back to bikes, sadly. To ride a motorbike you have to be young and invulnerable. It also helps if you're immortal.

• • •

According To Hoges ...

The Bullworker

When I was a kid, I was a sucker for magazine ads for mail-order goods like X-Ray Specs and Whoopee Cushions, as well as all the so-called self-improvement courses. Ads like 'Know the Secret Kill Techniques of a Tibetan Monk'. It didn't matter what it was, I sent off for it all, but my absolute favourite was an ad featuring a ninety-pound weakling who goes to the beach and a big bully kicks sand in his face and takes his girlfriend. As a teenager that happened to me so many times that if I saw someone bigger than me on the beach I'd grab a handful of sand, throw it in my own face and hand over my girlfriend.

It was embarrassing and I got so sick of it that I sent away for a thing called a Bullworker. I exercised with it every single day and, look, I don't usually give free plugs, but they are terrific! The very next time I went to the beach, right on cue, this bully came along and kicked sand straight in my face. I jumped up and flattened him. Knocked him out cold. Yep, you hit someone with a Bull-worker, I'm telling you, and they don't get up in a hurry.

I also had a real teenage problem with pimples. It got so bad that I was going around for a long time with a bent neck, because when I went to bed at night I had so many creams and lotions on my face my head kept slipping off the pillow. I walked around the streets all bent over. Drunks used to pat me on the head and give me a couple of bob.

Then I saw an ad that said, 'End the misery of haemorrhoids – with Malloy's Suppositories'. It had piles, as in P-I-L-E-S, in brackets under the word 'haemorrhoids', and through desperation or stupidity I thought that was an abbreviation for pimples. Away my order went. A week later they sent me these dirty big capsules. I choked the bloody things down three times a day for weeks but to no effect on my pimples at all.

The pills were pretty expensive, so I sent them back with a little note telling the company where they could stick them. They then sent me a letter that explained that was exactly where I should have stuck them. I replied, 'But that ain't where I got the pimples.' Didn't even get my money back.

My sister, Wendy, also left school early, even though she was so gifted academically. She went on to become a pathology technician and did outstanding research work. Smart cookie. Not only that, Wendy married Johnny Devitt! Who is that? Johnny Devitt, my brother-in-law, was the fastest swimmer in the world! Johnny trained at the Granville pool and he went on to win gold at the 1956 Olympics in Melbourne and again in 1960 in Rome.

All in white and emblazoned with wings, we were the Parramatta Swimming Club. I'm third from left in the second back row. My future brother-in-law and Olympic gold medalist Johnny Devitt sits in the centre, second row from the front.

Johnny held the world record for the 100 metres and the 50 metres, and the 100 yards and the 55 yards. But he'd never tell you. He was so low-key, such a gentleman. You could know Johnny for years and never even be aware he could swim. If that was me, I'd have gone around everywhere with my Olympic medals. I would have worn them to work. On dates. I'd have gone to bed with them on my chest. But no, not Johnny. A really lovely man.

• • •

Next stop after getting rid of the motorbike was the army. Like most young blokes in the late 1950s, I was conscripted. There was no war on at the time, so at least it was going to be less dangerous than riding motorbikes.

I didn't take my national service at all seriously. Instead I did what every young recruit did, and tried to beat the system. Sometimes you had to do it in very subtle ways.

After basic training, I went into heavy artillery. This was anti-aircraft or 'Heavy ACAC'. The biggest gun in the world at the time was a 3.7-inch anti-aircraft gun. It weighed nine tons and jumped a foot off the ground when fired. And that was with three people sitting on it.

We were divided into gun crews, each of ten people, and told to give our gun crew a name. The other crews came up with things like 'The Fighting Tigers', 'The Killer Rats', 'The Deadly Anacondas' and all these other macho names. Our gun crew was a ragtag bunch, pretty much a mob of Westies. We thought we'd enter into this macho competition with the name 'The Rose Petals'. We were excited by this, but then this country guy we all called Farmer Brown came up with the perfect name. Right away we knew it was the one for us. Our gun crew became 'The Prairie Flowers'.

The army drill sergeants, well, they'd seen too many movies and were almost comically over-the-top, butch, bravado types. We'd do a drill and our guy would be barking out orders and spitting and cursing. When we finished he'd always say, 'That was a brilliant and precise military movement, THOROUGHLY FUCKED UP BY YOU PEOPLE!' The first time I heard it, I thought it was hilarious, but he said it again and again. It was his one line.

Our name was some type of revenge. Our drill sergeant mocked us when we first announced it, but he was the one who had to stand in front of everyone and announce in his most butch and macho voice, 'Okay, Composition 1, The Fighting Tigers; Composition 2, The Deadly Death Adders; Composition 3 … The … um … Prairie Flowers …'

It certainly didn't make our lives any easier, but it made us laugh.

• • •

According to Hoges …

At the Dentist

I came back from national service one weekend with a sore tooth, so I went to the dentist. It was the first time I'd been for years and I was really pleased with the way dentistry had progressed. I mean, everything had changed except the *Reader's Digest* in the waiting room. I was reading one with a story about why Hitler wouldn't invade Poland.

The biggest change was that you could now have gas. It made the dentist's almost pleasurable. Instead of getting a needle, you breathed in the gas and it made you sort of remote from the action. You hovered around the ceiling above the dentist, looking at the galah in the chair with his mouth open. *Go on, drill holes in him, who cares.* It was fun.

Actually, a mate of mine, Lofty Taylor, used to go twice a week for a check-up just so he could have the gas. We called him Lofty because he was always high. One thing as a kid that used to scare me about the dentist was the prospect of drowning in your own saliva. It would sort of build up in your mouth. That stopped being a problem when they invented that little vacuum cleaner thingy they hook over your lip. I then started to worry, though, that it was gonna suck my tongue right out of my head.

Anyway, I remember going to a dentist in Granville years ago and this bloke had the most stunning, beautiful nurse you'd ever seen in your life. I thought, *Righto, I'm gonna make a big impression on this girl.* So I swaggered into the surgery, plopped myself down on the chair and announced, 'It's okay, Doc, no needles, no gas, just rip her out.' I was being the ultimate wanker.

But it turned out I needed just a simple filling. I reluctantly let him persuade me to have a needle. So he did it, and my whole mouth went numb. I was sitting there in the chair, looking up at the nurse and smiling and winking at her and doing my best to chat her up, which isn't easy when you have four fingers and a pound and a half of junk in your mouth.

What I always love with dentists is when they start working and put all the junk in your mouth then ask, 'So, how's it been going lately?' You go, 'Nngnts baad thnnnqks', and they understand you perfectly.

Anyway, this bloke did a fine job on the filling and soon finished and I was pretty proud – I'd handled it. Not so much as flinched. I'd been really cool and suave and smiled at the nurse the whole time. I knew I'd impressed her. The dentist then said to me, 'Okay, spit in the bowl.'

It was a fairly simple request, only the needle had done its job too well, and I knew the way my lips were feeling I couldn't spit in the Pacific Ocean. Undeterred, I was still trying to smile at the nurse, but it wasn't working. Suddenly I realised my jaws had disappeared. I couldn't feel them or any other part of my face.

Even I started to realise at this point in time that I probably didn't look all that suave to this girl. Nonetheless, undaunted, I took my little bib off, wiped some more dribble off my chin, looked her straight in the eye and said, 'Lyssmn, whet arrme yooffa dooooningz oof SsssSat ... Woooota yyooof ddddoning oof Saaaat, ooon Saaaaata? ... Oh, doesn't matter.'

O ur sergeant was constantly frustrated by our incompetence and lack of interest, but the fellow that really broke his heart was a private we called Crazy Kosiboski. If ever there was a misfit in the army, it was Crazy Kosiboski. Right from the first day you could see he wasn't going to make it. He had one of those round faces and innocent round eyes like babies have. And he'd walk around all day singing to himself and playing with a yo-yo.

This kid was totally uncoordinated. He couldn't march to save his life. The mean old sarge would drag him out of line and shout, 'All right, Kosiboski. Watch the demonstration. Left and right, quick march. Left, right, left, right, left, right. Try it.' But Kosiboski somehow managed to do left, left, right, right. The sarge would go ballistic!

Soon it was the day of our parade. A big event in the army. Three thousand soldiers on display and all rigidly at attention, frozen, like human statues, waiting for a flyover by twenty-four jet fighters. No one moved a single muscle. The planes went hurtling over the parade ground and Crazy Kosiboski broke ranks and waved at them.

Another day we were on the rifle range with the Owen gun, which is a light machine gun and a serious piece of equipment. The sarge shouted, 'All right men, face the front. Firing in five-second bursts. Commence firing.' *Bang, bang, bang, bang.*

Suddenly Crazy swung the gun around at us. 'Hey, Sarge, this gun's jammed.' *BANG!* Missed the sarge, as Maxwell Smart would say, 'by *that* much!' The sarge understandably lost it. I was pretty worldly, but even I heard some new expressions as he delivered them rapid-fire.

Days later on the grenade range, we had to throw a grenade and then drop down behind a brick wall, or shelter, so you didn't get hit by shrapnel. Crazy lobbed his grenade but then jumped up on the wall so he could see the explosion.

Understandably the sarge went ballistic, again. It was the final straw. The following week when we moved out for a forty-eight-hour full-scale mock war, Crazy had to stay behind in camp alone. I can still remember his face when we pulled out. He looked like a kid who'd come up empty on Christmas Day. We almost felt sorry for him.

Meanwhile, with the rest of us away, and everyone trying to make sense of this nutter, headquarters was doing some investigating. Suddenly Kosiboski's lieutenant was looking for him. They'd discovered his name wasn't in the files anywhere. They had absolutely no record of him. Apparently, he had just wandered into camp with us, thought, *Oh I like this*, and stayed. And now he'd disappeared.

When we heard the news, we all fell about laughing. We were ordered to help find him. We turned the camp upside down then finally went down to this old ammo shed where we would sometimes hide to play two-up or cards. As we opened the door the laughing suddenly stopped. There, pinned to the ceiling, was a sign: 'Crazy Kosiboski strikes again.'

He was crazy. But crazy like a fox. You see, there's a rule in the army that says when you go into a battle zone, you leave all your personal effects behind. Watches, wallets, cameras, transistors – stuff like that stays in the barracks.

Crazy had shot through all right, and along with him had gone every bloody thing in the camp that wasn't nailed down. He got me for a wallet with money in it, a watch and a radio –

all up, about £200 worth. But, if you're still around, Crazy, I just want to say, mate, that the entertainment you gave us made it worth every penny.

3

The Boxing Groom

In 1958, on one of Sydney's hot summer days right before Christmas, I got married. I'd just got out of the army and suddenly I was a married man. I was still only nineteen, a child bridegroom really. One of my wedding presents was a Meccano set.

I'd met my bride back when I was working at the swimming pool, back when I was having a ball and being a massive flirt. Back when I was a real poser too and thought I was oh-so-cool.

This girl simply stood out from the rest. Her name was Noelene Edwards. She was a few months younger than me and was blonde and pretty and smart. She said she was impressed by my diving and we really hit it off.

Noelene was also a local and laughed at my jokes, and I was really taken by everything about her. So, not wasting any time, we tied the knot. The ceremony was at the local church, and the reception was in Noelene's parents' backyard in Granville. We laid it on as best as we could manage. I made a speech of sorts and also got up and sang an Elvis number. There was no entertainment or band as such, but a mate brought his guitar and I did my best to serenade the crowd, as did my mates Les and Jack. None of us went on to release an album, but we could hold a tune.

Being married as teenagers seems so ridiculous now, but all our friends were getting hitched too. Remember we're talking the late 1950s, when you'd hear someone say, 'Hey, you see that bloke over there, he's twenty-two and he's not married yet.' You know, he'd be the odd one out!

At first Noelene and I moved into her parents' place (living with your mother-in-law was just about the only birth control there was in the fifties), then over the following year or so we moved into a succession of what were little more than shacks, in places like Homebush and Villawood. For a while after that, I was working for the Department of Roads, and that job came with a little house in Gymea. Finally we settled in a Housing Commission cottage in Chullora. Well, Chullora Heights, which sounds a bit posher. We were right next to the railway goods yard.

We were still only nineteen when our first little boy, Brett, was born. That's a scary thought now, but, again, most of my Western Suburbs peer group were in a similar situation. I didn't know how I'd take to fatherhood, but I just loved it! I was so proud, I remember one of the first things I did was take little

Brett in a stroller down to the Dog Trap Gauge Hotel, next to the railway crossing near where I lived. Just wanted to show him off to all my mates, being nineteen and all.

I could see at once what a wonderful, strange innocence little kids have. They're so open, just the best kind of human beings. Maybe that's why I had three of them – Brett, Clay and Todd – by the time I was twenty-two or twenty-three. And maybe it was my distant relationship with my own father that made me want to be such a rough-and-tumble, hands-on dad.

I was totally involved with my kids. We'd muck about together and go skateboarding. I'd watch them play rugby league on a Saturday, then they'd come watch me play on a Sunday. Afterwards, I'd spout all types of tips and advice about what they'd seen me do. They'd hang on every word, but then I started to realise they were better at sports than I'd ever be. At that point, I couldn't let them watch me play any more, or they wouldn't listen to my advice.

· · ·

According To Hoges ...

Of Mice and Blokes

One of the unpleasant duties that comes with being the man of the house is the job of executioner. You see, for some reason it's nearly always the man's job to kill any unwanted pests and crawlies that come inside.

Soon after we got married, we moved into a little one-bedroom shack in Gymea, south of the city. It was on the edge of a national park, so sooner or later every hairy-go-wobbler known to man paid us a visit. Now I didn't mind killing rats, cos rats are arrogant. These rats were like a bikie gang. They'd storm into the kitchen. Some of them down there even had tattoos. And they'd look at ya and sort of demand food. 'Give us a taco or we'll break your leg.' I didn't mind killing something like that.

But I couldn't kill mice because mice are sort of humble, polite little fellas. When a mouse goes through the room, he always goes along the edge, right against the wall and it's like he's saying, 'Excuse me, just going through to the kitchen to get some crumbs and that. Don't get up, don't get up, I won't be long, I won't be a pest.'

Then if you corner them with a broom, they look up at you sort of pleadingly: 'Don't hit me with the broom. Can't we talk this over? All that mess under the fridge, it wasn't me. It was the other guy.' You can't kill something like that.

And women, women are funny with mice. My wife used to jump up on the chair because she thought the mouse was going to run up her leg. Which is ridiculous. The last recorded case of a mouse actually running up a woman's leg was in 1957 and it was at Mascot aerodrome and it was a Yugoslav lady trying to sneak through customs with a fourteen-pound slab of Gorgonzola strapped to her thigh.

Spiders, I also hate killing spiders because spiders are bad sports. I mean, you kill a spider that's about as big as Joel Garner's hand and as soon as you kill it, it curls up to the size of a sultana and you can't brag about it. They deny you the trophy.

But the scariest creatures of all are the unknown creatures. This is true. When I lived in that little house in the scrub, one night when I was going to bed and just about to turn the lights off, I heard this noise out the back. It was sort of like ... 'What the hell's that?'

I went out the back to have a look and whatever it was quickly went round the front, making the same weird noise. It was a sound like no creature makes – not quite animal, not quite human – a swirling sound, and trying to make it now has me spitting all over the page here and I still can't find a way of writing it down. Just know it was weird.

Anyway, I'd go out the front and it'd go around the side. And it was scary. The place was quite remote but we felt so exposed. I decided it was either a black panther, or a Tasmanian devil.

I ordered the family to lie down on the floor in the bedroom. I got the old rifle out and started stalking the beast. I crept out the back door, cos it had been circling the house, and I lay there in wait, gun ready. After what seemed like an eternity there was a rustle in the bushes near the dunny and then that noise again ... *Bang!* I fired. Not wanting to kill anything, I aimed at the base of a tree. In the still of the night in the bush, a .22 rifle goes off like an army cannon.

There was a moment's silence, and then the thing went scarpering off so fast into the scrub that I knew I was right, it had to be a panther.

A week later Noelene and I were coming back from the shops, walking towards the house, and this weird, goofy fellow came riding past on a pushbike. He was about thirty, wearing a cowboy hat, and had two toy guns and a marshal's badge on his chest. As he rode past us, and just as he went to turn into this big clump of scrub that went up behind our house, he looked back at me and ... yep, he made the exact same noise.

I went cold. I could have accidentally shot the poor bugger.

I continued to work at all sorts of strange, weird and wonderful jobs. Life was what it was: get up at quarter to six in the morning, get on the bus and train, go to work. Then come home to see the kids, who'd be playing footy and wrestling around in the backyard. We'd have the standard meat and two vegies for dinner and, as a treat, sometimes a bread and butter pudding.

Financially it was always a struggle, but I didn't know any other life, and I had no real desire to change things. And because we were such young parents, we were all learning and growing up together and I was loving every minute of it. Our little girl, Loren, arrived four years after Todd and, as she got bigger, she started to join in the fun. She was tough and determined, but the boys still protected her like all good big brothers do. It was just wonderful to have my own tribe.

There were a few hurdles along the way. I developed a bad temper soon after I was married. I'm not sure what it was. Maybe it was just surly, late-teenage frustration coming through, but things would set me off, violently. One day my temper got the better of me. I was trying to mow the backyard in Granville. With every pull at the fraying cord, the lawnmower would start, but then, by the time I had straightened up and grabbed the handle, the bloody thing would promptly stop. After twenty or more goes, I got so frustrated I picked the stupid thing up and threw it over the fence into the neighbour's yard. I felt good for about twenty seconds, then I looked down at the still unmown grass. With my tail between my legs, I had to knock on the neighbour's door and do my best to explain why my lawnmower was embedded in their backyard. I was a little embarrassed, but their kids fell about.

It was around that time I took up boxing. I'd dabbled in it a bit as a kid, but it was Muhammad Ali, or Cassius Clay as he was known then, who inspired me to get serious about it. He was the most exciting boxer in the world in the early 1960s and became world champion in early 1964. Suddenly boxing became a significant, respected sport. Ali was the first heavyweight who fought like a lightweight. The rest were like they are now: clumsy oafs. But he moved about like he weighed nothing at all. So quick, so graceful. He made the others look

Hogan 1. Punching Bag 0. My early boxing training stood me in good stead when filming *Almost an Angel* (1990). *(Alamy)*

like they were just big and slow and tired. He was the greatest showman too. I idolised him.

Boxing took away all my anger and frustration, as I needed self-discipline and focus to do it. It was the best thing that could have happened, and it completely changed my temperament.

I trained in a boxing gym in Granville. It was a proper gym, not like the ones today. It smelt of old socks and jockstraps, like all good gyms should. But while it was a professional boxing gym six days a week, on Saturdays it was one of the biggest illegal SP bookie joints in the Western Suburbs.

One day, old Billy Moran, who was my trainer and taught me to fight, pulled me and my mate Phil aside. 'Look, do you boys want to make some easy money on Saturdays?'

'Yeah,' we replied.

'Well some of the joints have been raided by the cops of late,' he said, 'so I want you two to come in, put your gear on, and sit in opposite corners of the ring. Then, if we get the warning buzzer from our cockatoo, you two jump up and start sparring, and whatever punters are in here will gather around the ring and watch you train. You know, that'll be our cover.' He added, 'And I'll give you a day's pay for two or three hours.'

Naturally, me and Phil took it on. And for about three or four weeks, that's what we did. Sat around the gym, got paid for it, had a bet. Then on the fourth week, the buzzer went. The cops were coming.

Everyone panicked, the bookies covered up their sheets. Phil and I jumped into the ring and all the punters gathered around it just as seven coppers burst in. There were three plain-clothes detectives with a big boofhead sergeant leading them, and three uniformed guys. They made a semicircle so none of us could get to the door. Of course nobody looked at them. We pretended they weren't even there. All the punters were giving their full attention to us as we got our gloves on.

'Well, well, gentlemen, what do we have here?' asked the big boofhead sergeant.

'Oh, we're just watching the boys work out, you know,' said one of the braver punters.

The sergeant went, 'Hmm,' and looked around. There were at least sixty punters in the gym, jammed around the ring, all looking at Phil and me, like we were gods.

'I doubt,' the boofhead said, 'that at the very peak of his career, Sugar Ray Robinson had this many people watching him work out. Who are these two palookas?'

Now, old Billy, he was pretty quick and as he finished gloving me up he said, 'Well this is different. This is very personal. Both of these lads are undefeated, and this is a grudge match. And it could get quite nasty.'

I was like, *What? Did he say 'grudge match'?*

Then Billy leant in close to me. 'Just throw a lot of arm punches.' (Arm punches are when you throw your glove out with speed, but you don't really put your weight into it.) 'They won't know the difference,' Billy said, 'but don't forget, it's meant to be a grudge match. You got to look fierce.'

I looked over at Phil, and Phil was standing totally relaxed and almost in a daze. I could almost hear him humming 'Theme from A Summer Place' – you'd know it if you heard it; it's the calmest bit of music ever.

'Phil, Phil!' I growled at him. 'I'm going to take your head off your shoulders.'

He snapped out of his daydream. 'What? Oh yeah, right, right. This is a grudge match.'

We started giving a great performance, glaring at each other. I tried a mixture of Muhammad Ali and John Wayne.

Billy said, 'All right, gentlemen, you both know the rules, we're all professionals here. Keep it clean. May the best man win. When the bell rings, come out fighting.'

Ding. Out we came. Me and Phil. Lots of movement, dancing around. Little quick, flicking punches. Exactly the sort of slapping, sparring session that we'd been asked to provide.

We're looking pretty convincing, I thought. But about twenty seconds in, Phil suddenly propped and threw a perfect right hand with all his might, and it went right between my gloves. I felt my nose break, then blood running down the mouthguard and dripping off my chin. And I thought, *Well that's not acting*.

It really annoyed me because, to be honest, deep down, I'd been pretty sure I could take Phil. I thought, *I'd better remind him of that*. And about twenty seconds later, I saw my chance, slipped aside, and *boom*. I threw a beautiful left hook, got him right on the ear, which quickly turned purple.

That's when the problems started, because deep down Phil was also pretty sure he could take me. And that's when it all turned to shit. Knees, feet and everything. It was so ugly. At one stage I had Phil in a headlock, and I was pounding away on his kidneys. He was trying to get out by kneeing me in the nuts. Then we went to the canvas, still kneeing and kicking, fists and feet going everywhere.

If I could've got my mouthguard out, I'd have bitten a piece out of his arm, but old Billy came to the rescue, rang the bell and dragged us apart.

'No, this is nonsense,' he said, 'I won't have this in my gym. No contest. It's no contest.'

The punters had all been cheering us on in the ring, but now nobody knew what to do. It had all gone deathly quiet. Finally the big boofhead cop went, 'Ha' and looked at the other cops, and they left.

That was it, they all simply walked out of the gym. We all looked at each other. *Did we really get away with it?* It remained deathly quiet and then we heard the buzzer sound, meaning they'd gone. At that point, all the punters burst into spontaneous applause.

Old Billy, quick as a flash, picked up a spit bucket. 'Gentlemen,' he said, 'I think the lads here saved us from some heavy fines and a ride in the paddy wagon. I think we should show our appreciation.' He pulled out a fiver and dropped it in the bucket, before passing it round the punters.

As it turned out, that was the biggest purse Phil and I ever got in our boxing careers – about sixty quid, after Billy took his fiver back out, of course.

• • •

According To Hoges ...

A Fighting Chance

At the time when I was really into boxing, there was a well-known standover man around town, Randall. Now, the name Randall sounds more like he'd be your friendly local accountant, so everyone called him by the much more fitting name of Horsehead. Mind you, no one ever said it to his face because he was big and tough and a real thick-headed bully. One day he stood over my little brother, Pat, for money and my brother told him to get stuffed and got well and truly thumped for his cheek. Knowing what I'm like, Pat thought it was probably best not to tell me, but I found out from a mate of his some time later. He said, 'You should do something about Horsehead, Hoges, cos you can fight, can't ya?'

'Yeah, I can fight.' *If he crosses my path, I'll sort him out all right,* I thought. *How tough can Horsehead be?*

The very next day I was working out in a gym in Granville and some of my mates came rushing in, saying, 'Hey Hoges, we found Horsehead! He's over at the Royal Hotel. You're going to sort him out, aren't you?'

'Um, yeah, that's right ...'

So we headed over there. It was only two blocks away and two of my mates from the gym, Phil and Ronnie, were with me, just in case Horsehead had backup there.

On the way, I was working out in my head exactly how it would play out. *He's a big oaf but I'm very fast,* I thought, so I planned that I'd jab him, move back, then swing a right hand over the top, followed by a left hook. I was getting excited, thinking there was no way he'd be able to handle that combination. I knew this was going to sort the buffoon out.

The Royal Hotel didn't have swinging saloon doors like in an old western, but my entrance gave the impression it did. If there'd been a piano player, he would have stopped mid-tune. I quickly sized up the room and spotted the big lump holding court against the bar. Without missing a stride, I walked straight up to him and said, 'Hey, Horsehead.'

A few people scattered.

Slowly this man mountain turned to me. He knew who I was. As I peered up at his bloodshot eyes, he slowly took his beer in his hand. This was a trick that standover merchants used in those days. They'd drop their beer and you'd automatically look down to see where it smashed and right then was when they'd hit you. I knew about this. I'd seen that trick done. I wasn't falling for it.

'I believe you thumped my young brother ... Horsehead.'

His eye started to twitch and I watched as his hand started sliding the glass towards the edge of the bar.

I was thinking, *Bang, I could send a very fast lefty to his mouth before he has a chance to drop the beer. He's then gonna swing wildly at me and I'll have to block that and then quickly hit him again.* I was feeling confident – I think because I'd just come from a workout. I was already pumped and primed. So, I went for it.

Bang. I hit him in the mouth. He hardly moved.

There was a moment's silence and then in an instant he came at me with his left. I thought, *I'll parry that with my left. Then I'll clobber him with my right hand.* But the big oaf didn't throw a punch at all. Instead he threw his whole body at me! Now, I was barely a welterweight, about 140 pounds, or a bit over 60 kilograms. Horsehead was about 240 pounds! That's nearly 110 kilos. He was a genuine heavyweight. Down I crumbled with him on top.

Legend has it that we hit the floor and then I knocked him out, got up, dusted off my hands and walked out. If only that were true. You see, what actually happened was this. His giant mass was almost suffocating me. Not being one to give up, I was still desperately attempting to hit him from my squashed, winded position when suddenly he grabbed my head and was about to drive it right through the tiles of the hotel floor.

At that point my mate Ronnie Beekin stepped forward. Now, Ronnie was a very promising fighter who, a year or two later, would turn professional and eventually be rated about fifth in the world in the middleweight division. A really good bloke to have onside was Ronnie. As he saw my head about to be driven through the tiles, he just stepped in and, whack, delivered a very short, sharp right to Horsehead's huge jaw, knocking him out cold.

From the other side of the oval bar, the stunned patrons only saw Horsehead and I go down and then me, moments later, get up, dust off my hands, wink at the publican and walk out with the boys. It gave me a short-lived reputation as a good street fighter, which I wasn't, though Ronnie Beekin certainly was.

Once again, it was clear: I wasn't John Wayne.

Inspired by Muhammad Ali, I later turned professional. For a moment I believed that one day I could become the welterweight champion of the world. But unfortunately I was never more than somewhere between average and mediocre and soon found out that I could barely be the welterweight champion of my street. I had only six professional fights. Won five, lost one. But it wasn't exactly world-class opposition. I was certainly no Ali.

Phil and I remained the best of mates. In fact, he got me a job just after that fight. He was working at Crest flour mills in western Sydney. 'Come on over,' he said. 'They're always hiring casuals. It's an easy job, money's not bad.'

I was out of work, so I went over there in the middle of the week, saw the boss.

'I haven't got anything at the moment, son,' he said. 'No, actually, wait a minute, do you think you could run a bagging machine? It's pretty simple, it's just two levers.'

'Well, yeah.'

'Okay,' he said, 'I've got to sack the clown that's running it now. I'll be getting rid of him on Friday. If you come in on Monday, half past seven, you've got a start.'

'Okay, beauty.'

As I was leaving the joint, I thought I'd better check out this bagging machine, to make sure I could work it. I followed the signs, and finally, there it was. The guy who was running it turned around, looked at me and waved. It was Phil.

4

The Bridge Calls

It was 1961. My parents had saved and scrimped for a *Women's Weekly* World Discovery Tour. It would have been the first time either of them had ever been outside Australia – and it was just months away. They were so excited about finally getting to see the rest of the world, but shortly before they started packing their bags, my dad, Jack, dropped dead. He was only fifty. It was a heart attack that killed him. If he had the same thing today, he'd be fine. They'd just put a couple of stents in him and he'd be all good.

While he and I didn't have a close relationship, his death obviously shook the whole family. I was a new husband and father and maybe I'd always hoped that in my later twenties or thirties we would have learnt to understand each other better, and perhaps even become close. Sadly, that hope disappeared.

I was already very close to my own kids, but Dad's death probably changed my attitude to life a little bit in other ways. I was someone who'd try to do handstands on his motorbike and dive off anything, but now, probably for the first time, I realised that we're not indestructible, that we all have a limited timespan.

I was just twenty-one but realised that anything I felt like doing or got the urge to do, I should probably do now. Not that my horizons were that wide. I stumbled from one job to another, collecting various tickets as I went, qualifying me to use various machines and work in different areas. But, in the end, I settled on the construction game.

There was a boom going on in Sydney. High-rise stuff. And I thought, *Well, that's where the big money is.* So I went to technical college and got my scaffolder's – or rigger's – ticket and headed into the city to get hold of the money.

At one stage I even worked as a dogman. A dogman is the guy who stands on top of the load of building materials on a crane and rides it high up into the sky. They're like the glamour boys of the building game. But it can be hazardous if you don't follow the rules. There's a correct way to ride that load: grasp the main cable, strongly. Feet apart. Your other hand, which has the walkie talkie to talk to the driver, is wrapped around the other cable. This is the safe way to ride, and the only way to ride the load up forty storeys.

Except, of course, if you're working next to another high-rise building with office girls watching from the window. I mastered this situation too. Walkie talkie in the belt, one hand for holding on and the other one free for waving at the ladies. Have I mentioned I was a bit of a poser?

Anyway, after a couple of years, the building boom ground to a halt. I needed to find steady, permanent work. I heard they were looking for riggers on the Sydney Harbour Bridge and thought, *Well, that's pretty permanent. That's not going anywhere.* So I got a start on the Bridge.

I hadn't been there long when suddenly I was recruited to be an organiser for the Ironworkers' Union. It happened after some bigwigs involved in this arbitration thingy came down to the Bridge one day and asked me to show them around. In doing so I had some fun and dramatised things a bit. In my sincerest voice I said something like, 'You know, every day of my life, we're here, us workers, with our lives depending on the grip of one hand.' Which was true. 'We all hang on as best we can,' I added, 'but if we make one small mistake, if we let go for even a second, we fall to our death.' The bigwigs listened sombrely then ... we got an instant raise!

They weren't allowed to call it 'danger money', so they called it 'height money'. The workers' union got in touch with me right away, thrilled, and suddenly I was working as a union organiser. But the new job just had me going around to little factories and I soon realised that I was actually little more than a debt collector. I was going to the places where someone hadn't paid, or someone didn't want to join the union, and that wasn't for me. I only lasted a couple of months, then threw it in and went back to the Bridge.

Now I've often read or heard people saying that I was a painter on the Harbour Bridge. I wasn't. I couldn't hack that at all. Imagine being a painter on the Sydney Harbour Bridge?

Going to work every day and asking, 'What colour are we doing today, boss?'

'Grey.'

No, my job was to put up the working platforms and the stages and keep the painters safe. And I was a good rigger. I know that because sometimes I'd go weeks without dropping a painter. Actually, to be honest, I never dropped a painter.

It was great, with sea breezes and the best view in Sydney, and there was satisfaction in every day you kept someone alive. I was enjoying life, and seeing a lot of humour in the things and people around me.

But I think a bit of Crazy Kosiboski must have rubbed off on me, at least the Crazy bit, because about ten years after my nasho, or national service, I decided I wanted to go to Vietnam. Why? Firstly, because I wasn't very bright and, secondly, I figured I'd already done nasho, so to sign up only made sense.

I must have been listening to that part of my brain again, the part I call the Wombat. I was a young family man, with a houseful of kids, so absolutely no one else thought this was a good idea, including the people recruiting for Vietnam. I was also in my late twenties, and it was the younger men they were keenest on signing up.

They did let me join the supplementary reserve, however. I was called an engineer, but mainly I just used to blow stuff up. I really enjoyed it. We worked a lot with high explosives, though I never added 'High Explosives Expert' to my resumé, because I thought they might end up not letting me on commercial jets or something.

Anyway, I wasn't an expert, but I was good enough to make things disappear. I remained an active reserve for quite some time, and I was involved in training some of the younger men who were heading overseas for service too.

One day we headed away on a mock battle. We went out into the bush where we were split into two groups. Ours had to set up camp and protect ourselves from any potential ambush. The other group were dropped in the scrub miles away and had to use their knowledge to find our camp, sneak up on it and overrun us.

I'm not sure how many miles away they were dropped or if they got disorientated, but we could have grown a vegie patch in the time we were waiting for them. They still hadn't arrived by 3 a.m., when it was my turn to be on lookout. I was leaning against a tree, staring out into the darkness, bored. It was cold and raining and when I thought I couldn't be any more miserable I found my trusty old cigarette lighter had given up the ghost.

Suddenly I had a brainwave that Crazy Kosiboski would have been proud of. I'd noticed on night training that when our rifles fired a small flash appeared at the end of the barrel. I thought, that's the answer. I'll use this flash to light my cigarette! So, I carefully placed the butt of my rifle on the ground and the tip of my hand-rolled cigarette over the end of the barrel and … *bang!*

It blew my cigarette to the shithouse. The rifle jerked out of my hands and, for a brief moment, I was embarrassed. But then, one by one, heads started coming up out of the scrub, some of them camouflaged with mud and sticks. Others with hands in the air. Surrendering. Totally believing that Ol' Eagle-eyed Hoges had spotted them. Soon I was surrounded by my group, all of them patting me on the back for my laser vision. And at night!

Up on the Bridge moments after my shirt apparently blew off.
(*Russell McPhedran*/Sydney Morning Herald)

The other group, already horribly tired and frustrated, were marched back out into the wet scrub to try their ambush again. And I don't think I ever did get to have that smoke.

• • •

Through all this I was still working on the Bridge. In the very late sixties, I got a bravery award for stopping a young guy from dropping himself off the side. But it shouldn't have been an award for bravery, it should have been for being fearless and stupid. Bravery is when you get into a dangerous situation and you're afraid, but you overcome your fear and do the right thing. I never had the fear, the Harbour Bridge was my home. It never fully occurred to me that I could fall four hundred feet to my death. As I said, fearless and stupid.

Unfortunately, we did occasionally get suicide jumpers on the Bridge. The most popular spot for this in Sydney was a place called The Gap, which is a cliff in the Eastern Suburbs where people almost regularly did themselves in. At other times they chose our bridge.

One day, we were working in the crane cabins on top of the Bridge. The cranes have a big tray under them and you lower the painters down and they can walk right through the cabins and across the arches. I was in one of these cabins and suddenly there was a phone call saying, 'Listen, we're pretty sure there's a jumper on his way up the arch. Can you intercept him or something?'

This young guy had blasted past a couple of painters and was walking up the arch towards the top of the Bridge and towards the cabin we were in. Sadly, we were used to it – well, as used to it as you could be. As I hung up the phone I looked out the back of the crane to see this guy, focused and very determinedly walking towards us.

There were three other guys in the crane who I won't name because it could be embarrassing for them, but I said, 'Listen, there's a jumper coming up here. He's just brushed off the painters and he's coming fast. This is what we'll do: when he gets in the cabin we'll jump him, because it's contained. It's safe in here.'

'You go out the back and work with the cables,' I said to one of the guys. Another guy was already driving the crane and I said to the last bloke, 'Just sit either side of the driver and pretend you're helping or something, and when the bloke comes in I'll confront him and try and engage him in conversation, and that's when you come in behind him. This'll then mean there's four of us around him, and when I nod, we'll all jump him at once and secure him in the cabin.' That was the plan.

Anyway, the guy advanced up the arch and the closer he got, the bigger he got. He was a huge, strapping young man, probably no older than his mid-twenties, and the look on his face told me he was set on jumping and ending it all.

But we were ready. 'Okay, when he gets in the cabin,' I said, 'I'll give the nod, right?'

The boys were not as enthusiastic as I was about it, mainly because I was about twenty-eight. They were all a bit older, and this didn't sound like a brilliant plan to them.

Sure enough, the guy came up the small ladder and stepped into the cabin. I stepped right in front of him before he could get past. 'What the hell do you think you're doing up here?' I asked. 'You're not supposed to be up here doing this kind of thing.'

'I'm up here cos I'm going off the side,' he replied. 'And don't try and stop me, or I'll take you with me.'

'Oh really,' I said. 'Well that's not going to happen.' And I started nodding my head, the very obvious signal for everyone to jump him. I told the young bloke, 'You can't go any further.' And now I was really nodding my head desperately. The guy at the back hadn't come in behind him, and the other two guys were sitting either side of the cabin. One of them was looking out the window, while the other one was having a scratch and pretending he was doing something with the motor.

I was standing there like an idiot in front of this guy, nodding my head in vain. Suddenly the guy glared at me and quietly said again, 'Don't try and stop me,' and pushed me out of the way as though I was nothing and carried on up the arch. I was furious with the blokes, and called out, 'The signal. The signal!'

They all started making lame excuses that they didn't know he was the guy, or they never noticed that I was nodding. But, simply, they had chickened out. I turned back to watch the guy as he kept marching on up the arch. My brilliant plan hadn't worked.

I watched for another moment but knew I couldn't let it end like this. I followed him up the arch, where he now stood on the outside of the rail and I got hold of his shirt. He was poised right on the rail's edge. Then he looked at me and said, 'Take my hand.'

'I'm sorry,' I said, 'but I'm not going to take your hand.'

'Please mate, just hold it.'

So I did. I grabbed hold of his wrist, but I had a fifty-pound grip on it and about a two-hundred-pound grip on the steel rail. He leant back and looked me in the eye and said, 'Let me go.'

'No, mate.' I shook my head. 'I'm not going to let you go.'

'Let me go,' he said more desperately. 'I just want to go.'

What happened next is a bit of a blur, but we talked and he ended up walking down off the Bridge with me. I learnt he was just twenty years old, a uni student who had been on something and was having a weird trip, a trip that had led to him standing on top of our most famous bridge, ready to kill himself.

I remember that as we walked down the arch he grabbed hold of my shoulder. 'You shouldn't have done that,' he said, 'I could have taken you over the edge with me.'

It was true that he could have. 'You're a good guy,' I said. 'Why would you want to do that?'

And I just kept talking to him. We got down off the arch onto the deserted railway deck where the trains go over the Bridge. As soon as our feet touched this solid ground, police and rescue guys burst out of nowhere and jumped on top of him. At one stage four cops were engaged in an almighty struggle with him. One of them had a hold of his legs, but the big guy was thrashing about and throwing this copper around like he was a sock. I was like, *Yeah, he could have taken me over the side with him.*

Finally, they got him down and into the office, where he asked for a drink of water. He proceeded to bite a big chunk out of the glass and try to swallow it. The cops stopped him. Beyond that, I don't know what happened to that young man, but at least we didn't let him kill himself that day.

As for the weak bastards I was working with, to be fair I think one of them maybe did try to follow us up the arch. Once I started talking with the young man he probably thought that now that I had his ear, he shouldn't interfere.

Despite this not being their finest hour, the guys on the Bridge were actually a great bunch who helped many other desperate people. Sadly, though, we weren't able to save everyone. Suicides would happen a couple of times a year but were generally kept quiet. There was no counselling for the workers, no additional support. And it was always unnerving.

In the end I spent about ten years crawling all over the Coat Hanger. I knew every inch of it. And it was funny all those years later when they started doing tours up on the Bridge. I used to walk up there to rig up a stage, with a sixty-pound cable over my shoulder, sometimes cursing every step. Now people pay money to be able to go up there and just walk about and take in the view. I look up at them and think, *You're galahs!*

· · ·

According To Hoges ...

Rescue Work

When I first started on the Bridge, I didn't realise one of the duties of a rigger was to also rescue co-workers who got themselves into difficulty.

One morning me and some other riggers were working up near the top of the arch when the foreman came rushing up. 'Race down to the dock,' he said, 'Persil has had a heart attack and you're going to need the Robinson stretcher.'

We were pretty excited as we rushed down the arch, not because we didn't like Persil – he was a beaut bloke – but because this was going to be our first chance to use the all-new Robinson stretcher. It was a bit of an odd thing, sort of like a cross between a full-size cricket pad and a straightjacket, especially designed for rescue work.

We found Persil lying on the cold steel railing. He was a bit of an alarmist, and he'd diagnosed a pain in his chest as a heart attack, probably fatal, when, as we found out later, what had actually happened was that in his haste to wolf down his counter lunch, a chicken bone had lodged in his throat.

Anyway, Persil was carrying on with his 'prepared-to-meet-my-death' speech, so we decided to take him down to the bottom of the Bridge. We strapped him into this terrible straightjacket-like stretcher and started the long descent. Of course, he was still putting it on, playing the part of the calm, brave hero, looking death in the face. And he kept saying things like, 'I've had a good innings. Don't take any risks for me boys, I've had it.'

Then, while we were making our way down a steel ladder, one of the other riggers accidentally trod on my hand. I instinctively grabbed at his foot but in so doing let go of my handle of the stretcher. The stretcher was on safety ropes, and Persil literally swung out of our hands, turned upside down and found himself hanging two hundred feet above the harbour. Suddenly all his calm composure in the face of death deserted him and he screamed like a banshee.

After quite some effort and a volume of screaming none of us had experienced before, I got hold of him again and we set him back upright and carried him down the ladders and then up through a trapdoor and onto the railway deck. Now he was in comparative safety, he resumed his calm 'hero-in-the-face-of-death' act, just as the first-aid man arrived. Well, what we called a first-aid man; that's to say a guy who had a regular job around the place but had also done a five-day course in band-aids and bruises. The only first aid he was normally required to do was when someone cut a finger or needed an aspirin after a big night.

Our first-aid bloke was a ripper, a painter named Ron. He was tall, grey-haired, distinguished-looking, and he used terms like 'lower lumbar region' and 'angina'. You couldn't help but call him Doc.

We decided we'd better get Persil off the railway deck, over a fence and onto the road, where the ambulance was going to arrive. This was a difficult operation, as it involved getting the patient over a six-foot-high fence. Persil lay frozen in the straightjacket as Dr Ron took charge, taking care of his patient and saying 'steady, steady, higher on this end, watch his feet' and responsible things like that. Unfortunately, Dr Ron was so engrossed he failed to notice the open trapdoor we'd come out of. No lie. There was a brief scream – and then he was gone.

Fortunately, Dr Ron didn't fall two hundred feet to the harbour, but he did fall about seven feet onto a steel girder on the railway line and suffered severe bruises and lacerations. So we quickly dropped Persil and rushed down to rescue Dr Ron, helping him back up to the railway deck and then quickly off the line – just as we saw a train coming. This is when scream number three reminded us that when we'd dropped Persil, we'd also left him on the railway line!

Anyway, we got him out of the way in time and onto the road without further mishap. We then took him out of the Robinson stretcher and put him onto an ordinary one. By the time the ambulance arrived, he'd regained his composure to such an extent that he was lying there making out a verbal will.

Now Persil's goods and chattels were of little interest to anyone, with the exception of a beautiful tailor-made and expensive-looking overcoat he had. It could only have come into his possession from falling off the back of a truck. Unfortunately for Persil, calm and brave now, he chose to say, 'My overcoat is in my locker. So, anyone who wants it can have it,' just as we were lifting him into the ambulance.

Even more unfortunately for Persil, the two blokes most interested in the coat, me and Tight-fist Doyle, were on the same end of the stretcher. We dropped everything and broke into a sprint. Persil protested as he slid gracefully back onto the road.

The result of all this was that Dr Ron had severe bruises and lacerations from head to toe, probably in the lower lumbar region, and angina too for all I knew; I had a cracked bone in my finger from when the guy stood on it; and Tight-fist had a badly sprained ankle from me tripping him on the way to Persil's locker. As expected, Persil turned up at work the next morning with only a sore throat, I'm sure as much from the screaming as from the chicken bone.

So we killed him and threw his body off the Bridge.

5

The Tap-Dancing
Knife Thrower

The moment had come. The little jazz dancer with her
trembling lip and teary eyes had to be avenged. I walked
out on the stage, under the bright lights where the *New Faces*
host, Frank Wilson, and his judges were sitting, smug as all
get-out.

I don't remember exactly what I said. It was just bagging the
judges. You know, 'We appreciate you professional entertainers
coming here and giving us your time. And particularly the
gentleman that told the kid about the diet, that was very helpful.
You could've gone a step further and given her the diet that

you're on, cos we've noticed you're in great shape, and you've lost all your body fat. Pity it didn't work on your head.'

Sophisticated stuff like that. I did this for a couple of minutes and got some good laughs. 'Okay, that's me,' I said. 'I'm done.'

Then, the panic hit them. 'No, no. Tap-dancer? Knife thrower?'

'Oh, almost forgot. Okay.'

Then I got a little inspiration when I took the knives out of the bin. I looked at them and announced, 'Ladies and gentlemen, for the first time anywhere in the world, I'm going to do the act tonight blindfold.' And I put the bin over my head. 'Right, here we go. Tap-dancing and knife throwing at the same time.'

I jumped up and down on the spot for about five seconds, threw the knives on the ground, took the bin off my head and bowed. And that was it. The crowd clapped and I tried to leave. 'Oh wait, wait,' one of the judges yelled. 'You have to wait for our comments and marks.'

'Nah, that's all right,' I said, 'I don't need it. I know I'm good.'

I walked off before the judges could judge. The audience loved it. They could see what I was up to. Everyone else on the stage, though, was a bit mystified. I didn't care. I went and got my appearance cheque, and left.

With *New Faces* going live to air, it should have been my national humiliation. But, amazingly, a lot of people found it hilarious. A lot didn't. And the guys at work thought I was an idiot, except the ones that had put me up to it. At home, Noelene and the tribe treated me messing about on the telly as a harmless, fun diversion. None of it mattered, and that appearance would be the start and end of my show-business career. And I was quite happy with that.

• • •

I went back to work on the Bridge the next day, as normal. And this is where the odd taste of the Australian public comes into it. I learnt they had an expression in television. They say 'the switchboard lit up'. That means a lot of people rang up to complain or talk about something, or make a comment on what they had seen on the box.

Well, the *New Faces* switchboard, they tell me, lit up like a Christmas tree. There were thousands of people ringing up and saying, 'The tap-dancing knife thrower should've won,' and 'The guy from Lightning Ridge was the best thing on there.'

I didn't know this until a week or two later. I was up on the Bridge and I kept getting messages like 'Someone wants to talk to you from Channel 9.' One lunchtime, I took a call and it was Desmond Tester. 'Now Mr Hogan,' he said, 'I'd like you to come on the show again.'

'Well, I can't,' I said. 'I didn't win. It's against the rules, isn't it?'

'I'm the producer,' Tester said, 'I make the rules. And I'd love you to come on the show again.'

'Well, I can't do the same trick. I've done the knife throwing bit. I'm not that interested.'

'You can do anything you like,' he said. 'You can just have a talk, or whatever. But I'd just love you to come on again.'

'Well, will I get paid again?'

'Yeah, I'll give you double what you got last time.'

'In cash?' I asked. He agreed and I accepted the bribe (and of course I declared the income – we'll talk about tax a bit later, I promise) and prepared to go on the show again, a week later.

'What are you doing this time?' the contestant coordinator rang to ask.

'Well, one of my other talents is I'm a shovelist.'

'A *what*?'

'I play the shovels. Don't you ever listen to classical music?'

'So you're a … shovelist?'

The next day I turned up at Channel 9 with my 'instruments'. Desmond Tester came around. 'What the hell are you doing with those?' he asked.

'I'm playing the shovels, for God's sake.'

'Let me guess: you don't want to rehearse.'

'No,' I replied, 'they're delicate instruments. I don't want to risk them, as I've just had 'em tuned.'

He was a beaut little bloke, Des, and he just sort of looked at me then smiled. 'Yeah, I've got to see this one too. He's not rehearsing, crew. Let him on.'

I went out and gave cheek for five minutes, threw in a joke or two, and told one judge he was 'a shining example of *it's not what you know but who you know*'. And then with great fanfare, I played the shovels. The piece I selected, which was to be played by the Geoff Harvey Orchestra, was the 'William Tell Overture'. It goes da da da da da da da da daaa da da – you know the one. So the music struck up and I just stood there and did absolutely nothing until the final note, when I simply banged the two shovels together, once.

And I won.

True story. And then I was in the final in November, which required heading off down to Melbourne. It was my first-ever commercial flight. The only time I'd flown before that was in a Caribou cargo plane in the army. This trip to Melbourne was also the first time I'd stayed in a flash hotel. It was in the city and had a queen-sized bed, a hairdryer on the wall and drinks in frustratingly little bottles in the fridge. Everyone referred to me as Mr Hogan.

For my grand hurrah I needed another gimmick, so I decided I was going to play the thunder box. There was no such instrument of course, as 'thunder box' is slang in the army for toilet or dunny. I went to the props department at Channel 9 and got hold of a big tea chest, essentially a big plywood box, and wrote Thunder Box across it with a marker pen. I now had my instrument.

Once again, they said, 'Time for rehearsal,' and once again I said no. But this was a different crew from the one in Sydney. They protested that they needed to know what I was going to do.

'Put it onstage there,' I responded. 'Put the Thunder Box down there and I'll stand here and I'll talk, and when I'm ready to play it I'll run across the stage to where the box is and I'll play it. Simple as that. But it's important that I run over there. Okay? You'll need to be ready.'

They shrugged and said okay and wandered off. I assumed they'd heard about my tap-dancing knife throwing act from the Sydney producers and so knew I was weird.

Once again I came out and took the mickey out of the proceedings. I opened with something like, 'Sorry, ladies and gentlemen, my act tonight was going to be axe throwing, but

I had a bit of practice out the back and, anyway, act number three won't be appearing tonight.'

One of the judges had his own restaurant that he sang at, so I asked him if it was the only place where he could perform without getting fired. I remember also telling one of the catty, arrogant judges at one of my three appearances (they blend a bit into one in my mind), 'You're such a lightweight the automatic doors at the supermarket won't open until someone with more substance comes along.'

Anyway, I finished talking and, with the anticipation high, I ran across the stage as fast as I could and drove my head right into the thunder box. I then claimed the sound it made was in A flat. It was stupid, but so was I.

Unfortunately, or luckily, there are no recordings of my *New Faces* appearances. They were all in black and white and, in those days, videotape was expensive, so they'd just re-record over it for the next show.

While I don't think what I did was that funny, it was outrageous at the time that someone like me would be on the idiot box in my work clothes, rabbiting on, among beautifully presented singers and musicians and people who really could tap-dance. To go on there and take the piss out of the judges was the sort of thing that a lot of people probably wanted to do, but never had.

Unsurprisingly, I didn't win that time. I came second to someone playing a cello, or something with strings, and I was sort of relieved. I thought, *Finally, that's the end of this silly nonsense.* And back I went to my normal world. Back to Noelene and the kids, back to my mates on the Bridge – and more than happy about it.

The New Faces talent show has discovered some worthy television performers, the latest of which seems to be Sydney comedian Paul Hogan.

RIGGER WITH

~~PERSONALITY~~ OF THE WEEK

A VIEW

PAUL HOGAN FINDS HEIGHT HELPS HIM TO THINK

A rigger on the Sydney Harbor Bridge, Paul captured public interest when he first gave television viewers a taste of his dry, self-written Strine humor on New Faces.

He moved up into the final of Australia's New Faces and dressed as a dinkum garbage man he once again won the judges' favor when he sent them up in his disarmingly natural manner

The Nine network must have spotted the potential. Since the New Faces final he has appeared twice on A Current Affair and once on Stuart Wagstaff's Tonight show.

This week GTV-9 announced that Paul will be seen regularly on A Current Affair (week-nights at 9.30 p.m.) to comment on topical social issues when humor is required.

The show's producers say Paul will be used as a television cartoonist in the verbal sense, and he will be used "as often as a newspaper cartoonist."

Paul had never appeared publicly or on television before he performed on New Faces and apart from being very funny, he brings a refreshing ethnic touch to the comedian's role.

It may be to early to speculate, but he could be ripe material for grooming as a compere for a Nine show.

Poor and famous.

But once again, the public interfered with my life. Apparently, after my Melbourne appearance, the switchboard didn't just light up, it caught fire. People rang from all over the place wanting to see even more of the weird comedy guy.

Again, I had no way of knowing any of this, but when I walked down off the Bridge on the Monday afternoon there was a camera crew at the pylon, waiting to interview me. A guy named Mike Willesee had just started up a new half-hour show called *A Current Affair*, and he'd asked one of his reporters to talk to this novelty performer who'd caused a ruckus at the switchboards of his station, Channel 9.

The guy he'd sent was Tony Ward, a well-known actor who played a secret agent in the hit television show *Hunter*. He'd left acting to work as a producer-reporter on *A Current Affair*. I suppose I should have been all respectful, but when he stuck a microphone under my nose and hit me with questions, I just started talking … and talking.

The funny thing is, I didn't realise back then that you could stop filming and later edit the shot. It had never occurred to me. I thought once they started filming that was it. So, we were under the Bridge and I could see a train coming from a long way off, and I thought, *Shit*, and started talking faster and faster to get through the interview before the noise hit.

Anyway, despite this, and the fact that I ignored all of Ward's questions and did nothing but take the mickey out of him and his preened-for-television hair, they put the interview to air that night in late November 1971.

A few days later I was back on the Bridge and got another shout from the office. Someone was after me again. This time it was the Willesee guy himself, and he wanted to meet me.

I thought, *What now?*, but agreed to drop into Channel 9 on my way home from work.

Mike Willesee was a bit younger than me, and had apparently captured 2 million viewers for his new show. *A Current Affair* did a lot of serious stuff: politics, union disputes, feminism and the Vietnam War, where lots of young Australians were fighting. And Willesee admitted to me that his show wasn't really interested in who was doing well on *New Faces*. But the reason he'd sent Tony Ward to the Bridge was to do a sneaky job interview. 'What we've been looking for is a working man who can give his opinion on particular items that turn up in the news,' Willesee said. 'We tried an actor or two, but it didn't really work. You are obviously a working man, and obviously a little strange. Would you do that, you know, on your way home from work from time to time?'

He said they could ring me at the Bridge during the day and give me a subject. It might be the Queen's birthday or the price of beer, or some union problem or whatever. If they did that, could I stand in front of the camera after work and give an opinion?

'Oh, yeah, I've got opinions on everything,' I replied. And I did.

'I'll gladly pay you,' he said. 'It'll be the equivalent of about a day's pay.'

Bloody hell, I thought, *that's all right, and it's only going to take me a few minutes.*

That's how it started. I'd be at work on the Bridge and every now and then they'd ring me. Nobody had mobile phones, so one of the boys would just sing out from below that Willesee had called, and the subject was *blah blah blah*. At the end of the day, they'd have a camera out in the yard at Channel 9's Willoughby headquarters and I'd turn up in my work gear, often filthy dirty, look straight down the barrel of the lens, and give whatever galah opinion I had on that particular day.

It resonated with viewers because I was no different from most of those watching the show. I was just another joker from the real world. A punter. I knew what it was like to be struggling to pay the rent or to have five open bottles of milk in the fridge and exactly one pint of milk divided between them. I was used to having wet nappies hung up around the house because it was raining outside, and having kids that ate like starving steel workers. I couldn't get up from the table, cos when I'd come back, half my tea would be missing.

After I'd dispensed my words of wisdom, they'd give me $30, and off I'd go. It was only going to be an occasional thing, but it was a nice little top-up to my wage. In fact, in those days, $30 wasn't the equivalent of a day of *my* pay as Willesee had said it would be. It actually took me nearly two days to earn that much. So it was pretty cool.

The only person who wasn't happy was Mum. 'Why don't you dress nice?' she said. 'Other people dress nice on television. You go on there in your torn shirt.'

6

Enter Strop

On *A Current Affair* I was billed as 'The Man on the Street'.
There was no script, no rehearsal and sometimes they
would change the chosen subject at the last moment. Then I'd
only have a few minutes to prepare.

I was lucky because I never got nervous. Not then, not
since. Of course I worried about the wellbeing of my kids
and family like everyone else and sometimes got a bit nervous
on their behalf before one of their big occasions, but one
thing I never lost sleep over was my career. I was bulletproof,
because I never really had anything to lose. Showbiz was
never the most important thing to me. That's been the gift
of my life.

Anyway, from December 1971 onwards I produced comedy spots for *A Current Affair* as a sideline to my main gig as a rigger. It was a good little earner for me, and they thought themselves pretty lucky too.

'I just couldn't find an Australian actor who could play an ocker,' Willesee later wrote about the sheer coincidence of exactly the sort of bloke they were looking for turning up, out of the blue, at exactly the right time. 'It was as if anybody who'd ever been to drama school had had the Aussie vernacular ironed out of them. Even the ones with working-class roots couldn't seem to get it back.'

With such a big ready-made audience, I quickly became popular. After just two or three appearances, *The Age* newspaper in Melbourne declared me 'Personality of the Week'. I had to love their quote: 'Paul had never appeared publicly or on television before *New Faces* and apart from being very funny he brings a refreshing ethnic touch to the comedian's role.'

A Current Affair was produced in this old cottage within the Channel 9 complex at Willoughby. We'd film in the yard, except when it was raining. Then we'd be inside the cottage in front of this ugly two-tone plastic sofa.

I started to get a bit inventive. For one piece I decided that, rather than just having me talk to the camera, it would be better to have a conversation with someone else. That someone had to be like a friend of The Man on the Street, but not very bright. That was important because I never came over as very bright, and I wanted someone who was even dumber so I could get this particular point over.

'Do you have any actors here?' I asked.

'No,' Willesee said. 'But one of the producers of the show,

With Mike Willesee and *A Current Affair* producer John Cornell – soon to be known by all as 'Strop'.

John, does this Marlon Brando impression. I think he got it from *The Godfather.*'

That producer was John Cornell. He was about twenty-eight and was a good-looking, dapper sort of guy, so it didn't seem promising. He put a cap on and stuck his jaw out to distort his face, and started talking. 'I don't see Marlon Brando there,' I said. Nevertheless, he had a good dopey way about him, so I said, 'Yeah, he'll do.'

We decided that his name would be Darryl, but everyone would call him Strop, or Stropper, because in Australian slang that meant a wanker. So from then on, whenever I'd do a little piece that needed more than just me, I'd get John to put a hat on and help.

When I started, my gig on *A Current Affair* was supposed to be maybe once a fortnight. But then it was once a week, then twice a week or more – if they could get me to do it. Within weeks I went from being a totally unknown, mind-your-own-business rigger to, well, kind of famous.

This was becoming awkward because *A Current Affair* was a national show and hugely popular. And, for the audience, it was a great novelty that this guy who worked on the Harbour Bridge would pop up and talk about everything like he was an expert.

It was around this time that I realised that being rich and famous might be pretty cool: you could come out of the theatre after a show, sign a few autographs, wave, then get in your limo and off you went. But poor and famous, wow, that really sucked. I'd be on TV on Thursday night, then Friday morning on the train going to work with my audience – and my critics. There'd always be some prawn saying, 'Hey, you're Hoges, I saw you on TV last night. You know what you should've said …'

A few months earlier if I was in a pub and there were a couple of guys staring at me I'd be up and ready to take them on. But now it would happen and I'd be on my feet about to thump some guy when suddenly I'd remember, 'Oh, he might have just seen me on the telly, I'd better sit back down.'

It takes a bit of time to get used to being a recognisable head. One time I was in some odds-and-ends store and two women in their fifties, who I'm sure were quite lovely, came and stood staring at me, only inches from my face. And by 'inches' I mean I could feel their breaths on my neck. After a moment I sort of smiled and said, 'Can I help you?'

'No, we're fine,' one of them said.

'We're just having a gawk at ya,' the other added.

And that's what they did. For the next five minutes. They followed me around the store and then one of them cheerily said, 'Okay, we've had our gawk. See ya later.' And they left.

Eventually this started to wear a bit thin. There was another problem too. People driving across the Bridge would be gazing up, looking for the joker off the telly and … *bang!* Happened more than once. Not a good thing. So the Bridge people weren't happy with it either. I remember looking down at the harbour and out to sea from my amazing vantage point on the Bridge and thinking, *Yep. Enough. Time to give it away.* The next day I rang Mike Willesee and said, 'It's all become too silly. Sorry, but I'm not going to do your show any more.'

• • •

The powers that be at Nine weren't happy with me quitting. John Cornell, who was still a producer and my occasional sidekick, explained to me one day that while my segment might not be very important to me, it was becoming increasingly important to them, because whenever I was on, the ratings went up. In those early days I'd only see John briefly when I ducked into Nine and he was in Sydney (he was mainly Melbourne-based at that stage). But on this occasion he sat me down on that two-tone plastic sofa in the *Current Affair* cottage.

'Look, just answer me a couple of questions,' he said. 'Everything you do here, it just comes off the top of your head?'

'Yeah,' I said.

'Do you think everything in the world's funny?'

'No. Just the people.'

John smiled and started to nod. 'You should have your own show.'

I just laughed. 'I'd have no idea how to do that.'

But he was insistent. He said, 'We can work it out. You and me, between us, we can do it! It'll be fun.' John was sophisticated and slick. Not the type of person I'd worked with on any of my other jobs. I liked him but wasn't sure if I could fully trust him. 'Just keep thinking about the funny side of the things you see, whether it's on television, in real life, on the news or whatever,' he said, 'and we can get it into script form.'

I thought it was a mad suggestion. But this bloke's enthusiasm and faith in me, and the lure of my own show somewhere down the track, were enough to convince me to stay on at *A Current Affair*. I gave my notice at the Bridge. If it wasn't for John Cornell and that chat, I would probably have spent the rest of my life up there.

John and I were about the same age, but he had lived a totally different life. He was born on the other side of the continent, in Kalgoorlie, the elder son of a tough, Depression-era father. He had a compelling drive to succeed from the get-go, and huge self-confidence. He was the London editor of the *West Australian* newspaper when he was about twenty-two.

He was far more worldly than me, but still had an earthy sense of humour. And, I would soon learn, he was an absolute larrikin and a tough little rooster. He would have a go at anything or anybody, completely fearless. And John saw far more potential in me than I ever did.

7

Doctors Recommend

My comedy spots on *A Current Affair* were starting to gain a lot of attention, and various offers from the advertising world started to appear. To begin with they were just little things, here and there: a local mechanic or a small construction company. Still, I was flattered.

Mike and John, though, said I should hold out for the 'big hit' and it came within months. A bloke named Allan Johnston got in touch. He was a young copywriter at the Hertz Walpole advertising agency.

Allan thought I'd be ideal as the face for a television and print campaign for a new cigarette that Rothmans was launching. I liked Allan and his ideas. Back then, cigarettes were still good for you – you know, 'Doctors recommend Chesterfield' – so I didn't hesitate the way I would have done just a few years later. I signed up to launch this new brand called Winfield, and from the middle of 1972 I mixed meetings with Allan Johnston and his boss at Hertz Walpole, Jim Walpole, with my ever-larger duties at *A Current Affair*.

Cigarette advertising in the early 1970s was all exotic locales, jet-setting and ski resorts. Peter Stuyvesant was 'Your international passport to smoking pleasure'. Benson & Hedges used Stuart Wagstaff, with his clipped English tones, saying, 'When only the best will do'. And in keeping with all that, from August 1972 there I was, on television in a dinner suit, with the fifty-piece Sydney Symphony Orchestra playing Tchaikovsky in the background.

'G'day,' I began. 'I've been asked to talk to you, see, and being the suave, sophisticated man about town I thought I'd do the job with a bit of, you know, polish and a touch of class.'

The ad ended with me saying, 'Anyhow, have a Winfield', which introduced a completely new brand of cigarette. I'd cut the slogan back from what they originally wanted, which was 'Anywhere, anytime, anyhow, have a Winfield.' Just thought that was too much of a mouthful.

It's hard to imagine nowadays what a huge stir this ad caused. And the outrage wasn't about cigarettes, not at all. It was about the way I talked. Sure, an Australian working man's accent might have been heard on television before, but it had never been used to sell a product. It was considered a negative, not a positive. The television stations, the newspapers and talkback radio were immediately deluged with letters from angry people. I was lowering the tone of the whole country, apparently.

The people who weren't angry were the ones at Rothmans and Hertz Walpole. Even though they'd told me rather plainly at the start that 'the trade needs a new cigarette like a hole in the head', the forty-cents-a-packet Winfields were flying out the door. Within days of the ad first airing, I'd hear people saying, 'Anyhow, have a Winfield', and 'Let her rip, Boris, old son', which was a line I'd ad-libbed to the conductor behind me.

Winfield worked its way up to become the leading brand on the market, and it completely obliterated Tartan, the cigarette that W.D. & H.O. Wills had released two weeks earlier as their forty-cent competitor. The Winfield ads also led to a surge of 'ocker' advertisements for all kinds of products. Most of these failed, but the Winfield ads themselves went from strength to strength over the next few years. They were terrific, too, even if what they were selling wasn't. And I enjoyed them because I got to do all sorts of interesting stuff. I sailed yachts, rode horses, played concert-standard piano (okay, that involved a bit of trickery), swung on a trapeze wire, fenced, and dived off cliffs. In that last one, the skills developed at Granville pool were useful. In one ad I was to dive over a waterfall and into a river, and then Strop would dive in afterwards in a ham-fisted attempt to rescue me. I did my dive and, once everyone was happy, I stuck on Strop's gear and doubled for him.

But the best thing about the Winfield ads was the way they allowed me to spend more time with my younger brother. Pat was a happy-go-lucky bloke who'd left school early like me and pretty well everyone we knew. He'd become a sheet-metal worker and was bloody good at it. Tragically, though, when he was about twenty he was engaged to a lovely young nurse and she was killed in a car accident. Understandably this really shook Pat up and he decided to get away for a while. He moved to the United States and then settled in Canada.

When Rothmans was launching Winfield Blue, a milder cigarette, I had the idea of introducing Pat as the type of bloke who'd go for them. So they flew him out to Australia and we both got dressed up in blue dinner suits for the Winfield Blue TV, print and cinema ads. 'Meet me brother, Pat,' I told the audience, 'who likes stuff a bit more mild than me.'

We got into medieval get-up for a sword-fighting scene. That was the most memorable ad. At one stage it was me and Pat crossing swords against three others. As it turned out, two of them were stuntmen and the third was an over-excited extra. The extra rushed at me and stabbed me in the hand. His sword pierced my hand between my recently broken thumb and forefinger. I ended up with quite a few stitches and can still remember the pain.

Pat enjoyed the novelty and extra money from doing those ads and I loved him being involved. He never worried about anything. He was so low-key, great fun and easy to be around. He didn't get the acting bug but decided to move back to Australia anyway and I was able to introduce him to the construction guys at a movie theme park up on the Gold Coast, and they immediately signed him up. His talents with sheet metal saw him build sets for dozens of TV shows and movies. But every so often I was able to lure him away from the tools to appear with me in a new ad.

• • •

There was one Winfield ad in which we were doing aerobatics in a Pitts Special, a double-wing stunt plane. My pilot, Jim Scott, would sit in the seat in front of me and get us up there among the clouds for each take. But then, at a certain point, he would drop down low in his seat and pull a special sliding panel over himself that the TV people had made, so that he couldn't be seen. I would then turn on the camera and the sound gear and, looking like I was flying the plane by myself, do my spiel flogging the ciggies.

Then I'd go into a dive and while we were heading down towards the ground I'd pull the slide open and Jim would pop his head out and take back control of the plane. All went smoothly the first two or three takes. Then on the fourth one I pulled the slide back, he stuck his head out, saw where we were and simply went, 'Shit!'

When he said 'Shit!', I almost did. We were quite a bit closer to the ground than he thought we should be, and it was coming up fast! He pulled the plane out of the dive with the sort of G-forces that drag your stomach somewhere down between your ankles, and ultimately all was fine.

The director, the crew and the pilot kept telling me that the Pitts Special was the finest stunt plane there was, that they never had accidents, and all that. I was pretty calm in the plane – well, most of the time – and generally didn't worry much about myself. But maybe I should have worried about the plane a bit more.

About six months after we shot those ads, the Pitts Special we used was smashed to pieces against the ground. Luckily the pilot bailed out and was okay. But, sadly, a few months after that, Jim Scott crashed a different plane into the ground and

Loving being a dad. With Clay, Noelene, Brett, Loren and Todd.
Two more kids were yet to appear.

died. It was all supposed to be so safe, but the plane and the pilot were both gone within the year.

Looking back, of course I regret my role in flogging cigarettes, even if it was the 1970s, and even if I myself did smoke the things. Within a few years they were putting ever bigger health warnings on the cigarette packets and the ads, and I was less comfortable with the whole thing. And if I'd known what I know now, I never would have promoted or supported the awful things. I had too many young fans to be selling cigarettes, to be dealing drugs.

• • •

According to Hoges ...

A Day at the Races

I've had some terribly embarrassing times. When I first had some success, I fell into one of the biggest traps in show business, and that's believing your own publicity. I went down to Port Augusta once. I had to go down there for a charity race meeting. I was supposed to present the Jack the Slasher Cup, raise money for the hospital and all this sort of thing.

When I got down there I found I'd been entered in a horse race for amateur riders, though even being referred to as an amateur rider was probably overstating my abilities. As a kid I'd ridden draught horses that lived in a paddock down the end of our street, but they never moved faster than a steady stroll. I thought the race was going to be a bit dicey, but the secretary of the race club came up and said, 'Well, listen, I knew it'd be all right because I've seen those Winfield ads, with you riding a bucking Bronco and sticking to that horse like chewing gum to a blanket.'

'Umm ... yeah,' I said. 'Put me on whatever nightmare you've got and I'll ride it.' Suddenly my big mouth had me climbing up on this little grey bag of bones I think had just escaped from the knackery. The race began and we jumped out of the starting gates and everyone was all sidewards and backwards. They were all mugs in the saddles and inside the first twenty yards two riders hit the dirt. I was happily bouncing along at the back of the field with nothing to lose, so, just to keep my horse awake, I decide to give the bag-of-bones a couple of gentle taps. Well, I suddenly found out how it had got away from the knackery! This little thing could run like a hairy goat. In the twinkle of an eye, I'd passed most of the field and there was only one horse left in front of me with a hundred yards to go. *This is terrific*, I was thinking. *'The Man from Snowy River'* rides again.

I really scrubbed this thing along and about four or five lengths from the winning post it was obvious to everybody that I was not only going to win this race but was also going to win it right on the line! It was real hero stuff and a big roar went up from the crowd. Naturally, I rose up on my stirrups to acknowledge the waves and cheers of my adoring fans – then I shot up over the nag's head, did a somersault with a half twist, and ended up hanging underneath the horse's belly. And that's how I crossed the finish line. I got second place because they figured I was still in contact with the horse. Well, it did have one of its hooves in my mouth.

I continued doing my *Current Affair* gig through 1972, plus the Winfield ads and quite a few other things, including a tour of pubs with Tim Connor, a really good Irish singer I'd met through *A Current Affair*. He sang, I talked.

It was a period of transformation. Gough Whitlam's Labor Party was odds-on favourite to take government in the December election. We'd had twenty-three years of very conservative Liberal government. There was a lot of bottled-up energy and Gough was promising huge changes.

Meanwhile, I was busier and more famous than I could have believed possible. I was receiving bags of fan letters and even got an invitation to get my kit off as the centrefold in the new *Cleo* magazine ('I'm not egotistical enough to think I'd turn anybody on,' I told the media, though that may just have been modesty), and to appear at universities to speak on 'Australiana or a subject of my own choice'. There was an R-rated film someone wanted me in. I said no because it could have killed my family appeal immediately and wasn't really my thing. There was also a Crawford Productions television series, but that would have taken up all my time.

But not everyone was on board. Plenty of viewers wrote in saying I was boring and talentless and a yob and was giving Australians a bad image. Such people wanted us to be third-rate imitation Poms or Americans, presumably. They certainly wanted to pretend that the basic Aussie labourer didn't exist. But he did. And I was one of them.

With all this activity, I'd gone from making $70 a week to, well, a great deal more than that. With the top tax rate at 66 percent, I wasn't nearly as rich as the tabloids claimed, but I was able to go straight from renting a small and rundown home in Chullora, way out in the Western Suburbs, to buying a big house in Mosman, in what those same tabloids called 'the Riviera end of the North Shore'. Mosman overlooks Sydney Harbour and was, and still is, a desirable address. I'd really only seen it from up high on the Bridge. But my mum lived in Dee Why and my sister was in Manly and the Channel Nine studios were nearby, so I thought it would work well.

Some people thought my living in Mosman meant I was no longer a 'man of the people', but I thought otherwise. When people win the lottery and then say, 'I'll still keep my job and nothing will change, I'll live in the old house,' I always think, *Take the money back off them! Give it to someone who will enjoy it!* If you win the lottery, make the most of it.

Noelene and I certainly took to this more scenic part of the world, but I think moving may have been a little harder on the kids. And we now had five of them following the arrival of Scott, or Scotty. While we were obviously still in the same city, their mates' houses were no longer just a block or two away. And settling into new schools is always hard, but it's even harder when your dad's on the telly.

I remember Todd coming home one day and telling me that his new teacher had made him stand up in front of the whole class and told him, 'You won't be treated any differently here just because your dad's well known.' Obviously the poor bugger was already being treated differently. But they were an amazing bunch of kids and, before long, all seven of us had settled into our new environment. I guess it helped too that my act was popular with kids. I was effectively a nice guy on telly and wasn't doing too much that would embarrass them in front of their classmates.

Generally I didn't make too many stupid decisions with my newfound money, but I did replace the nine-year-old station wagon with a bright orange Charger, the sporty two-door Valiant. Probably not the smartest buy for a man with so many kids, so it didn't last very long.

Meanwhile, with John Cornell being John Cornell, he fairly quickly convinced Channel 9 to back his crazy idea that this Hogan bloke should have his own show. But first, I had a rock concert to appear at.

The Wider World

Things were changing really quickly in the early 1970s. Youth culture was the big thing. Sex, drugs, rock 'n' roll and all that. No surprise then that Australia had a few attempts to create its own Woodstock, which is to say, a giant outdoor music festival where everyone camped out over a long weekend. The biggest took place in Sunbury, on the outskirts of Melbourne.

The first Sunbury Festival was in 1972. For the second, held in January 1973, Channel 9 decided they wanted me to go there and do a bit of mock coverage for television and also MC the event. It was big. We ended up with something like 30,000 late-teenagers and twenty-somethings sprawled out across the paddocks. There was a lineup of twenty-five bands or more, and it was definitely the scene to be at in Melbourne that summer. And of course this was the early 1970s and Australia was really, really into dope. Or grass, as they also called it. All weekend there was a permanent dense cloud of the stuff throughout the whole valley, so much of it that everyone was stoned whether they were smoking it or not. At times the security, and even the cops, just stood around giggling.

For me, this was a whole new experience on a number of fronts, and I was learning as I went in front of this simply massive crowd! Talk about a baptism of fire. They were all in their hippy gear – or nothing much at all – while I was in my stubbies and sleeveless shirt. The whole crowd was so stoned that I'd go out and say something funny and then would have to wait two and a half minutes for the laughter to stop. Even if the gag was mediocre. I started thinking I was the funniest man in the world. *I just said this and, look, they're still laughing!* I'd walk over and have a chat with the drummer. And walk back and say the next line.

Anyway, the Australian headliner was Johnny O'Keefe. Johnny was a legendary old-time rock 'n' roller. He'd been a huge star when I was a teenager: the first local rocker to top the charts, the first to tour America, an amazing showman. But he was thirty-eight years old and now found himself having to compete with Madder Lake and Blackfeather and all sorts of current prog and heavy metal bands that the younger audiences were into.

When Johnny appeared the crowd started laughing and booing. They didn't want him there because to them he was so un-hip. I was upset by this because Johnny was such a classic

Making it up as I went along in front of 30,000 stoned festival goers.
The giggling never stopped.

hellraiser. It probably didn't help that his backing band – which was really a rock group – was called the Eden Park Orchestra. That wasn't what this Sunbury audience was looking for.

Fortunately, whenever I went on, they would listen to me because I was the only one making jokes. So, I went up there and sort of made fun of Johnny as though he was a struggling amateur. I said, 'I've been working with this young man in his tent, and he's trying to get it together.'

Even though I was like the crowd in most ways, I was in my thirties, which made me a senior citizen there. So I would talk to them like I was one of their parents, and they thought it was hilarious. At one point a completely out-of-it and entirely topless young woman jumped up on the stage with me. 'I'd appreciate it,' I said through the microphone, 'if the parents of this poor lost boy would come around the back of the stage to claim him.'

Later that day I took to the microphone again and in my most parental voice said, 'Listen up. I've been talking to the police and they told me there was a lot of highly illegal *mari-juana* here. But, I have promised the police and your parents that I would do my best to put a stop to this. So, here's your big chance. If you've got illegal *mari-juana* down there, outside Johnny O'Keefe's tent there is a 44-gallon drum. And if you drop your *mari-juana* in there, the police will not arrest you. No one will say anything. And me and Johnny O'Keefe will see that it is all burnt. And we will all be in the clear.'

Everyone was falling about laughing. All those youngsters who thought they were so hip and cool, just because they were smoking a bit of weed. Anyway, after all that, Johnny O'Keefe finally came on and did his old-fashioned 'Shout' and 'Wild

Child' and that kind of standard rock. And despite the fact that the younger, so-called hipper crowd didn't want to know at first, eventually they couldn't resist JOK's classic energy and he absolutely killed them! He was terrific, the highlight of the whole turnout.

I also had an interesting encounter with a bunch of 'Bovver Boys'. This subculture was picked up from England and didn't last long in Australia. They were basically hooligans with shaved heads and hobnail boots who loved to cause trouble. They were out in force at the festival and at one point about thirty of them came to the back of the stage.

'We want to see Hoges,' they demanded.

'What the hell for?' someone in security asked.

'Just tell Hoges to come out here and give us a wave at the back of the stage.'

So I walked out the back and waved, and suddenly they all roared and yelled, 'Good onya, Hoges!' I realised they were all looking and pointing at my boots. In those days I was still wearing my big hobnail boots from the Bridge with my footy socks and so, as far as they were concerned, I was one of them. It was terrific. The security all suddenly started to relax and the Bovver Boys continued to wave and say, 'We love ya, Hoges, yer wearing our boots!'

It was a wonderful experience, Sunbury. All those people were so laid-back and blissful because of the permanent cloud. Even with the Bovver Boys, there were no fights, no brawls, during the whole festival. It was just a giant ad for dope.

Those were the good old days, when drugs just made everybody laugh and fall about and giggle. Gradually in the seventies in Melbourne, drugs turned into horse tranquillisers, and when people got stoned, they just got boring. But that summer of January 1973 was magic. It was our Woodstock.

. . .

Our TV idea was pretty simple: a travel show in which 'Hoges' would travel to other countries and do his thing. Channel 9 agreed to put up the money, with the idea that John would produce and we'd go on the road, first to Singapore. I'd be meeting the locals, learning new customs and habits and generally making good-humoured fun of the experience.

The Singapore show was called *Hogan Abroad* or 'How to Travel Overseas without Makin' a Mug of Yourself' and to be honest, I totally just winged it. I didn't really know what I was doing. I just had blind faith in John Cornell's judgement.

We wandered around and took in all the odd things Singapore had to offer. I danced with a snake and ate all types of crazy food I'd never seen or heard of before, even though Strop had thoughtfully brought fourteen sandwiches to save us from the perils of local cuisine. We went to temples and the Tiger Balm Gardens and generally had fun, although one night we visited Bugis Street to film the Billie Boys, who were the famous transgendered dancers of what was popularly called 'Boogie Street'.

They came to this big open-air restaurant and paraded around and we caught it on film. They saw us and decided they wanted to charge us. We paid some of them something, but then others kept coming and started asking for money too. Corney, never one to be bullied, told them to go jump, and suddenly we were approached by the Tong, the local organised

This TV caper is not too bad. Filming in Singapore.

crime outfit. They started appearing all around us and looked threatening, to the extent that I lifted the camera tripod over my head, ready to whack people. Our cameraman, Greg Hunter, had his camera ready to belt people too.

Then the Tong, having circled us, started to move in. There was a mob of British Royal Navy guys there. 'Are you Aussies all right?' they yelled out. 'Do you need a hand?'

'No, we're all right,' we called back, 'but thanks.'

It was probably a stupid thing to say, but luckily, at that moment, our driver came in and translated and begged and made it all go away. I'm not exactly sure what he said, but I was loving every moment! It was, after all, not only the first time I'd filmed something like this, but also the first time I'd ever been overseas, and it was first class! I'd gone from crowded trains and cut lunches to large reclining seats and plenty of money almost overnight – without that striving period in between.

Looking back, that Singapore show probably wasn't great, but it rated very well and Nine agreed to another. We made a much better fist of our second effort, *Hogan in London*. It was my first trip to my ancestors' old country and I quickly realised that the great city of London was ripe for the taking by two wise-cracking Aussies.

We had an absolute ball. Warren Mitchell did a bit for us as Alf Garnett and was very funny. We even had Germaine Greer come along and do a sketch as Strop's sister. There she was, the ultimate intellectual feminist with her jaw stuck out, dressing down Strop like a big sister: 'I'm sorry Darryl, I'm going to have to tell Mum.'

Something even funnier: afterwards, John and I went to this large, posh restaurant in Soho with Germaine and a lot of pretentious people. There was this rather annoying Irish poet sitting opposite me. He'd had a skinful and he was spouting away, making disparaging remarks about Australians.

This got right up my nose. I said, 'What did you just say then, dickhead?'

He started to reply but before he got a whole sentence out, Germaine, who was sitting next to him, just went *whack* and backhanded him clean off his seat and down onto the floor.

'I just saved you from a vicious beating,' she said. 'So just shut your mouth and get back on your chair.'

'Ah, okay,' he meekly replied. And he bloody well did. He didn't move and hardly spoke for the rest of the night.

On another night, we all went into this popular Aussie pub in London. When we were leaving, a lot of Australians were watching me and Germaine. So as we were walking away down the street I put my arm around her and immediately she put her hand on my bum – knowing we were being watched. She was great, a real stirrer with a wicked sense of humour. I love Germaine.

So now we'd made two travel shows, but in between them, there'd been an almighty ruckus. After Singapore was screened, Clyde Packer summoned us to a meeting.

Now the Packers not only owned the Nine Network but also newspapers and magazines and were among the richest people in Australia. The patriarch, Sir Frank Packer, had handed control of the family business to Clyde in 1970, having decided that he, the eldest son, was smarter than his brother, Kerry. So although he was fairly new to the job, Clyde was running the Packer empire and the Nine Network. And he was a really big man, probably weighed three hundred pounds in the old money. That's over 135 kilograms. And Clyde used to wear kaftans. It was the 1970s and a lot of big fat guys wore kaftans.

Anyway, we turned up at Clyde's office and had only just walked in the door when he started ranting about how our latest show was over budget. He started accusing John of being either an incompetent producer or of pocketing some of the production money.

John most certainly wasn't guilty on either front. Though with all the travel and accommodation costs and with John being very generous and always making sure the crews were well taken care of, both financially and with meals and drinks and so on, there wasn't a lot left over at the end of the day.

Big Clyde then started poking his finger, trying to make his point. And I was just watching this argument between Clyde and John get hotter and hotter. They were standing very close, face to face in fact, and Clyde's poking finger was getting closer and closer to John. By now, I knew John well enough to realise this wasn't good, and I thought, *Any minute now that finger's going to land and this is going to end up in an almighty blue.* The thing too was that although John had boxed as a teenager (thirteen wins, two losses), he was a bantamweight, whereas Clyde was like André the Giant. I thought, *I can't let this happen.*

My John Wayne gene kicked in and I rushed in real close to Clyde, thinking to myself, *I'm just getting started in my new career on television and here I am about to thump the guy that owns the whole network.* But it was unavoidable. Or so I thought.

Before I could throw a punch, John grabbed Clyde by the shirt front and dragged him right across the room and shoved him hard against the wall. It was the bantamweight against the super-heavyweight champion, but the bantamweight was going for it! Clyde, a rich powerful magnate, wasn't used to anyone manhandling him and didn't know what to do.

'That's an effing lie, take it back,' John said.

Clyde sort of mumbled an apology.

'Louder! I didn't hear you!' said John. By now Clyde was starting to slide down the wall with John still holding his shirt front. Instead of thumping Clyde, I had to restrain John! I pulled him off, and we left the office.

From then on, somewhat unsurprisingly, John was wiped. Clyde and Mike Willesee told me that I was still welcome at Channel 9, but not John. I probably surprised them a little because I said, 'Nah, if John leaves, I'm going with him.'

They told me I was mad. They told me it'd be the end of my career. But John had always stuck up for me, and staying loyal to him was worth more than any promised new contract from the Packers and Nine.

• • •

John, who may have also been surprised that I left too, said, 'Nine's not the only network.' And we ended up over at Channel 7 mid-1973 with our London tapes, which we owned (John was smart like that!), and a new contract. In August, *Hogan in London* appeared on Channel 7 and rated hugely.

Our new station was delighted, but they said what they really wanted was us in the studio. They wanted a regular sketch comedy show, something that was vastly more ambitious than anything we'd done so far.

John sat me down. 'Do you think you could write sketches?' he asked.

I really didn't know the answer. The only things I'd written since I'd left school were kids' lunch orders on brown paper bags – oh, and that letter to *New Faces*. Writing things down wasn't really my thing. Until this point, I'd just walked in front of the camera and whatever came out came out. It worked in little snippets in the travel shows, but I could see it wasn't going to sustain thirty minutes or an hour in a studio.

John and I started to talk about what I thought was funny or what was happening politically or what was on television that I could send up. He would then have to virtually prod me with a cattle prodder, because I was such a lazy bastard, to get me to write this stuff down.

'What have you read? What books do you read?' I remember John asking.

'I read *The Merchant of Venice* at school. Nothing since. I read the paper but never read books.'

'Well, don't start now,' he said, 'If you suddenly start reading books, it might change the way you think. And the way you think is what's going to make us successful.'

That experience at the Sunbury Music Festival earlier in the year also had an influence. It made us realise that we could take the piss out of people and point out the funny peculiarities of Australians, but in an Aussie way, where we were all laughing at ourselves together and there was no malice.

A lot needed sending up, yet there was almost no Australian comedy on television. We had British and American comedy but nothing much homegrown. So, with John's guidance, I began to discover that I could sort out all this rubbish in my head and put it on paper after all. Bit by bit, I could build a whole comedy show made up of sketches and monologues.

Another bloke who had a huge influence on our show was a producer we knew at Channel 9 by the name of Jimmy Fishburn. Jimmy had worked on the travel shows and when we went to Channel 7 he decided to come with us. Jimmy was also the producer of 'Les Girls', the famous drag show in Sydney, and when he joined us he said he would be in charge of 'tits and feathers'. He was a true showbiz guy and he really taught us how to do all the stuff we had no idea about, like how to structure things and put a full hour of comedy and variety together. We simply couldn't have done the show without Jimmy.

The Paul Hogan Show was launched in November 1973. It would have been earlier if I hadn't had an emergency appendectomy in Mosman Hospital just after the London show went to air. Anyway, the new sketch show, believe it or not, rated really, really well and drew encouraging reviews.

That first year brought such skits as 'Pierre Hogan on Aussie restaurants', 'Picking up a sheila for Strop', 'Australian sex habits on film', 'Teaching the Chinese to play Aussie Rules', and the regular appearance of Luigi the Unbelievable, an appallingly bad magician who became one of my best known characters. In one episode Luigi took up knife throwing.

Our guests included such actors as Rebecca Gilling, Noel Brophy and Leonard Teale, and the singers Stevie Wright, Marcia Hines and good ol' Johnny O'Keefe. There were sports stars too. We had the Socceroos on in mid-1974, to celebrate them participating in the soccer World Cup finals.

Along with producing our show, John was now officially my manager. I say 'officially', but we never had any sort of contract, we just shook hands. Yep, this bloke I'd first met courtesy of his absolutely awful *Godfather* impersonation, and hadn't known whether to trust, was now not only my manager but also my co-writer, subeditor, chief motivator and best friend. And separate to that, 'Strop' had already become something of a legendary Australian character in his own right.

John had two rules. The first concerned quality. 'If we make anything, let's make it well,' he said. The other rule was, 'Let's never do anything that's just for money. It has to also be fun.'

And it was fun. We cruised along happily at Channel 7, and became a lot more organised. We had to deliver a studio show every month, which took a lot of planning and also meant we had to do a lot of writing. Or, more alarming for me, I had to do a lot of writing. But I was actually enjoying every moment.

I never took any of it for granted, though. I kept my union ticket, my rigger's certificate and my crane driver's ticket all current, just in case someone came up and tapped me on the shoulder and said, 'You shouldn't be here on television. You're a construction worker. Go on, off you go.'

9

Frankie and the Drunk

It's hard to imagine today just how big a shock it was when I first arrived on television – with that accent! In Australia in the early 1970s everyone on the radio including all the DJs tried to speak with an American accent, whereas everyone on television, particularly newsreaders, tried to speak with what they thought was an English accent. Or a proper accent. So, it was like *Who's this yobbo, with the Australian accent? That's so uncouth!*

I reckon even people with accents that were worse than mine were appalled. In fact, I remember thinking that I had the exact same accent as the union leader Bob Hawke. But it was just the way I spoke and it's the way I still speak. I didn't put it on, or take anything off. I had a regular Australian accent. Yet to some this was horrifying.

Now, I've never been a darling of the critics and very rarely read reviews, but I remember early on that one of our Channel 7 shows got yet another damning write-up from a critic at one of the Sydney papers. I was okay with that, but when we read it aloud in the office it was obvious this clown hadn't even seen the episode he was heaping shit on – he critiqued a couple of things that were in one of the station promos, but not in our show. And that did annoy me.

Soon after, I was on the radio with the presenter Mike Gibson and he mentioned that review and how nasty it was. 'Come on Mike,' I said with a laugh, 'the guy's probably just some failed actor whose career hasn't worked out, so he makes himself feel better by dumping on others. I actually feel a bit sorry for him because, having read his review, he's certainly no writer either and, from what I hear, he also doesn't have a sense of humour and apparently can't even make his own wife smile.'

A week or so after that I got a very formal letter from some fancy law firm threatening to sue! They would only call off the proceedings if I went back on the radio show and apologised to the TV critic, and also paid for advertisements in the press in which I would say sorry and withdraw my critical statements. I thought this was pretty pathetic: a professional critic gets criticised and immediately calls his lawyer.

I told John about it, and he reached for the typewriter, saying we'd better respond.

'Nah, that's all right mate,' I said. 'I can do it.' With that, I grabbed the lawyer's letter and wrote 'GET FUCKED' right across it. I then stuck it back in the original envelope, marked it 'Return to Sender' and dropped it in a postbox.

Never heard from the critic or his fancy law firm again.

Then there was a journalist named Jimmy Oram, or James Oram if he needed to sound important. Early in my career he wrote a story for the *Daily Mirror*, one of the Sydney afternoon papers, which had the headline 'Get This Ugly Australian Off the TV'. A week later he saw me somewhere and came up to tell me how we were a great double act, with me new to the TV and him getting me all this publicity.

'I gave you a full page with a picture,' he said. 'It's the best thing that could happen to you.'

I didn't understand why he thought I should be pleased. He was a bloody weirdo and I wanted to thump him. In fact, Clyde Packer encouraged me to thump him, which made me a bit dubious.

One night I was with friends at a pub in the Eastern Suburbs and Jimmy Oram came strutting up to me like a cockroach in a top hat with this big grin on his face, expecting me to greet him like a long-lost mate. We talked – or maybe *he* talked – then he asked for a lift back into town. I don't know why we said yes, but on the way back we went past some cops who had pulled a motorist over. Oram wound down the window and yelled, 'Ya Gestapo bastards! Leave him alone!' He thought that was the funniest thing in the world, and when he wrote his next story, he said it was *me* that had wound down the window and yelled at the coppers.

Years later, Oram wrote a whole book about me, apparently often taking crazy things he'd done in his life and attributing them to me. I never bothered reading it.

• • •

Then there was the Frank Sinatra incident …

Ol' Blue Eyes did an infamous tour of Australia in July 1974 and had various run-ins with the local press. He told his Melbourne Festival Hall audience, after a few shandies I'm sure, that Australian female journalists were 'hookers'. 'I might give them a buck-and-a-half, I'm not sure,' he slurred.

This led to union bans that briefly prevented Cranky Frankie giving any concerts or even travelling within the country. When he finally left Australia, in a great huff, he vowed never to talk to another reporter as long as he lived. By coincidence I flew to London on the same plane as him. Sinatra snubbed the reporters, as he'd promised he would, but some journo had seen me boarding. 'We've got a man on the plane, his name's Hogan and he's in television,' the journo wired ahead to London. 'Knowing what he's like, he'll probably talk to Sinatra and can give you a story when he arrives.'

I knew nothing of this. And the reporter waiting for me in London knew nothing of me. He was sitting there waiting for a Mr Hogan, Television Journalist. But I'd discovered, a year or so earlier on my first-ever international flight, that the bars on planes are open twenty-four hours a day. So, when we landed in London, the first thing this man saw was a Mr Hogan, Television Journalist, Pissed as a Fart, staggering down the gangplank.

He rushed over to me and asked, 'Did you talk to Mr Sinatra, Mr Hogan?'

My head was spinning. I looked around and thought, *What?!*

'Did you talk to him?' he asked again.

'Did I talk to him?' I said. 'We only sang duets nonstop

between Hamburg and Frankfurt.' He started writing this down. I thought, *Bloody hell, I've got a live one on the line here.* 'Yeah,' I continued, 'as a matter of fact I was telling Frankie – oh, by the way, he likes that with an "ie" and not a "y" – I was telling Frankie that I'd noticed how his voice cracks on some of the slower numbers and that he should do what me and Johnny O'Keefe do: sing faster and louder and no one will notice.'

The guy nodded and lifted his pen. 'How did Mr Sinatra react to this advice?'

'Well, actually,' I said, 'he was thrilled about it. As a matter of fact, he asked me to join the Rat Pack and he wants me to work with him in the United States. He even said we'll probably end up doing a double act, Hogan and Sinatra. I said his name should go first but he insisted it be alphabetical.'

I went on like that then completely forgot about it. Two days later I got a telegram from the network back in Australia, saying, 'Congratulations on the big break', along with a copy of the front page of Sydney's *Daily Mirror* newspaper. Above separate photos of Frank and me, merged so it looked like we were arm-in-arm buddies, was the headline 'Hogan and Sinatra! U.S. tour talks'.

The article described how Frank and Hoges had really hit it off. On it went. And on, and on. All of page one and then onto page five.

Here's the truth. Frank and I did talk. Sorta. Just as I was coming out of the dunny, he was about to go in and Ol' Blue Eyes himself looked straight into my eyes and said, 'Ugh.'

That was it. The entire conversation between me and Frank. He effectively said, 'Get outta the way, stupid, I'm busting to go to the lav.' Great headline but.

HOGAN AND SINATRA!

U.S. tour talks

Frank Sinatra has shown interest in Paul Hogan's brand of ocker humor and will help him break into show business in the U.S.

This follows a chance meeting on the Qantas jet taking the Sinatra party to Britain.

Hogan and his manager, John Cornell, who plays Strop on television, were on the same aircraft as Sinatra.

Hogan said on his arrival in London today he spent a considerable time talking with the Sinatra party.

Hogan and Cornell are in London for talks with scriptwriter, Johnny Speight, the creator of Alf Garnett, with a view to doing a television series for the BBC. Hogan will fly to America from London.

What 'Oges thinks of Ol Red Eyes — P5

COBBERS . . . This is how Paul Hogan imagines his relationship with his new mate Frank Sinatra.

The best headline ever! If only it had been true.

• • •

Back in the 1970s, most people who were on television had started in theatre or clubs and worked their way up. I did the opposite. I was on telly but wanted to go off to some clubs and try stand-up. I wanted to know if I could make real punters laugh because I always had the suspicion that studio audiences would laugh at anything. I'd done the earlier pub gigs with the singer Tim Connor, but those had been small and low-key. And remember, talking to the crowd at Sunbury and at another huge rock concert I'd emceed in Brisbane didn't count. They were all off their tits.

So, in late 1974 I got booked into some clubs and pubs and put together a show. Interestingly, a lot of people seemed to think I was doing this new live tour so I could say all the things I wasn't allowed to say on television. They were wrong; there were never two versions of 'Hoges'. As I told the press at the time, 'I don't think you have to be blue. I think if you can't be funny without being smutty, you shouldn't be there at all.'

I mostly enjoyed it too. To get laughs because someone thought what I'd said was funny, knowing there was no sign telling them to laugh or clap, was a great thrill. And a relief in a way. It wasn't totally without incident, however. I remember being booked into a hotel in Melbourne. Before I went there, I was told it was a comic's graveyard: 'It's a rock pub and they want rock acts. They'll heckle the shit out of you and won't give you any time to be funny.'

I thought, *Well, that'll be good training.*

So I was doing my stand-up act and the place was chock-a-block. I soon realised it was also a well-known Melbourne bikies' club. Right down at the front there was this whole pack of toothless, mean-looking guys in leather. I kept doing my act and it was going over pretty well. Then some guy down there sitting among the bikies yelled out something. I had a comeback. I don't remember what it was, but it got a laugh and on I went.

But then he sang out again. I pulled out a second-level insult and thought, *That'll put him in his place*. But he hadn't finished. I'm thinking, *Geez, what have I got to say to this clown?* Then, *bang*, one of the bikies stood up, turned around and flattened him. Belted him something rotten. Now bleeding, the guy slowly came to and attempted to get up off the floor. Meanwhile the other bikie sat back down and said, 'Sorry, Hoges. Keep going.'

I tried, but it wasn't easy standing up there being funny while some poor bugger was writhing around on the floor with blood coming out of his mouth.

That was only the second-most off-putting experience in my early attempts at stand-up, however. Luigi the Unbelievable was perhaps the most popular character from our early TV episodes, so I decided to take him on the road. Luigi used his sister-in-law, Maria, as his assistant. The gag was that Luigi would do some sort of magic trick onstage then he'd say, 'Keep-a dancing, Maria,' and she would have to dance around to distract the audience from the fact that the magic trick had once again failed.

Maria, played by the wonderful Marion Edward, wore bad tutus and fishnet stockings with holes in them. She was not your classical ballet dancer. In fact, she wasn't really meant to be a dancer at all. Just Luigi's sister-in-law. It was just a tasteless, bad magician act.

Luigi the Unbelievable trades his magic tricks for a squeeze box.
Now it was the audience who wanted to disappear.

On this occasion in the club, Luigi was going to catch a bullet with his teeth while inside a large hessian bag. The gun was fired but, as always happened with Luigi, something went wrong and he was (supposedly) wounded. While he was lying there, groaning in pain, the stage hands ran out to drag the bag, with Luigi in it, offstage. As they were doing this, Luigi shouted from within the bag, 'Keep-a dancing, Maria.' Poor old Maria, as usual, had to dance around badly to cover up for his apparent misfortune – and allow me time to get Luigi's costume off.

I then headed back out onstage as Hoges and started talking about Luigi and how bad he was. But this time the audience were all just looking at me. No one was laughing.

I was thinking, *What the hell?* Then I looked down. Maria was laid out flat, moaning, with people gathered around her performing first aid. While I'd been in the wings, she'd pirouetted off the stage and fallen two and a half metres to the floor.

She'd broken her leg and was in enormous pain, yet I was still standing up there ignoring her completely and trying to be funny. People must have thought I was such an arsehole.

We took Dancing Maria to the hospital and she was there on a gurney in the corridor with her ugly, garish costume on, and her fishnet stockings with the big holes in them, saying, 'I'm a dancer.' People were going, 'Ah yeah … okay.'

Poor Maria.

10

Delvene Joins the Crew

We were into our second year at Channel 7. Over at Nine, Sir Frank Packer had recently died and Clyde Packer had wisely decided he wasn't the right guy to be running a media empire. He never had enough mongrel in him. He enjoyed the party life too much, and preferred having fun and supporting the arts, rather than sitting in boardrooms and chasing the dollar.

Despite our falling out, and Clyde's crook taste in kaftans, John and I both still liked him. Clyde was a big, soft, warm-hearted man. His brother Kerry wasn't, and Clyde had just sold all his shares to him. Although Sir Frank had always thought Kerry as bright as Clyde, he got that wrong. Kerry was smarter with money and more competitive and ruthless than Clyde and just about anyone else. Frank had been a legendary bombastic bully and Kerry had that in him in spades too. But Kerry also had a gruff charm and was desperate to take his television station to number one. So, soon after he took over, Kerry made a big offer to bring us back to Channel 9.

We accepted and our move was announced in September 1974, but Channel 7 contested it, saying we had agreed verbally to make more shows with them. It went to court and, as a result, we stayed at Seven. They were good years there, and the show (under all sorts of weird names, including *Paul Hogan – Anyhow, Have a Streak*) went from strength to strength and settled into a routine of monologues, sketches and musical acts.

We usually had two musical acts per show. Dozens of good singers and bands appeared, including Little River Band, Dr Hook, Dragon and Marcia Hines. We staged their songs elaborately and they loved it. I was actually driving along one day and heard Air Supply on the radio. I stopped the car and rang Jimmy Fishburn, who was producing the show with me then, and said, 'We need to get these boys on.' It turned out to be Air Supply's first-ever television appearance. It was a thrill to be a part of so much great music.

● ● ●

The Strop character famously wore a lifesaver's cap because he thought that would make him more attractive to women, but he was a perennial virgin and gormless nitwit. Most of the Strop sketches would be about Hoges trying to get him women, or trying to improve his lot in the world. People who

121

knew John thought this was hilarious because in real life he was good-looking and a terrible pants man. All over the place.

Anyway, in a memorable sketch from the 1970s, Strop announced to Hoges he had the perfect hangover cure. Strop called it 'the bomb' and made it up in a glass during the sketch. It started with a couple of fingers of room-temperature Foster's, a teaspoon of salt, a teaspoon of pepper, a dash of tomato sauce, a raw egg and an oyster, all stirred with a spoon dipped in Vegemite, and he was supposed to scull it all down. However, on a stool just behind the table, was a matching glass with a banana smoothie in it. It was the same size and colour as the horrible concoction he'd made, and John was supposed to do the switch. But, it turned out he was a method actor. He got so into doing Strop, that he forgot the switch and just drank the crap he'd concocted. He had iron guts.

● ● ●

The Paul Hogan Show

The Hangover Cure

Strop hovers over two large glasses. He pours some beer in them.

STROP: First of all, a dash of the hair of the dog (*Foster's beer*), room temperature.

HOGES (*watching*): It's flat.

STROP: Then, add about a teaspoon full of salt. A teaspoon full of pepper. Oh,

```
too much. I'll have that one. Then a
dash of tomato sauce. Raw egg. And an
oyster, mate. Then, hold it, me secret
ingredient.

HOGES: I get it. Go on.

STROP: Stir it with a spoon, dipped in
Vegemite.

HOGES: I know this, mate, the old gag,
right? You stir it up. You tip it down
the sink and you won't have a blocked
drain for six months, right?

STROP: No, mate. No, you drink it.

He chokes it down.
```

It was certainly unusual for a successful businessman to regularly come and make a goat of himself on television. But John's an extraordinary human being. In the hangover cure sketch, eternal virgin Strop was moping because he had no chance of winning the heart of a beautiful girl in a fur coat, who, after an outrageous party at Hoges's place, just happened to be lying unconscious next to him on the floor.

That girl was Delvene Delaney, from Geebung, in Queensland, where she'd been the local TV weather girl. After being declared Model of the Year in Queensland, she'd had a small star turn on a slightly racy soapie called *The Box*, then done a few other bits and pieces, including a daytime TV show called *High Rollers* and a film called *End Play*. I met her at a television function and said to John back in Sydney, 'Boy, have

Amazing eyes. Beautiful bone structure. And how gorgeous was Delvene!
(*Bauer Media Pty Ltd*/Women's Day)

I found the girl for you.' In early 1975 he finally met twenty-three-year-old Delvene and quickly offered her a role in our show. With no ulterior motives I'm sure …

As it turned out, Delvene was a terrific asset for *The Paul Hogan Show* (by now in colour too!). She quickly became a really important part of our lineup. She had great comic timing and, for someone as pretty as she was, no vanity. You'd often get a pretty girl saying, 'Oh, no, you gotta have the right angle or lighting.' With Dele, there was none of that.

As I predicted, John and Delvene were a match made in heaven! They hit it off immediately and were in love only days after I organised their introduction. But Delvene's mum was horrified when she announced she was dating Strop. 'What,' she said, 'that disgusting yob on the telly?' But, as we all knew would happen, Dele's mum changed her mind the instant she met John. Charming bugger.

The move to colour in early 1975 was interesting. Colour TV was such a novelty that the network had a colour consultant who would come onto the set to make sure we were making full use of it. 'Oi, you're not using any purple,' he'd say, and some assistant would have to run around trying to find a purple pillow or bunch of flowers. The whole colour wheel was expected to be represented at all times.

One of the worst, or possibly the best, pranks we ever pulled was in one of our earliest colour episodes. There was another very popular show at the time called *This Is Your Life*. This would involve a celebrity of some form, or maybe a veteran, being surprised at their place of work by the show's host and told that that night's episode would be dedicated to them. The guest and the presenter would then front up before a live studio audience and, through anecdotes, photos and video clips, go through the highlights of the guest's life. Sometimes an important person from their past would deliver a line from behind a screen, and the guest would have to try to recognise the voice. The person would then come out, surprising everyone and causing tears to flow. It was often an old teacher who had sage advice, or a football coach or an old boss.

Anyway, we heard that one of our crew knew Australian tennis great John Newcombe, who'd just beaten Jimmy Connors to win the Australian Open. I'd always loved Newk as a player and wanted to meet him, so we approached him with the ruse that I would be hosting a special episode of *This Is Your Life*. We said the network was keen to have the show appeal to a younger audience and felt the teaming of me along with Australia's brilliant tennis champion, him, would be a ratings bonanza. Newk, being a good bloke, agreed.

Without him knowing, one of our researchers, Shelly, got in touch with his parents. She found out what sort of car he used to drive, where he used to go and generally what he did as a teenager. The following week we got Newk in the studio and I said 'This Is Your Life' and he grinned, and probably felt a little silly about the whole thing, but we were underway.

'Now let's see if you can recognise this voice from your past,' I said to him about one minute in. The voice, which was offstage, was a young lady and she started to describe how Newk used to come and pick her up in his little blue Volkswagen, and how they used to get fish and chips, and he'd take her to Dee Why beach and it was there he declared she was the first girl he'd ever truly loved and that he would remember her until the day he died. Yet, sadly, they had drifted apart.

'Do you remember that voice?' I said to Newk, and he started to squirm.

'Er ... um ... um ... no.'

'Well, she's an old girlfriend of yours and she certainly remembers you.'

She then poked her head around the side of the set and waved at him.

'Do you recognise her now?' I asked. Newk still looked dumbfounded, so I added, 'Mate, it's Gloria!'

Of course, Newk had never seen or heard of her before. But he's a real gentleman and didn't want to embarrass her. He was looking at me like, *Shit, what do I do now?*

'Surely,' I said forcefully, 'you must remember Gloria.'

He was really pained now. 'I'm so sorry, but no, I don't.'

At this point a man in the audience stood up. 'You just humiliated my girlfriend!' he shouted. 'How dare you say you don't remember her?'

Gloria's 'boyfriend' – who was actually an actor we had planted in the audience – was now fuming with anger, and stormed up onto the set towards Newk.

Everyone was getting extremely nervous – except me. I waited until the angry boyfriend was only a few feet away, then stepped in front of him and threw a vicious left to his solar plexus.

He instantly fell face-down on the floor and began groaning and writhing in pain. Poor Newk was looking on, totally horrified. And I, without missing a beat, turned back to him and said, 'So, this next tournament, it seems like you might be coming back up against Jimmy Connors. How do you think you'll go?'

Newk was just staring at me like, *Are you completely insane?* But he was absolutely unable to say a word. He had been rendered completely speechless. Then the boyfriend on the floor rolled onto his back and started laughing and Newk smelt a rat. He was almost ready to attack me.

It was one of the funniest bits we ever did. Fortunately, Newk was not only a world-class tennis player, but also a world-class bloke and never held a grudge about this prank. In fact, many years later I ran into him in Las Vegas. He was there for a champions' tournament, and we both liked blackjack so we propped ourselves at a table in one of the casinos. When we walked out, the sun had come up. I was able to go to bed, but John had to go and play a championship.

He lost. And he blamed me. He told anyone who would listen that Hoges kept him up all night. I don't accept that blame because he might have lost at tennis but he won at blackjack. I didn't.

• • •

John and I had a TV production company and our office was in the Hertz Walpole building in Sydney. It was about as 1970s as a 1970s office could be. I know this because I recently found a description of it in an interview a *Women's Weekly* journalist did with me there: 'It's Seventies Executive, impressive. There is pale grey carpet, burnt orange curtains, fat brown corduroy velvet settees, a huge good timber desk with black leather chairs, small umbrella trees standing in Hong Kong baskets, telephones to match the carpets. I sank down in a black armchair and his secretary gave us coffee in fashionable stoneware cups.'

One day I was visited at that very office by a group of businessmen who'd been involved with the Variety Club in the United States. The Variety Club sounds like a social club for old tap-dancers or something, but it's one of the most successful children's charity organisations in the world. It had begun in the United States, among show-business people, and these guys now wanted to start a Variety Club in Australia. They asked me to be the founding president, known to them as the Chief Barker. Because their track record was so good, I agreed.

When you start a new charity, you have to get your bona fides out there, so everyone knows that you are on the up and up. Reg Watson, who was the driving force behind Variety Australia, as it became known, had a connection through his army service with Louis Mountbatten, who was an Earl, and Admiral of the Fleet, and had been a huge figure during World War II. He was also related to the Queen and Prince Philip and happened to be in Australia at that time. He agreed to become the royal patron of the club. Royal patronage granted immediate legitimacy and gave you a high standing in the fund-raising community.

We quickly organised a dinner for Lord Mountbatten at Government House. I was less than four years off the Bridge, yet found myself at this exclusive event, sitting right next to Lord Mountbatten himself. An odder couple never existed, me and him.

He started quietly questioning me about some of the jokes he intended to tell – 'Would this work here …?' – and generally running his act by me. In the end we decided to get up together and do a bit of a double act, playing up our different social levels. It went over gangbusters. I think people loved it because we were two people from such opposite sides of society.

At that dinner, in 1975, we raised $100,000, even though there were only about thirty people there. Back then, that sort of money would be enough to buy several good houses. So it got us off the ground. Variety Australia is now one of our most respected charities and gives out millions every year to underprivileged kids in various stages of grief. The fact I could play a small part in helping it get established in Australia is one of my proudest accomplishments.

Sadly, four years after my dinner and double act with Lord Mountbatten, he was assassinated by the IRA. They blew up his boat when he was holidaying in Ireland. It was at the height of The Troubles, as they call it in Ireland. I think it was a great loss.

• • •

In 1976, John Cornell, Delvene Delaney and I went to Hollywood for a scoping trip and to film a few 'Hoges in LA' bits for a Channel 7 special we'd agreed to do in the spirit of our early travel shows. We were staying at the Beverly Hills Hotel and one day I was walking down to the pool when I looked up and saw, climbing out of the water and heading back to the hotel, the man who had influenced my whole life. The man who had given me a complex that had got me into trouble – and also propelled me to where I'd ended up.

It was John Wayne. As in, *the* John Wayne!

He looked at me and I nearly froze.

'Ahhh, oooh, g'day, Duke,' I finally blurted out. Like an idiot.

'And a good day to you too, young fella,' he drawled.

It was such a tiny exchange, but I can't remember a time in my life when I've been so excited. It was my biggest brush with fame, ever, and it completely blew me away.

And if that wasn't enough, on that same trip, John and I, as Strop and Hoges, sat down and interviewed Hugh Hefner on camera at the Playboy Mansion! For the mad virgin Strop, this was almost too much. In fact, that night was almost too much for both of us because Hugh invited us to one of his famous parties. Though, to be honest, it wasn't everything they were cracked up to be. All it was, was an amazing, or some would say spectacular, home, on an amazing, or some would say spectacular, summer's night, with fifty or so amazing, or some would say spectacular, Playboy Bunnies in bikinis. Where's the fun in any of that?

I remember John and I swimming in the grotto, surrounded by bunnies who were fascinated by our accents and hanging off our every word, then looking over at Delvene and thinking, *I'm glad she's with us to keep us in line.* Actually, we would have behaved either way, but if there was one place that was ever going to tempt a couple of young guys in their thirties it was the Playboy Mansion. Mind you, the best America had to offer was on display, and none was a patch on our Delvene.

As for Hugh Hefner himself, I've never met anyone like him. He was the ultimate host. He was surrounded by people but made each and every person feel as though they were the most important person in the room. John and I were nobodies, just a couple of characters from an Australian comedy/travel show yet he laid on the world for us. A charming man.

Hoges, Hugh Hefner and Strop – no more needs to be said.

11

Changing Channel, Again

In late 1976 Kerry was on the phone again. 'I want you back home,' he said. 'Come back to Channel 9, that's where you belong.'

'We're quite happy where we are,' John replied.

'No, you're not,' Kerry said. 'You need to be back with us. What would it take?'

John was pretty quick with an answer. 'Even more money.'

Kerry agreed immediately. He had so many other successful ventures, he was already Australia's richest man. All he cared about was getting his channel in the number-one slot, whatever that took. Moving back to Nine wasn't really about money from our point of view. It was about freedom. We all sat down together one day and John said to Kerry, 'Look, we can't churn out shows as fast as you are going to want, because Hoges has to write each one. He thinks in a peculiar way, and we haven't yet found anyone else who thinks that way. We can only do a show when he's thought of enough funny bits.'

The reason for saying this was simple. Management always had dollar signs in their eyes and wanted to turn our show into production-line television. They thought this would give them higher ratings for more weeks of the year. People would approach us and say, 'We've got these really good writers so you can have more sketches.'

Even Clyde at one stage came to us with a pack of scripts and said, 'This is how you do a series. Here are the scripts for this show's next four episodes. They have a whole writing team, not just one man – who hates to write!'

The scripts for the show Clyde handed us weren't funny, or at least they weren't my idea of funny. Their style would never have come across as authentic 'Hoges'.

'The show has to stay with Paul's point of view,' John now said to Kerry, 'otherwise it won't work.'

'Okay,' Kerry said, 'how many can you write?'

'I don't know,' I replied. 'It might take me a couple of weeks or it might even take me months to come out with the next one.'

Kerry knew that, even if he didn't get as many Hogan shows as he wanted, by luring us across he was stopping Channel 7 from getting any Hogan shows at all.

'Well, that's all right,' he said. 'Any time you make a show, I'll buy it. If you make twenty, great. If you make ten or three, if you even make two, that's okay.'

'So there's no deadline, no restriction, none of the usual "pilot and thirteen episodes needed"?' we asked.

'Nah,' he confirmed. 'You think of enough funny stuff, write it down. As long as it keeps rating, we've got a deal. Shake hands.'

That was the sort of bloke he was. Gruff and ruthless, but absolutely of his word. I never had a contract with John, and we never had a contract with Kerry. I threw my lot in with Nine based on nothing more than that original handshake. With Kerry that was enough. He was the last of the great moguls.

So we started making *The Paul Hogan Show* at Nine, this time filming it in Melbourne, with the terrific Johnny Ladd as our producer. The first 'special' appeared in March 1977. The new shows were called 'specials' because they were never monthly or weekly; they were whenever I had enough funny ideas to make a whole show.

The critics and experts predicted the show would be a disaster because not only did we not have a regular time slot, we'd also just changed networks. They said a show gained a following at a certain time on a certain channel and if you broke that combo, you'd be in big trouble.

Nah. The first special we did at Nine set new ratings records. As in, it rated the house down. In 1977, the year our show joined the lineup, Channel 9 finally reached the number-one slot in Australian television. We certainly played our part in that, and, as the show went on, it was never beaten in a ratings survey for the seven or so years we were there. It was always number one.

As for the cast, we had a regular bunch who did the show with me for years. Delvene, of course, but also other hilarious

On the set of *The Paul Hogan Show*. Judging by the look on my face, we were clearly filming one of those heavy, emotional scenes.

people like Roger Stephen. He played everything from gormless teenagers to heavy metal rock stars. I'd get a call from him asking, 'So when are we going back to work boss?' and, no matter when it was, he'd be there and he'd be brilliant. Same went for Andrew Harwood and John Blackman and Karen Pini and others.

We also had plenty of guest stars in sketches. The Little River Band singer Glenn Shorrock always insisted that, when he was on the show with the group, he'd be in a couple of sketches too. He was good – very good!

We always knew we had an audience who were keen to see a new show, so that made writing it and putting it together exciting for all of us. And Channel 9 used every new special like a battleship. They would wait until one of the other channels would have a major series making its debut, or something else big, and they'd put a Hogan Show special up against it.

Remember, most people didn't have recorders or any form of catch-up TV in the 1970s. So if they missed the first episode of, say, a new series on Ten, they were less likely to go looking for it the following week, making it more likely they'd stick with Nine. That was the theory, anyway, and it seemed to work. Nine dominated the ratings.

● ● ●

When John Cornell put on his lifesaver cap and stuck his jaw out, he was Strop, the dumbest guy on the planet. John had no vanity and this can be a key ingredient in comedy. But in reality John was always the smartest guy in the room, and when he took off his cap and pulled in his lower jaw, he could go toe-to-toe with Kerry Packer, Australia's most powerful media tycoon, and have him eating out of his hand.

Kerry was physically big. He was loud and larger than life and extremely opinionated, and he was a top-shelf bully. I could never work for someone like that but, thanks to John's excellent deal-making, I didn't have to. We owned *The Paul Hogan Show* and were producing it ourselves and then selling it to Kerry. He didn't own us and this forced him to treat us differently.

Kerry admired how tough John was, how he would never kowtow to anyone. John treated Kerry like he was just another guy. He may have owned the channel and he may have been richer than God, but that didn't mean he could get away with a single thing. As for me, I don't think Kerry Packer had ever met anyone who not only had a blue-collar background but didn't care who he was or what he did.

We became unlikely friends. Kerry seemed to really like hanging around with John and me. I remember him going off bombastically at some meeting or other and John saying to him, 'Kerry, if you're going to carry on like that, you can't knock around with us.'

Kerry said, 'Oh, okay, sorry guys.'

• • •

Noelene and I had both coped well when we'd become parents in our teens. Fortunately, we'd both really liked it, were right into it. But then came fame. It was tough on Noelene and all the kids. I was thrust into the limelight, something they didn't invite. Before then it was Struggle Street, but we just accepted it – I never, ever thought about trying to keep up with the Joneses. But then suddenly I went way past the Joneses and everyone wanted to know all about our lives.

A journalist asked me, early in the piece, if my marriage was solid. Like it was any of their business. 'People who have marital troubles are mostly blokes who read their own publicity and believe it,' I replied. 'They think they're too good for one person and should share themselves around. A lot of fellas who find themselves more attractive to the opposite sex think it comes from within them, instead of facing the truth, that it comes from without – from the TV set.'

I was never anything like the Hoges character at home, nor was I ever the star. My family wouldn't let me be like that, for a start. There was no way you could get carried away with yourself with that lot. Wouldn't try, wouldn't dare.

Having four sons and a daughter really helped me keep my feet on the ground and, in return, I always tried to keep a low profile with the family. I didn't want them to be pointed out wherever they went. It didn't always work, though. My eldest son, Brett, once said to me, 'I feel like my name is Brett Hoganson.' That was because people would always refer to him as 'Brett, Paul Hogan's son'. I thought, *Yeah, that's pretty terrible to go through life, always being pointed out as someone else's son or daughter or wife, rather than who you are.*

Over the years I've worked hard to keep my family out of the spotlight so that they can be their own people. It's worked pretty well, though it wasn't always easy. In the seventies, Noelene and the kids and I promised to go to a screening of a little movie one of our neighbours had made. We sat on hard wooden chairs for what felt like an eternity in a local church hall as this incomprehensible film played and played on the wobbling screen onstage. Finally, it came to an end and me and the family were attempting to make a quick exit, but word had got around that the comedian off the TV was there.

There was a bunch of journalists with video cameras waiting at the door to hear what me and the family made of this new production. The kids and I looked at each other and decided to change direction and dive out through the back. This didn't help much, as we were surrounded by fences and backyards on all sides. I thought, *Bugger it, I'm not going back in there.*

I got hold of Noelene and hoisted her over the closest fence and into the nearest backyard, followed by the kids. We ended up running through three backyards, a couple of vegie patches, a compost heap, past one or two yappy dogs and a couple of their not-so-friendly owners till, finally, we were in the safety of a parallel street. After we all got our breath back, Noelene looked at me and said, 'Okay, you're so smart. Where did you park the car?'

It was back at the bloody hall.

12

Creating Characters

Icertainly never set the world on fire as a performer in the 1970s. I think my real strength was comedy writing. Or, initially, comedy thinking, because, as I've said, early on I never wrote anything down.

You can learn to write, but you can't learn to write comedy. I think comedy is the way you look at the world. If you see ordinary everyday stuff and think it's funny, and you have a funny way of putting it, and you share it with other people, and they laugh too, you're a comedy writer. If they don't laugh, you're just a lone weirdo.

For years, this comedy was just playing out in my head as I went through school and into my various jobs. I was never a comedy fan as such, and I certainly never imagined being a comedian. If someone had asked the young Paul Hogan who his idol was, he'd have said Muhammad Ali or perhaps Sugar Ray Robinson. It wasn't until I was in my thirties that I realised other people thought the way I looked at the world was funny too.

The early Paul Hogan shows were basically Hoges, the know-all working-class Australian, telling stories and appearing in sketches. He was the character I had played on *New Faces* and was, I guess, an exaggerated version of me or, in a sense, me as my loud-mouthed seventeen-year-old self.

As well as telling stories, Hoges sent up various television personalities, but there were only four channels then, and we quickly ran out of Aussie personalities to have fun with. So, in time I started to invent characters loosely based on people I'd met in my various real-world jobs (another reason it was good to have had a life before showbiz!). I thought, *Yeah, if this character was a bit like so and so, he'd be funny.* Early on, I created Luigi the Unbelievable, then Sergeant Donger and Arthur Dunger, and on and on it went.

I don't think many of the people who provided my inspiration actually clocked that they were the starting point for my character. I certainly never ever named them or pointed them out, as I didn't want them to be ridiculed. Still, I think Luigi the Unbelievable recognised himself. He used to work on the Harbour Bridge and at lunchtime he'd try and do magic for us. Badly. Like really badly. But he was very entertaining.

Sergeant Donger was based on the boofhead cop who'd raided the training gym when I was a young boxer. After the first Sergeant Donger sketch went to air I had a lot of young constables say to me, 'You obviously know our sergeant.'

Leo Wanker – legend!

Perce the Wino. Some thought of him as a drunk. To me he was just a really good drinker. (*Newspix*)

'Trevor' Shakespeare.

Proving that
cricketers aren't the
only ones who need
to wear a box.

People really liked Perce the Wino and Nigel Lovelace, the leather-jacketed eleven-year-old skateboarder. But my favourite character, and one who became an unlikely legend of his own, was Leo Wanker. Leo was the world's worst stuntman and wasn't a million miles away from his inspiration, Evel Knievel. If I bump into women in the street, they'll often tell me they loved *Crocodile Dundee*, whereas guys will drive past in cars and shout 'Leo-o-o Wanker!' He was so full of himself. I loved him.

Arthur Dunger was also a favourite of mine. On television these days they're always advertising some sort of weird and wonderful exercise machine or some diet drink that'll help you lose weight and get fit. The world's become a little obsessed with fitness, and I feel a bit guilty because I sort of started it.

I produced one of the first regular exercise segments on television with my very good friend and athlete Arthur Dunger. It's a sketch near-on impossible to explain, other than by saying you can watch it on YouTube. Arthur resonated with people everywhere because we all know an Arthur, or are one ourselves. One of my proudest moments was turning on the cricket and seeing Bay 13 at the Melbourne Cricket Ground filled with people dressed as Arthur Dunger. It was like seeing one of your kids on the telly.

I don't exactly know why people loved these characters as much as they did. All my writing and performing was just based on instinct and what I personally found funny and that never changed – even when the budgets got bigger. I always went with my gut, because that's what got me into this mess in the first place, and, to be honest, I didn't know any other way. Also, there weren't any gurus when I started on television,

Playing hard man
Charlie Bronson.
It took even less
acting than usual.

Rocking out as Rod
Stewart. Apparently
the nose was too big ...
according to Rod.

no wise old men I could go to and say, 'Is this funny? Will this work? Should I do this?' Nor was there a comedy school or entertainment school or anything like that. You just did what was in your gut, what made you laugh and you felt would make others laugh too. You got up and did it and hoped for the best.

The show was all scripted, but because I generally wrote the sketches – in pencil on a legal pad in block capitals – and was also in them, I would often change things or make it up as I went along. The only sketches that were fully improvised were Hoges and Strop. John and I would decide roughly what the scene was going to be about and then go out there and make it up on the spot, just chatting and hamming it up like there wasn't a camera for miles. That was cool.

One thing I particularly loved to do was to send up ads off the telly. Things like the 'I can't get by without my Mum' deodorant ad, the French male model selling us Bic razors, and, a personal favourite, the mongrel dog breeder spruiking Pal. But the one people most often ask me about is for Fold-A-Way Timber. That was a product we invented, basically a length of bog-ordinary four-by-two with a hinge halfway along for added convenience. Every home should have one …

When I sent up other Australian television personalities, they seemed to enjoy it. Talk-show host Don Lane even lent his singing voice to the clip I did about him. We also had fun with quiz-show host Tony Barber, cricketer and commentator Richie Benaud and *60 Minutes* journalist George Negus – I called him George Fungus.

Then there was the new host of *A Current Affair*, Michael Schildberger. Mike was a little bloke, a lovely man, and had a great sense of humour. When he heard I was doing an impression of him, he turned up to the taping and sat in the front row, about twelve feet from me, and just stared. It was almost impossible to keep a straight face.

I added some international flavour by impersonating American stars like *Hawaii Five-0*'s Jack Lord and Hollywood action heroes 'Clunk' Eastwood and Charles Bronson. I did a skit about a movie festival of Charles Bronson's biggest hits. I had him as the impassioned priest in *Going My Way* and singing and dancing 'his way into your heart' in *Singing in the Rain*, and also playing the upper-class Harvard law student in *Love Story*. With a wig and makeup, I actually looked a lot like Charles and always had him playing it exactly the same way. No matter what the role was, Charlie just stood there, carved out of stone.

What we didn't have, back in the 1970s, was MTV. The only time we ever saw any international music acts was on *Countdown* on Sunday nights, with dear old Molly Meldrum doing the hosting duties. So I decided to have some world-famous acts on my show too. We had some real legends, if you didn't look too closely. I did everyone from Tom Jones and Bryan Ferry to Elvis and AC/DC, as well as Molly himself. I once had 'Rod Stewart' swinging his microphone stand around and knocking the blocks of the other members of his band. Somehow Rod saw the sketch and rang me. 'You nailed it, mate,' he said, 'made me very proud.' Though he did add, 'But the fake nose was too bloody big!'

I later interviewed Rod Stewart at his house for one of my specials and we sort of clicked because he came from the real world too. At one stage he'd worked as a gravedigger, so he was used to being around people like me. I think we both felt we were now playing roles, me the role of TV personality and he the rock star. He was a nice bloke with a great sense of humour and, best of all, a man who never forgot how lucky he'd been.

Even though we often had international guests, I never considered the overseas market when writing *The Paul Hogan Show*. I never thought about America. Although we'd sent Hoges to the United States to do a travel show, that was just taking the piss out of the place a bit. I never knew if my humour would work there, never cared. John thought about it, though. As I've said, he always had much more faith and ambition than I ever had.

Still, when the Hogan shows were up and running smoothly, John figured I didn't need him as much because I had such a good crew around me. So he went off with Kerry Packer and revolutionised sport.

In the mid-1970s John had been approached by some members of the Australian cricket team who were keen for him to become their manager, because – hard though it is now to believe – none of them had one. And John found out – well, we found out – that these national heroes were getting no more money playing for their country than the guy running the scoreboard. It didn't matter if they were a demon fast bowler, world-class wicketkeeper or champion batsman, they got a pittance, because the game was controlled by the Australian and international cricket boards.

John thought that was unfair, so he agreed to manage them and negotiate their deals. At the same time, Kerry Packer, who was smarting because his beloved Channel 9 couldn't get exclusive TV rights for cricket, had an idea. He was going to sign up the top players from around the world and set up his own competition. Kerry wanted more colour and movement than in the regular game, primarily because his station was now broadcasting in colour, but also because he wanted control. And Kerry knew the key was to offer more money – decent money – to the players.

So, in 1977, Kerry and John together devised World Series Cricket. This put them in direct conflict with the International Cricket Conference (now the International Cricket Council), which had been running the game for about seventy years and wasn't about to give up control easily.

Kerry had the money and the will, but the innovation and everything that gave it excitement – that was all John. Thinking outside the box is what John does better than anyone. And with the little company we had, John ended up signing the best cricketers from around the globe. One of them was a Pakistani fast bowler named Imran Khan. He is now Pakistan's prime minister – and he was also on our company payroll.

World Series Cricket was the forerunner of night cricket, Twenty20 and one-day games. It brought a far more professional approach to playing and televising the game. Other sports caught on and tried to copy many of the ideas. Once again Corney showed his brilliance. My only contribution was to tell them to let the players drink beer at the beginning of the game, not after. I found this always worked in our picnic matches.

With John fully involved in cricket, I was now producing our shows myself, with Peter Faiman, a whizz-kid of Australian television, as director and co-producer. Peter had been directing live TV for years on programs like the Graham Kennedy and Don Lane shows. He was a brilliant talent and made all the difference to the quality of our show.

I also used one or two sketches from the great writer Ken Shadie in each show, firstly because they were funny, but also because the show was an hour long. It was good to have some sketches that weren't driven entirely by me. I knew Ken from the Channel 7 days, when he'd submitted a couple of sketches for *The Paul Hogan Show*. He'd earlier written sketches for *The Mavis Bramston Show*, an Australian television comedy that I used to watch on the idiot box in the 1960s and really enjoyed. It had a fabulous cast – people like Ron Frazer and Carol Raye and Noeline Brown – and some really clever writing, though it was more English and quite different from what I was trying to do. I met with Ken and he was very laid-back and quiet and low-key. He was also able to quickly adapt his style to our show and wrote us great spoofs and send-ups of TV shows and commercials.

We also did stunts on *The Paul Hogan Show*. Amazing stunts that involved exploding motorbikes, rolling cars, crashes and high falls that were all shot quickly, on a TV budget and with minimum fuss. This was partly due to having a fantastic stunt coordinator called Graham Mathrick and my great stunt double, Chris Anderson. Both these blokes were fearless and, unlike Leo Wanker, the real deal.

Those were different times, health and safety wise. No one was ever there to say no to an idea. You didn't have endless meetings before doing a stunt, you just did it. At times, I'm sure, if we were a man short for one of the bigger set-ups, we'd simply recruit someone from the pub at lunchtime and they'd learn on the job. We were lucky that no one ever got seriously hurt.

There were other things you wouldn't do now. I remember that for a World Series Cricket send-up called 'World Series War' we had commentators giving a blow-by-blow description of a fiery battle, and we wanted to have smoke in the background. We simply doused a few old truck tyres in petrol and lit 'em up. We had black smoke billowing everywhere. Looked great. But, as I say, a different time …

•••

I was becoming more independent, but everything I knew about business I had learnt from the gormless virgin. That said, there was one bloke John Cornell wasn't looking after: himself. World Series Cricket was a great success in almost every area, but John was doing it for the love of cricket and wasn't getting much out of it financially. That seemed ridiculous to me. So, for the first and only time, we reversed roles and I became John's manager. I went to Kerry's office and gently knocked on his door and in true Kerry style he yelled, 'What the hell do you want?'

I walked in, made out I was a little nervous. 'I'll be back in a minute,' I said, 'I'm just going to have a leak.' I went and stood in the corridor for a little while. This allowed time for Kerry's imagination to run and, hopefully, wonder if I was about to announce that we were leaving the network again and taking our top-rating show with us.

When I reappeared, his whole demeanour had changed. 'Come in, son. Sit down. What can I do for you?'

'I'm not happy with what you're paying John,' I said. 'He's done my show and set up the cricket and is pretty well running this network.'

Kerry thought about it for a moment. 'Okay, what do you think he should be paid?'

I hadn't thought that far ahead and quickly plucked out a figure. Kerry immediately agreed. He agreed so quickly I realised I hadn't pushed hard enough. 'That's after tax, of course,' I quickly added.

He smiled and we shook.

• • •

John and Kerry had a big court case in London. The International Cricket Conference was trying to thwart their World Series Cricket plans and John and Kerry were fighting back. At Kerry's request, I went along too. He said, 'It'd be good if you'd come along and coach the cricketers in not playing bush lawyer. They might listen to you.'

A couple of the more prominent cricketers couldn't shut up. Kerry wanted to make sure they went on the stand, answered the questions and told the truth, but didn't elaborate on anything. I did my best to convince them to just sit there and keep their mouths shut as much as possible.

I was just a fringe character but saw Kerry, centre stage, being brilliant in court as the ICC's top-bracket barristers, or Queen's Counsels, all got rattled. They were sweating and their wigs were starting to slip around and they were dropping papers because Kerry had all the right answers, all the time.

During the court case we were staying in this hotel – I think it was The Grosvenor in London – and at the end of the day we'd all go back there and have afternoon tea or drinks or whatever, and talk about the court case. There'd be a roomful of us.

The hotel would bring up trays of pastries and cakes for high tea. Kerry Packer didn't drink, but he loved sweet things, especially those pastries called cream horns. One day, when the hotel staff brought the tea, Kerry was discussing the next day's proceedings with a couple of his lawyers, one or two of his executives and John. Although these were multi-million-dollar matters, Kerry kept looking over at the cake tray. I went over to it and saw that there were only a couple of cream horns on it. I picked one up and wiped the cream off the top. I knew Kerry was watching but couldn't come over. Then I ate it, with him glaring at my every move. I looked longingly at the second cream horn. I knew he wouldn't be able to help himself. Sure enough, he suddenly dropped all important business and came running over and grabbed it. There might have been sheep stations to play for, but he wasn't going to miss out on a cream horn.

Kerry was a funny bugger. One day we were all sitting around in his London hotel penthouse, even though we had our own smaller rooms downstairs, and Kerry said how much he liked the carpet and that it had inspired him to redo his offices back home.

'Get onto Harrods,' he told his secretary, 'and tell them to bring some carpet samples over.'

Harrods was the biggest and most expensive department store in London. Top of the line. A normal person would never go there for carpets. You'd go to Carpet Bazaar or somewhere like that. But Kerry was never normal.

Anyway, a guy turned up the next day with these foot-square carpet samples.

'I can't tell from that!' Kerry barked. 'Go and get me some big stuff. Get me some stuff that's as big as this room.'

Of course Harrods would have known of Kerry Packer, and

that money was never an issue for him, so they sent the guy back the next day.

'Come up on the roof,' he said this time, 'and I'll show you.'

So we went up to the roof and he had a truck parked on the street below. This was in the busy heart of London, but these guys pulled these huge rolls of carpet out of the truck and carried them into the park across the road and rolled them out on the grass. Kerry dismissed each carpet by yelling or waving. Or he'd get me to whistle, because I could whistle loud. Then the poor blokes down there would roll the carpet up then unload and roll out the next one. These were like forty-foot lengths of carpet. God knows what they weighed. Kerry went through six or eight before he finally liked one, and they had to put it to one side so he could compare it to the next one. Just a normal day for Kerry.

He had a mindset like no one else. Didn't understand your average person's view of money at all. But he certainly knew how to make it.

Oh, and by the way, John and I had the final vote on which carpet he should order. It had a nice block pattern, as I remember it.

As for the court case, Kerry chopped them to pieces. Eventually Packer and his World Series Cricket outfit secured a merger deal with the traditional authorities and reunified the game. The merger gave Kerry everything he wanted, including exclusive television rights, along with a few extra bonuses he hadn't even asked for, thanks to John.

Another thing I remember from that London trip: John and I were meeting some friends for dinner in a pretty fancy restaurant. We wandered in wearing our best attire and suddenly the whole

Tarzan and Jane.
Typecasting.

restaurant stopped. And stared. In particular I noticed every fine young woman in the place seemed to be suddenly sizing us up.

'Look at this, look at this!' I whispered to John. 'A couple of young, bronzed Aussies walk into the place and they can't get enough!'

Then we noticed that Roger Moore had walked in behind us. Roger Moore at the peak of his James Bond fame. Suddenly the two bronzed Aussies felt like ugly little mutants next to this six-foot-four idol.

• • •

Even when John was effectively running the network, managing half the Australian cricket team and generally being the busiest man in showbiz, no matter who he was with or what he was working on, or where he was in the world even, if I wanted to speak to him all I had to do was ring. 'Mate,' I'd say, 'I think it's time for a Hoges and Strop.' And he would drop everything and come running.

At the very end of 1977, literally at midnight on New Year's Eve, John married the prettiest girl on Australian television and possibly the most intelligent one too. Delvene Delaney was as smart as a whip, funny, tough and a match for John on every level. I'm not sure if I believe in soul mates, but if they do exist, John and Dele are it.

13

No More Dancing for Maria

The Queen came out to Australia in 1980, which was a really big deal. We still saw ourselves as part of the British Commonwealth, and sang 'God Save the Queen' as our national anthem and everything. A big Royal Charity Concert was held and I was on the bill to entertain. I walked out in the dark with a torch, swinging it around, mainly in the direction of the Royal Box, and asked, 'Where are they sitting, where are they? Just want to have a gawk at them. They're gawking at me.'

I'd decided I'd serenade Her Majesty with the 'Garbophone'. As you know, I was a qualified tap-dancing knife thrower, could play the shovels and specialised in the thunderbox, but I thought I should do something special for the Queen – so I invented the Garbophone. It was a big orange plastic rubbish bin with a tin whistle stuck in the side of it. After doing some silly stand-up, I started squeezing this big plastic bin and blowing into it for all I was worth, and everyone thought, *Wow, he's* …

Of course then I stopped and talked, and the music kept going, so everyone knew the music was coming from a sax player in the pit.

I decided that, while I had the bin, I'd have a bit of fun. So I announced a lucky door prize and drew a couple of tickets out of it for 'a fantastic four-course dinner for two at my place'. You can guess who won. I gave them the instructions to my place ('Just get yourself on the 174 bus from Chatswood Station') and took a bow. It went over big.

As per protocol, I was introduced to the Queen at the end of the concert. There's a great shot of her looking at me, smiling at my torn shirt, stubbies and footy socks. But what the photo didn't record was how she looked me straight in the eye and said, 'I'm terribly sorry, dear, but I don't think we'll be able to make dinner.' I think the Queen was taking the piss!

Standing to my left in that photo, and looking just a bit more glamorous than me in her gorgeous red formal dress, was Olivia Newton-John. That was when I first met Olivia and, believe me, I was more excited about that than meeting the Queen. QEII might be a majesty, but Olivia Newton-John's an angel. She was also one of the biggest stars in the world in 1980, a multi-million-selling country and pop music artist, and an actor. She'd starred in *Grease* with John Travolta and it had been the top box office film of 1978.

Soon afterwards I was told I needed makeup because we were going to be filming outside. Olivia asked if I had any and

I said, 'Oh, I don't wear makeup. I've got a tan.' Remember, all my views about television had been formed in the first half of the 1970s when everything was in black and white.

'No, you have to have makeup,' Olivia said. 'Here, sit down.' And with that, Olivia Newton-John made me up. She gave me some eyebrows and put some powder on my face and made me look better than I'd ever looked.

That was the first time I met Livvie and we've been great friends ever since. Someone asked me recently whether she was any good as a makeup artist. Don't know. Don't care. It was just: *Olivia Newton-John's painting me face!*

I told Mum I'd met not only the Queen but Olivia Newton-John as well. 'I hope you dressed nice,' she said.

'Of course,' I replied. 'As long as you think my rigger's outfit is nice.'

• • •

Hoges at ...

The Royal Charity Concert

Sydney Opera House, 27 May 1980

Would you believe, viewers, that some of the mob behind this bunfight tonight didn't want me on it? They reckon I got too much anti-charisma. That's the ability to lower the tone of the whole evening just by turning up … I said, 'Listen, this ain't no mixed-prawn night at the local footy

club, you know. This is the Sydney Opera
House filled with the cream of society.'
Cream, huh. There're one or two curdled
faces about … I'll admit there might be
the odd VIP here. I noticed one odd VIP as
I walked in. Neville Wran, the Premier of
New South Wales. How you goin' Nifty?

He's sitting up there in the dearest
seats, too. Must have had a big win at the
two-up, mate?

They said to me, 'Listen, this will be
a highly refined, sophisticated sort of
crowd.' What a terrible thing to say about
youse, viewers. Highly refined? You know,
what happens to sugar when they refine it,
don't you? They take all the goodness out
and leave it colourless and brittle. So,
my advice to you is, if you see anyone
near you that looks a bit refined, keep
away from them, they'll rot your teeth.

And sophisticated? Sophisticated means
false, but I think they was trying
to say it will be an intellectual
crowd in tonight. Well, I don't mind
intellectuals, I used to be one. My idea
of an intellectual is anyone with an IQ
over eighty-one, a vocabulary in excess
of thirty words and the ability to eat
with a fork without poking holes in your
cheek. And after watching you lot come
in, viewers, I'm delighted to report that
probably two-thirds of youse'd reach that
standard.

Practising on the Garbophone in the run-up to the big night.
(*Newspix*)

For the benefit of the other one-third, you probably have difficulty comprehending the complexities of fractions. Just look at the person on your left and the one on your right. And if they haven't got fork marks on their cheeks, you're probably the dill.

Now, there's a confident man, your Premier Neville Wran. He never looked to the left or the right to find out where he fits in. He knows what he is. Nifty, me son, we all know what you are. I didn't mean that, mate, I was gonna use that on Malcolm Fraser, but he never turned up. A scalper gave him 150 bucks for his seat.

Ladies and gentlemen, without further ado, when I first burst onto the show-business scene back in '72, well, I didn't really burst onto it — sort of leaked might be a better word, dribble — but I started out as a musician. I haven't played in public since then, so I thought tonight, as a special treat, a bit of nostalgia for people who have heard me play and a special treat for anyone that hasn't heard me play, like, you know, newly arrived migrants … (*looks up to Royal Box*)

You know, I'll give youse a tune tonight on the instrument that I helped make popular right around the world. So here we go with a little bit of colour and movement for the kiddies at home and those fraction people in the audience. Will you bring up the instrument, please. Give us a drum roll, Tom.

Hoges appears with Garbophone.

Ladies and gentlemen, as you're about to hear, the Garbophone is a truly beautiful instrument, unfortunately seldom heard these days outside of chamber music recitals …

This is a great pity because this is truly regarded as the musician's instrument. I mean, that Roger Woodward, who was out here before me thumping away at the ivories, he would give his eye teeth to be able to play this. It's a lot easier to get onto a bus than a piano, isn't it? Without further ado ladies and gentlemen, sit back and be thrilled to the back teeth as I play for youse now some of the better tracks off me last five albums.

Does everyone like Chopin? Good, here's a Beatles' number.

Hoges appears to play 'Smoke Gets in Your Eyes'. He stops but the music continues.

Yeah, I'll draw the raffle and get off. By the way, ladies and gentlemen, the fabulous door prize tonight is a fantastic four-course dinner for two at my place.

And the lucky winners, the lucky winning couple, are sitting in Box U, in seats 5 and 6. Now, I have no idea who the lucky couple are (*looks again at Royal Box*) but I'm no snob and they're welcome at my place. It's just get yourself on the 174 bus from Chatswood Station, tell the driver to let you off at Hoges' place.

Listen, if the dogs go for you, keep your arms folded and smile at them. And just one thing, please lucky couple, whoever you are, try and be there at six o'clock sharp because the missus likes to have dinner over with and the washing-up done by seven when *The Sullivans* comes on, okay? Good night, viewers. Play us off, Tom.

Noelene was a great mother and she always focused on the kids. We never battled or argued or anything, but we just drifted apart and then we broke up at the start of the 1980s. I accept all the blame for what happened. I was heavily involved with what I was doing, which left no time to be involved with what she was doing. Put simply, there was now a lack of interest in each other's lives.

Noelene had thought the fame and changed circumstances were a bit of a novelty to begin with, but towards the end she didn't much enjoy having to live in someone else's shadow. As with the kids, she felt she'd become someone's wife instead of simply being her own person, and that can be hard. And the marriage, I guess, had worn out, which sadly happens all too often.

So we decided to separate and get divorced. In the meantime I still went to all my kids' sporting fixtures and tried to be there for them. But then I suddenly realised I couldn't leave. Noelene and I could split up, but I couldn't divorce the kids! So, basically, I decided not to move out of the house.

And then, in 1982, we surprised everyone by remarrying because, well, we were a really close family. Still are.

• • •

Through this difficult time, I kept making my shows. The deal with Packer remained very loose. He said, 'Just do one whenever you like.' And I did, with Peter Faiman as my director and the great crew at GTV-9 in Melbourne. During this whole time, though, whether working on the show or not, John and I stayed best mates and fully involved in what each other was working on, if not always officially.

I must admit, though, that without John's prodding I didn't make a great many shows during this time. I was also getting restless, and Kerry was so involved in the cricket, and then other things, that he didn't seem to care. He'd lost interest in television to a certain extent. Up until then, he'd only cared about being number one and his answer to everything was to throw money at it. And it worked. Nine was comfortably at the top of the ratings, but now his attention was elsewhere.

We had a great relationship, me and Kerry, partly because, as I've said, I didn't defer to him. One day I was at a mate's place in Sydney and I was told that Kerry was at the house next door. I jumped the back fence and went inside and there was Kerry holding court. I snuck up behind him and got him in a mock headlock and started messing up his hair, giving him a bun, or swirly.

'Who the bloody hell is that?!' he growled as he was thrashing about.

When I finally let him see me, he said, 'I might've known it was you, ya prick!'

I don't know why, but I could get away with it. It probably didn't hurt that he needed John's smarts around Nine, so, you know, the relationship with us both had to work.

• • •

When I look back at *The Paul Hogan Show* sketches, I still find some of them funny but realise some would now be frowned upon as sexist. People, including my youngest son, Chance, say to me, 'You couldn't do that now.' And it's true. Things were a helluva lot different in the 1970s.

Some of the stuff is un-PC by today's standards but was quite acceptable back then – and maybe even tame by 1970s standards.

True, the show was usually packed with beautiful girls wearing very skimpy outfits. I'm not stupid: it added to my huge following of pimply teenagers. But the real point, when I had these girls on, was not for you to perv on them. It was to demonstrate what absolute melons we men make of ourselves over good-looking women, and the desperate, pathetic things we do to attract their attention.

So, I should probably take this opportunity to apologise for being sexist *and* for making the men always look like fools by walking into walls and falling over cliffs while gawking at pretty girls. In all seriousness, though, there was no malice in my humour and that gave it wide appeal. I never wanted it to be sexist or ageist or homophobic, or to deliberately embarrass people. Usually the butt of the joke was me, because there's no point in doing comedy in which most people are laughing but someone's sobbing in the corner. Forget about it.

I certainly don't mind people criticising what I did and saying it wasn't funny or didn't work or whatever, but I get annoyed when they suggest there was vicious intent. No, it was just meant as a bit of a laugh. Perce the Wino, if you put that on now, you'd get people saying that you're mocking the homeless, or ridiculing alcoholics. And to a certain extent, that's true. But in 1970s Australia, we never had alcoholics. We only had really big drinkers.

Some of the material still stands up well. On the other hand, the funniest comedy is often the really current stuff, but that's what dates the fastest. We had huge fun with Doug Anthony, the deputy prime minister, but nobody knows who he is any more. Half of what popular comedians say today will probably sound horribly un-PC forty or fifty years from now. We just don't know which half, because taboos change. But my characters were created out of empathy. Years later, I'd have non-Italians tell me they thought Luigi the Unbelievable was offensive, and then I'd get in a cab and have a driver from Rome or Sicily go on about how much he and all his friends loved that character. I think those cab drivers could see that I wasn't out to bag any people or groups. I loved Luigi in my own weird way, and wanted the audience to love him too, despite his complete lack of ability. Anyway, some of *The Paul Hogan Show* may not play to today's tastes or sensibilities but I also never expected that, fifty years after it was made, thousands of people could be watching and critiquing it on YouTube.

• • •

According to Hoges ...

Wreckers of the Lost Park

By the early 1980s I was getting to the stage of, *Well, I've sort of sent up everything. What'll I do now?* We made the last *Paul Hogan Show* in 1984. By that stage, I'd written about four or five hundred sketches, which I guess is not bad for a bloke who'd previously never written anything much down.

Although I didn't know it at the time, the idea for something far more ambitious, a full-length feature film, was quietly brewing inside my scone. The first inkling was the introduction I did to a parody sketch in one of the last editions of the show. The skit was a 'movie' called *Wreckers of the Lost Park*, and it featured 'Cootamundra Hoges' taking on a series of killer koalas and other dangers. This was the introduction:

HOGES: Seems like when you look through
the cinema ads in the paper nowadays
at least half of the films showing are
Australian. And that's terrific. But
if we want it to last, then our movie
makers need to be a bit bolder. We've
got to sell them around the world.

Despite what the film industry people
tell you, the rest of the world is not
sitting around breathlessly waiting to

see all about our history and folk law.
It's not really that fascinating. Let's
face it, even our legendary bushranger
Ned Kelly was really just a dim-witted
Irishman who went around robbing banks
with a bucket over his head.

Now, I'm a patriot, but fair dinkum, if
I see one more kangaroo hopping across
the screen in the movies I'll throw up.
What we've gotta do is, we've gotta give
the world an unforgettable adventure
story that is truly original.

14

Selling Australia

I was probably always a better salesman than I was a comedian or actor. With the advertising that I did, I was real, and it was real. That's why the ads were successful. The things I sold were things that I believed in: I really did eat those, drive this, drink that – and smoke that. Some advertising guru generously said that I made 'audiences feel better about themselves and, indeed, the advertised product'.

From late 1981 I made maybe two dozen commercials in the UK, promoting the Australian beer Foster's. It was a great, fun challenge because not only did the Poms have plenty of beer of their own, they'd basically invented comedy. Still, our ads were hugely successful. We weren't presenting a Bazza

McKenzie character, a drunken buffoon for the Poms to laugh at. No, this was a guy who knew what he was doing, and he was taking the piss, gently. They loved it.

I described the beer as 'The Amber Nectar', 'The Golden Throat Charmer' and 'The Liquid Lifesaver'. In one ad, I was in a yuppie pub where bright young things were talking on house brick–sized telephones, then the latest and greatest gadget.

'I've moved into a warehouse at the docks,' one yuppie bragged to me.

'Don't worry,' I replied, 'things'll pick up.'

The favourite line with audiences, though, was the one about Foster's tasting 'like an angel crying on your tongue'. I was often asked if I'd come up with that line. It was in reality a variation on a rather cruder Australian expression. So I guess I didn't write it, I adapted it.

• • •

According to Hoges ...

Foster's Beer 1

Outside the Tower of London

HOGES: Oh, ripper. Where are we, mate?

TOWER GUARD: The bloody tower.

HOGES: All right, sport, I only asked. Twit.

★ ★ ★

Foster's Beer 2

HOGES: You know, back home we'd have
to make our own entertainment. Long
evenings standing around the piano,
wishing someone could play it. Still,
we'd always end up running through some
old favourites (*drinks beer*). Music to
the taste buds!

When I was over there flogging Foster's, I must say, it was the first time that the Australian public let me down. I was selling *the* Australian beer, and they were buying it over there like it was going out of fashion, to the point where Foster's became the most successful foreign beer in all of Britain. But, then the Poms would come to visit Australia and discover, almost on arrival, that none of the buggers here drank it!

With those ads on air in the UK, I was becoming known there as the 'Foster's Geezer'. I started getting calls from British television stations saying, 'What about doing one of your shows over here?' I was a little nervous about it, you know, thinking 'coals to Newcastle' and all that because the Poms are so good at comedy. They have to be. Let's face it, if you lived in London, you'd need a sense of humour. Anyway, I went to England, and I made some shows there with John producing and Peter Faiman directing.

We had guests like the delightful Goodie Tim Brooke-Taylor, who so sadly died of COVID-19 recently. I also had musical acts including Dexys Midnight Runners and Dire Straits – and they were the real ones, not me impersonating them. These specials were with a brand-new network called Channel Four, which decided to include my show in the lineup for its launch day on 2 November 1982. To everyone's delight, the show rated gangbusters. Great fun and a thrill all round.

• • •

Not long after the shocking assassination of Lord Mountbatten, Prince Charles was travelling to Australia. Reg Watson got in touch with him and he agreed to replace his great-uncle as Royal Patron of Variety Australia. I had a dinner with Charles and he was very personable. We never ran out of things to talk about or laugh at.

Then, in 1983, Prince Charles and Princess Diana came to Australia. Prince William was a bub and they brought him out to show off the future heir to the throne. The powers that be decided they would put on a concert in the Royal couple's honour to officially open the new Sydney Entertainment Centre. I wasn't invited initially, perhaps because they still thought I was too rough around the edges. But when Charles heard about the concert, he said, 'Oh, wonderful, I hope Hoges will be on.'

'Oh yes, of course,' they said, and I got a last-minute, desperate call to appear. Feigning disinterest, I made them work, but finally agreed.

With Charles and Di having their little Prince in tow, I decided to come out onstage nursing a 'baby' before handing him off to a stage hand. We then heard some crying from the wings and I told them to 'give little William a drink … but not from the can!'

Most people laughed, but some diehard royalists thought I should have shown more respect. Charles and Di, though, both had a terrific sense of humour, so I tell myself they enjoyed it.

Actually, they must have, because they came to a Variety Australia dinner and I ended up dancing with the Princess, which was clearly an unforgettable moment (probably more for me than for her).

She was a sarcastic bugger too. She reached over to my bow tie – it was a formal black-tie affair – grabbed hold of it and wrenched it out. She looked at me and looked at it and said, 'These clip-on ones are really good, aren't they? Especially if you don't know how to tie a proper one.'

Noelene was over the moon about that dinner. Thrilled to the back teeth. Even more than me. She couldn't wait to get back home and tell everyone Princess Diana had flirted with her husband.

For Mum, too, it was really something. Like most people of her generation, she was a strong royalist. She couldn't believe Di was actually talking to her scruffy son, let alone dancing with him.

• • •

When I was in the UK and having a great time doing some new Foster's ads, John Brown, the newly appointed Australian Minister for Tourism, turned up and sought me out. He was part of the new Labor government under former union leader

The terrific Minister for Tourism, John Brown, presents me with an award for, um, tourism. (*Newspix*)

Bob Hawke. They had been elected in early 1983 and they were out to shake things up.

Brownie's a politician, but a real good bloke. I know that's an oxymoron, but he came to London and took Corney and me out for dinner and we liked him straight away. We could tell his heart was totally in the right place and he really wanted to make a difference.

'You're going well over here, Hoges, selling beer to the Poms,' he said. 'Back home we're going to have a couple of hundred thousand kids leaving school this year, and we've got no jobs for them. And the biggest employer in the world is the tourism industry. You sold beer to the Poms, do you think you could sell Australia to the Yanks?'

'Oh yeah, I'll certainly have a crack,' I replied. So off I went to the States to check out the target. I liked the Yanks, and while it's a very similar culture to ours, I was quickly reminded that there are a few accent and language differences, particularly in the early 1980s. The first time I got in a cab and gave directions to the driver, he said to me, 'That's a strange accent you've got there, buddy. Where are you from?'

I explained I was from Australia and he said, 'Australia? You speak pretty good English.'

Of course, me being a diplomat, I naturally said, 'Yeah, better than you, ya pelican.' But it was true there were a few words they pronounced differently or had different meanings for. Back then I liked to sneak out for a cigarette occasionally, but I soon learnt not to stand up in a crowded bar and say, 'Oh boy, I'd love to bum a fag.' I can tell you, I pretty quickly took those words out of my vocabulary. I now leave them for the bigoted rednecks.

Another thing I found out about the Yanks was that they were really into their politics and their social issues. They're very passionate, whereas we Australians, we're the exact opposite, apathetic. We're among the small number of countries in the world where they've got to force us to go and vote, or we wouldn't bother. So, there's a clash there. The Yanks are sort of famous for their passion, and we're sort of famous for our apathy ... but, then again, who gives a shit?

We found that almost every country in the world was advertising its wares in the States. They were all talking up their beaches, their forests, their fresh air. I learnt that other countries have beautiful beaches and waterfalls too, and we'd have to compete with them.

But we thought, *What if you go to a beautiful place, and find everyone there's an arsehole?* You'll never have a good time if that's the case. Whereas if I come around to your place and am keen to come round again, it's not because of the furniture. It's because of the company. Yet most tourism ads were all furniture, whether that meant beaches or waterfalls or mountains to climb.

So, what we decided was, instead, we would advertise the people. We'd say, *The best thing about Australia is Australians. They're friendly, they like their sports, drinks, parties, weekends. Don't like working much. And they're the perfect hosts. So come on down, you'll have a good time, and we'll be glad to see you.*

Up to this point Australia hadn't really done any serious tourism campaigns, and probably for a good reason. Sydney had not one decent hotel. The tourism industry basically didn't exist. It was time to change that.

Now, I'm from Irish convict stock. We lot originally came out in chains, and having been brought up in the Western

Suburbs of Sydney, being an Aussie was ingrained in me. If there's such a thing as an Aussie, I guess I'm about as much as you can be, unless you're Aboriginal. But you can also be an Aussie if you came out from Greece six years ago. It doesn't take long for it to get into you. People sometimes ask me what it takes to be an Aussie, and I say it's simple, 'Just wanting to be one.' It's true. I've met Italians who are as Aussie as I'll ever be. There's just something in the Australian lifestyle, or the air.

So it wasn't a big stretch for me, John and the boys from Mojo, the ad agency, to come up with a tourism campaign that was fun but also authentic. Mojo was just five years old but already recognised as the best advertising agency in Australia. It had been co-founded by Allan Johnston, that young copywriter who'd approached me about the Winfield ads a dozen years earlier. He was the 'jo' in the name. His co-founder Alan Morris was the 'mo' and was another titan of the industry. We all sensed we had the right formula, but there was a problem. The powers that be hesitated.

Those powers that be generally didn't like me. From the time I'd started on television, they'd considered me a national embarrassment. And now they were saying in their plum voices, 'You can't show that yob outside Australia. They won't understand a word he's saying. Can't we get Don Lane to do it? At least he's got an American accent. They'll understand him.'

Bugger that, we were determined to see it through. John Brown was genuinely concerned about building up an industry which until then had been third rate at best. But he admitted he couldn't get money from the Cabinet to fund the first ads.

I believed in it so much I made a twenty-minute video pitch that was then shown to the prime minister and Cabinet and, in John Brown's words, 'all those treasury officials with their eyeshades and quills', all sitting around a big L-shaped desk.

My message was, basically, 'Look here, if you get your fingers out of your arses and give Brownie the money, we can do something great.'

The pollies watched it and at the end they all turned to look at our prime minister, Bob Hawke. They all seemed concerned and certainly weren't convinced by me, except for Hawkie, and we all know how he talked.

'What's wrong with his bloody accent?' he asked them. And that was it.

• • •

According to Hoges ...

The Video Pitch

HOGES: The tourist dollar is quick, clean cash. They lob on Qantas, spend heaps on accommodation, tucker and zinc for the sunburn and then leave, and we're both richer for the experience. But you can't make this happen by being a quiet underachiever. Australia's not a bloody farm. We can't sit around the woolshed waiting for cardigans to come back into fashion.

ABOVE: My dad, Jack, and my mum, Florence, on their big day in 1936.

RIGHT: With my sister, Wendy, both with added rosy cheeks. At this age, getting my photo taken was a novelty. Boy, how that changed.

RIGHT: Pat, Wendy and me in our uniforms, ready for Catholic school. I asked a lot of questions. Too many questions. The priests were happy to see the back of me.

BELOW: I was a teenager when I married. A child groom. One of my presents was a Meccano set. The reception took place under an old tarp in my bride Noelene's parents' driveway.

RIGHT: Later in life when my success hit, people would remark that I was on top of the world. But no matter what heights I may have briefly hit, the view was never better than when I was a rigger on the 'Coat Hanger'.

BELOW: My little tribe, with two more still to come. We had 'em young and the kids and I all grew up together. A crazy, noisy, wonderful time.

ABOVE: As if the family needed more proof that I hadn't grown up. My true passion turned out to be downhill skiing, though I didn't see snow till I was in my fifties.

LEFT: With my daughter, Loren, after receiving a bravery award for a Harbour Bridge rescue. It would have been more fitting if the award was for being 'fearless and stupid'. *(Newspix)*

RIGHT: Thanks to Mike Willesee, I was off the Bridge and doing my best to look dapper alongside him. I'm not sure if my collar was big enough. (Newspix)

BELOW: A couple of deep thinkers, Hoges and Strop muse over all that's wrong in the world. While John Cornell could play the idiot like no other, he was as sharp a businessman as I've ever met.

ABOVE: Strop explains his hangover cure to Hoges on *The Paul Hogan Show*. We had no script. We were just two mates who made it up as we went along. Whether we were on camera as Hoges and Strop or off, as Paul and John, our approach never changed.

RIGHT: Sergeant Donger with the lovely Delvene Delaney. For years, every young copper I met told me I must have known their sergeant. I think there was a Donger in every cop shop.

LEFT: Me as Spock from *Star Trek*. The makeup people had their work cut out for them every week.

BELOW: John McEnHoges, the bad-tempered superbrat we all secretly wanted to be.

LEFT: Hoges goes to London. Debating our country's sporting prowess with the hilarious Alf Garnett, aka actor Warren Mitchell. *(Newspix)*

LEFT: I told Mum I'd met the Queen. She asked if I'd dressed nice. Luckily Roger Woodward and the angel who is Olivia Newton-John provided the glamour. Meanwhile, I appeared to be trying to hide things from the Queen's wandering eyes. (Wikimedia Commons)

BELOW: With the best friends a man could have: John Cornell and Delvene Delaney. If not for John I'd have probably spent my life on the Bridge. John is brilliant, and Delvene, his soul mate, is every bit his equal.

ABOVE: I was lucky enough to spend quite a bit of time with this terrific couple. Princess Di was like a regular girl, and Charles, when not having to play the Prince, displayed a fabulous sense of humour. *(Getty Images)*

BELOW: Back up on the old Coat Hanger and doing my best to make the Yanks feel comfortable about visiting Oz. It worked.

ABOVE: Me on the set of *Crocodile Dundee* with Linda Kozlowski and Johnny Meillon, clueless as to how much my life was about to change, both personally and professionally. *(Getty Images)*

BELOW: When I wrote the now famous knife line, I thought, *That'll do, unless I can think of something better.* Over thirty-five years later, it still gets quoted to me daily. *(Alamy)*

LEFT: At the Oscars in 1987, demonstrating the awful 'I'm-so-glad-he-won-instead-of-me smile' that nominees tend to do when they lose out. 'Give us a bit of variety,' I advised. 'Storming out of the building in a huff'd be nice … What's wrong with a bit of good old-fashioned booing?' I was never invited back. (AAP)

RIGHT: Some in the government were worried about me doing the Tourism Australia ads because of my accent. Then Prime Minister Bob Hawke, who's more Australian than me, said, 'What's wrong with his bloody accent?!' I must have been pleased, as I appear to be trying to kiss him in this photo.

ABOVE: *Dundee II*. Mick and Sue seem to be on the lookout for pesky paparazzi. *(Alamy)*

BELOW: Typecast, the God of Acting, Charlton Heston, played, well, God, in *Almost an Angel*. At one stage the Oscar-winning legend asked me if I was happy with his performance. He obviously didn't know I was just a rigger. *(Alamy)*

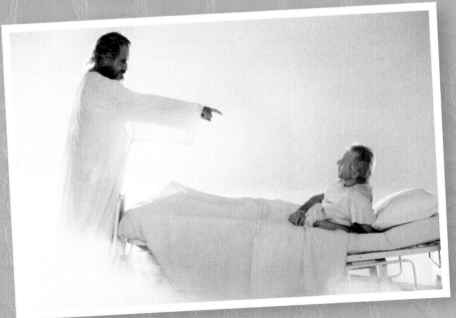

ABOVE: Playing cowboys with Cuba Gooding Jr in *Lightning Jack* – every boy's fantasy. Each morning was like waking up in a John Wayne movie. *(Alamy)*

RIGHT: Ten weeks in the Bahamas, a dolphin named Flipper and this terrific young actor, Elijah Wood – who wouldn't say yes? Elijah and me on the set in 1995. *(Alamy)*

ABOVE: With my youngest child, Chance, when he was a cheeky two-year-old. I've had a blessed life, full of incredible experiences, but nothing beats playing with your kids. If I was thirty years younger, I'd have more. *(Newspix)*

BELOW: Planning to scam the Tax Office with Michael Caton in *Strange Bedfellows*. Apparently some folks at the ATO thought the movie was real. *(Alamy)*

ABOVE: Having the time of my life filming *Charlie & Boots* with Shane Jacobson. It was so much fun I almost felt guilty that I was getting paid. *(Instinct Entertainment)*

BELOW: With farmer, friend and filmmaker Dean Murphy. We've done a dozen ventures together and having fun is always the priority. *(Instinct Entertainment)*

LEFT: Grab him before he dies. In 2016 I was honoured to receive the AACTA's Longford Lyell Award. I don't exactly know what it was for, but it was a great night! *(Getty Images)*

BELOW: On the eve of my turning eighty, art began to imitate life. *The Very Excellent Mr Dundee* saw 'Paul Hogan' failing to escape the Dundee legacy. In this scene an inflatable croc blows into the protagonist's arms in what a live-to-air reporter in the movie describes as 'the saddest thing I have ever seen'. My so-called legacy was in tatters and the media pounced. *(Clock Sounds Holdings)*

> Our tourist promotion is built around
> the kangaroo and the koala. People
> won't travel halfway around the world
> to visit a zoo. It's like you blokes
> are running a restaurant that sells the
> best food in town, but the sign in the
> window left by the previous tenant is
> advertising hardware. For Australia's
> sake, let us take that sign down and
> fill the joint with hungry customers
> every night.

Our 'America, You Need a Holiday' ads aired in the States from January 1984. John and I made it a condition that the government put the highest production quality into the commercials, and that they buy prime-time television in America. Otherwise we didn't think it was worth all the effort.

The ads said, in effect: 'We'd love to see ya, we're good fun people, come over to our place.' And Americans did. Australia went from the twenty-eighth 'most desired destination' to number one in a few months.

Tourism would eventually become our biggest industry and give tens of thousands of people jobs. Today, as I write this, I'm told it employs 3.5 million people. And all those pollies and bureaucrats who had opposed our ads went on to tell anyone who'd listen that they always knew how well they were going to work.

There was a fee for me in the budget, but I got them to pay it to Variety Australia. I needed to show the clowns in parliament

Ready to slip that extra prawn – I mean *shrimp* – on the barbie.
(Tourism Australia)

that we were all doing this because we believed in it, and that it needed to be done for the benefit of all Australians.

One day, standing down by the harbour, I was handed a script. It included the line, 'Come and say g'day. I'll slip an extra shrimp on the barbie for you.' That line was written by Allan Johnston.

'Shouldn't it be a prawn?' I said.

Allan laughed. 'We're not selling Australia to you, Hoges,' he said, 'we're selling it to the Yanks, so it's a shrimp.'

There was also a gentle irony in the fact that it was a tiger prawn and we were calling it a shrimp, making out like everything is bigger and better in Australia. One of the recurring things in my life is people coming up to me and saying, 'You should have called it a prawn.' They're just as wrong as I was.

Those Mojo blokes were great value and knew what they were doing! Alan and Allan were very funny and easy-going and full of good ideas. Their parties also became the stuff of legend, as all sorts of identities and TV people would go there on a Friday afternoon, just to hang out and have a good time. There have been plenty of stories about the excesses in the world of advertising in the seventies and eighties, and I think Mojo lived up to them all.

And the ads themselves? They went on to become the most successful tourism campaign ever in America. They still teach it in advertising courses on both sides of the Pacific. Actually, it's in the Smithsonian. If you check out the 'Power of Advertising' section, there it is: the 'Shrimp on the Barbie' ad from 1984, right in the Smithsonian, the biggest museum in the world. Pretty cool!

● ● ●

According to Hoges ...

The Land of Wonder

HOGES: America, you look like you need a holiday, a fair dinkum holiday. In the land of wonder. The land down under. Now, there's a few things I've got to warn you about. Firstly, you're going to get wet because the place is surrounded by water. Oh, and you're going to have to learn to say g'day. Because every day's a good day in Australia.

★ ★ ★

HOGES: G'day. Now it's come to my attention that some Americans still don't know where Australia is. Well, I'll tell you exactly where it is. Australia is where the sun shines on thousands of miles of the world's great beaches.

★ ★ ★

HOGES: Come on, come and say g'day. I'll slip an extra shrimp on the barbie for you.

In the mid-1980s, I went to the Melbourne Cup. I don't need to explain the Melbourne Cup to Australians but, for anyone else, it's not just a horse race. It's a national obsession, and a national holiday. It's bigger than the Kentucky Derby. It's pretty well bigger than anything.

There was this special, guarded VIP area which was full of personalities – the social elite of Melbourne and, um, me. I was surrounded by the well-heeled and those who desperately wanted to be, and many of them looked at me askance. To many I was still that rough bloke off the telly. I was known on the telly as the common man, but to this crowd I was too common a commoner to be in their area at this function.

Suddenly some officious security guards appeared and told us we all needed to move back, as Prince Charles would soon be passing through the area on his way to the presentation stand. Being good citizens, we all did as we were told and were on our best behaviour. Suddenly Charles appeared, looked over at the crowd, spotted me and broke away from the pack and headed in my direction.

'Hoges, how are you, mate?' he called out. 'Who are you going for in the cup?'

'Black Knight,' I replied.

We chatted for a bit and, after he headed off suddenly, I was the most socially acceptable person in Australia. People around me, socialites and others, were almost fainting because Charles had broken away from the parade to talk to scruffy ol' me. None of them would have known of our shared history through Variety Australia. They just thought I was terribly well connected. Black Knight didn't win that year. It came ninth, but it didn't matter.

I am very much pro-Royals. I've said so on television in Britain. They're always complaining about how much it costs to maintain them. 'If you don't want the Royal Family, we'll have them,' I've said. 'Send them out to Australia. Because they're the biggest attraction you've got in Britain. People don't come to your country for your beaches, you know? You don't go and sit on the gravel at Brighton or Blackpool and think, *Gee, this is the life.* Nah, your Royal Family is your biggest asset.'

They're historic and they signify a certain sort of pomp and pageantry. And basically the main job of the Royals is fund-raising for various charities and they do huge business in that department. They pay their way by helping out all sorts of causes. I think they're vital. They give Britain a history and a symbolism of sorts.

You can't top something like the Royal Family. If you look at America, they have no royals, so the media tries to create some. How else can you explain the phenomenon of the Kardashians or even the Trumps? When you look at that, you think, *Yeah, having kings and queens and everything is not so bad, compared to what it could be.*

15

A Hillbilly in NYC

When I was in New York doing a bit of tourist promotion in early 1984, some Aussie journalists there wanted to take some photos of me in classic New York places. I discovered that we just happened to be near the New York Yacht Club. 'If we can sneak in there,' I said, 'you can take some pics of their empty display case.'

They loved the idea and we managed to talk our way into that prestigious setting.

'This is where the America's Cup used to be,' I announced, posing next to a large glass cabinet. 'I'm not exactly sure where it is now, but if you want to see it, maybe have a look down in Australia, somewhere around Perth.' The Australian journalists all loved me taking the mickey, and afterwards we all went out for a drink.

When I left the bar that afternoon, I couldn't get a cab. It was five o'clock and it was clear I would have to walk. It seemed like everyone in New York was going one way and I was going the other. I remember thinking, *I've spent my whole life in cities but going against this peak-hour Manhattan crowd makes me feel like a hillbilly.* The energy of the city and the people and their fashion and fast talking was simply overwhelming.

So, as is my way, I started to write a sketch in my head. I thought it'd be a Hoges sketch, about how he'd react. But as I fought my way through the crowd, the sketch in my head grew longer and longer. I now started to think that instead of it being me, or Hoges, I should make it about a bloke from one of the remotest parts of the outback who'd never been to a big city. There were plenty of things to send up.

By the time I got to the hotel, my sketch, which normally would be about three minutes long, had stretched out to about twenty minutes. It was a jumble of random ideas but I sensed it had a future.

The following day I had to head back to Australia, as I'd been cast in the World War I TV mini-series *Anzacs*. This drama followed a group of young Australian men who enlisted in the 8th Battalion (Australia) of the First Australian Imperial Force in 1914, fighting initially at Gallipoli in 1915 and then on the Western Front for the remainder of the war. It was a story that needed to be told and a fantastic shoot, made with an absolutely great bunch of blokes – well, mainly blokes, as it was a war film. As with any television production, there were hours of sitting around. To keep myself busy I started to develop my 'sketch' further. It grew longer and longer until I thought, *It's not a sketch, it's a movie.*

With *The Paul Hogan Show*, there was always something of a rush to shoot things. When I was doing *Anzacs* I started to enjoy having more time; none of it was live or had to be ready for a show that week, so we could do as many takes as needed. It was also fun because I was allowed to write my own lines. That was the brief I got: if you don't like the dialogue or you want to change it, you know, go for it.

I didn't have to audition for the role of Private Pat Cleary, a fairly colourful character, and some wondered if that was wise. Could a comedian handle a straight acting role? I, for one, didn't have any doubts. If you can do comedy, you can certainly do drama. It's the other way around that often doesn't work. It's like Mel Brooks said: 'Dying is easy, comedy is hard.'

Anzacs was a good story, and a true story, and showed what made the Anzacs who they were, while also explaining how Australia came to have that sort of war-lover heritage we have. It seems like we've been in more blues than any other country on the planet: the Crimean, the Boer, World Wars I and II, Malaya, Korea, Vietnam. The only one we missed out on was the Falklands and, even then, the Australian navy was on its way when word came through the war was over. If there's a war somewhere, we don't want to miss out on it. Same goes for barbecues and sporting events.

In one episode of *Anzacs*, an Aussie digger remarks how much the French countryside reminds him of Daylesford, back home in Victoria, Australia. This was an in-joke, as some scenes were filmed near Daylesford, including a German counterattack scene. It was a twenty-week shoot and I had even more

On the set of *Anzacs*. I appear lost in thought. Probably thinking back to my time at the Playboy Mansion. *(Newspix)*

downtime than most other actors because I'd been in Nasho. The other blokes had to do some basic military training so they could look more like real army material. Anyway, I continued to write my ideas out like I always did, in my legal pad in block capitals.

While I was there, I met Alec Wilson, a genuine cowboy from South Australia. Alec had been brought in to *Anzacs* as a horse wrangler, but he had such a good rough head that they decided to get him to act a few times. So he knocked around with me, because I wasn't really an actor either.

By the end of the shoot, I'd not only made a great new friend in Alec, I'd written out my whole story and I knew it would be my first feature film. It was to be called *Buffalo Jones*.

I was a little unsure of the name at first, but then I started to warm to it. Luckily, common sense eventually prevailed and I realised it sucked. It was like some daft cross between Buffalo Bill and Indiana Jones. I needed a better name for a real outback character, someone who thought seven people was a crowd.

Meanwhile, although I had copious notes and scribbled ideas, the story wasn't really in the form of a screenplay. So I contacted Ken Shadie, who'd written some sketches for *The Paul Hogan Show* and he agreed to help out.

I'd ring Ken and read my notes to him over the phone and he would type them up and offer suggestions about things such as structure and pacing. Ken was a great collaborator, just the right guy, and together we turned my story into a screenplay. But we wisely dropped the name *Buffalo Jones*.

We called it *Crocodile Dundee*.

• • •

I'd only ever met one real croc hunter when I came up with my movie script. He was normally a professional roo shooter in Far North Queensland, but if there was a problem with an individual crocodile in, say, the Mossman River, they'd get him to go hunt it down and kill it.

This guy was toothless, heavily tattooed and had all the charm of a funnel-web spider. Awful. Smelt of death. I never even found out his full name, but the one thing I did get out of him was a black hat with crocodile teeth in it. I thought, *Oh, that'll do.*

Other than the hat, Michael J. 'Crocodile' Dundee was a completely made-up character. That hasn't stopped many people, even to this day, claiming they are 'The Real Crocodile Dundee'.

There was one guy in the Northern Territory who ended up dying in a gunfight with the police after he ambushed a cop. I still hear people claim the character was styled on him, and I was really annoyed by that suggestion. Because one thing I do know is that Mick Dundee would never ambush police, and he certainly wouldn't have died in a gunfight with them. Not at all.

To acknowledge that most of us older Australians are descended from the convicts, I chose the first name Mick for our hero, because that was very Irish, and Dundee for his second name, as that was very Scottish. The combination of Irish and Scottish convict blood seemed just right.

As soon as Ken and I had what roughly resembled the first draft of a script, I took it over to John.

'So what do you think?'

John smiled. 'I've done all I can do with the cricket. So,

yeah, let's make a movie!' Then he added, with all his usual certainty, 'It'll be a hit!'

I should mention another of John Cornell's roles. Not only was Corney always my cattle prodder, he was also the best subeditor around. I tended to overwrite, and John'd say, 'Oh, cut this bit out, you dragged on too long there, and leave that out. You can do better here – and here.' And he was always correct, you know. The writing credit for the script ended up saying: 'Screenplay by Paul Hogan, Ken Shadie and John Cornell; story by Paul Hogan'.

In the mid-eighties, there was no Paramount or MGM or any other big studios in Australia. You had to do your own thing, so I put up the original money, a hundred thousand or two, just to get us started. Feeling bullish, we then went to see Peter Weir. Peter is a world-class Australian director of such films as *Gallipoli*, *Dead Poets Society* and *The Truman Show*.

'I'm sorry boys, I've got too much on my plate,' he said. (I think he was working on the film *Witness* with Harrison Ford at the time.) 'Why don't you do it yourself,' he suggested. 'It's not hard.'

We thought this was an incredible thing for a world-class director to say, like it's no big deal. But we still thought we needed someone else. John and I looked at each other and then we both said, 'What about Peter Faiman?' Peter had directed *The Paul Hogan Show* and was certainly a phenomenal talent, but television direction and film direction are two different sports. Still, we thought, if anyone could manage it, it'd be Pete. So we went and talked to him.

'I've never done a movie,' he said.

'We know,' I replied. 'Neither have we.'

One of these is stuffed.

Peter came on board anyway, giving us a first-time director to go with our first-time film producer, John, and our first-time writer and lead actor, me. Now we just had to find the rest of the money – and convince the world that we knew what the hell we were doing!

• • •

As time went on, John and I became more and more confident that we had a good idea. Well actually, I was never as confident as John, who is confidence personified.

Most Australian films are financed by presales. This is where you sell the film all over the world before it is made. It covers your downside and gets the movie made. On the other hand, it often means the people who have staked the money try to tell you what to do. We didn't want to be told what to do. We had faith in what we were making and it was only going to be fun if we had complete control.

Our first port of call was Kerry Packer, who seemed to become monumentally richer with every passing year. We visited Kerry in his office in Park Street, Sydney. He looked at our proposal and said, 'Oh, you know boys, I don't know about making movies.'

Kerry went on to tell us it was near impossible to make money out of films and that we should stick to television, and that our idea wasn't strong enough and it simply wouldn't work. John, being John, just laughed and told Kerry not to worry. 'We'll raise our own money,' he said.

For a moment we considered meeting with the government film-financing bodies, but we quickly thought the better of it for no other reason than life's too short. Then, out of the blue I got a phone call from Denis Johnson. DJ grew up about a hundred yards from my place in Granville and was mostly a mate of my brother, Pat. His dad ran the local gas station. He was one of the few Granville lads that hadn't gone to jail. Instead he'd ended up as a successful stockbroker in Queensland. Probably should've been in jail if he was anything like other stockbrokers I'd met. Anyway, I hadn't seen him for years.

'Hey, are you trying to make a movie, Hoges?' DJ asked.

'Yeah.'

'Do you need any money?'

'Yeah,' I said, 'a few million.' I thought that might stop him in his tracks.

'Yeah, no worries.' DJ explained he had a lot of punters up there on the Gold Coast, 'who'd love to have a bet on you'. Whatever we needed, he said, he could supply it.

We ended up having all types of good folks investing, including three of the most famous cricket players this country's ever produced: Greg Chappell, Dennis Lillee and Rod Marsh. Thanks to good ol' DJ being true to his word, we were soon financed and ready to officially make a movie.

Now we just needed a crew. And actors.

• • •

Even though we were first-timers, we weren't complete fools. We knew we had to surround ourselves with the best possible people for the shoot. However, I've had a rule from when I first started in television and that is: I only work with people I like. I call it 'The No Arsehole Rule'. Now, some believe you shouldn't have fun when shooting, that you've got to have some drama and anxiety, otherwise the movie will be no good. I know that's crap. There are so many brilliantly talented people in this world who are also great people that there's no need to work with those who aren't.

At a party some years earlier, I'd met an actor I immediately loved: John Meillon. John had starred in about forty movies, including the legendary end-of-the-world film *On the Beach* with Gregory Peck, Ava Gardner and Fred Astaire.

'Mr Hogan,' John said to me, 'when you get around to doing movies, which you no doubt will, don't forget to ask your old mate.' So, I wrote the part of Walter Reilly, or Wally, for him. At the time I didn't realise that John, who came across as a rugged character, and was a bushman in *Wake in Fright*, the original outback horror film, didn't have much love for anything beyond the city limits.

'On another movie,' he told me one day, 'we were in some outback town and after work we all came out and stood on the pub's veranda and looked at each other. And we looked at each other again. There was absolutely not a thing to do. I walked around the pub a couple of times and came back to the veranda and everyone was still just standing there. So I wandered into what they called "town" and the only thing that was open was the vet's clinic. I went in and the vet said, "Can I help you?" I said, "I really just want to chat." And the vet said, "Oh, in that case we're closed."'

John endured the outback, but didn't like it.

I also wrote a part for David Gulpilil. Now David, a Yolngu man from the very top of the country, is another real actor with incredible range. I'd seen him do drama but had no idea he was so funny. I wrote him in as Neville, the reluctant son who has to attend a corroboree to keep his very traditional dad happy.

Then there was an old mate who was not only a wrestler but also a sometime bouncer at my old boxing gym and SP bookie joint, Steve Rackman. Steve was given the role of Donk, a huge, loud-mouthed barfly. Donk's favourite trick is balancing a beer on his head and seeing if anyone can punch him hard enough to make him spill even a drop.

My other casting contribution was my eldest son, Brett, by then in his late teens. We decided he'd come along and play a roo shooter.

As we built up our cast it became apparent that we needed to find a genuine New Yorker to play the reporter and love interest, Sue Charlton. At the time, Australian actors who could master perfect US accents simply weren't a thing, and we felt we couldn't have an actress from Wagga Wagga playing the role of a New Yorker without cheapening the film. The Australian Actors' Union felt otherwise and, for quite some time it battled us, demanding we use someone from Australia.

John meanwhile continued to do things his way, and searched the world for our Sue. Then Dustin Hoffman, via our shared US agent, suggested a Connecticut-born twenty-something New Yorker. Her name was Linda Kozlowski. Hoffman had been doing *Death of a Salesman* with her on Broadway, and rated her a huge talent. John met with Linda and immediately locked her in for the role.

Linda had never heard of me, had never seen the tourism commercials. Her agent at the time said to her, 'Look, it's only a little Australian movie. Do it for the experience, and if it's no good no one will ever see it.' Still, it was a big call for Linda to agree to travel on her own from the Big Apple to make a film with a bunch of first-timers in outback Australia.

The rest of the casting I left in the capable hands of John and Peter Faiman, and they filled the whole movie with great and memorable characters. We were now ready to begin filming.

• • •

Crocodile Dundee

The Opening Scene

A bush helicopter lands. Dust and chickens are tumbling in the wind. A man, fifties, stands trying to maintain his composure in front of his old ute. An outback town sizzles behind him.

A lady, Sue, late twenties, alights from the chopper.

WALTER (*offering his hand*): Hi. Walter Reilly, Never Never Safaris. I'm Mr Dundee's business partner.

SUE: Nice to meet you, Mr Reilly.

WALTER: Oh, please, call me Walter. We're pretty informal in the bush. (*He puts her bags in the ute as she tries to open the jammed door.*) No, uh, let me. (*He reaches in, opening it from the inside.*) There you go. You all right?

SUE: Yes.

WALTER: I'm sorry that Mr Dundee isn't here himself to meet you. But he is here in town ... somewhere.

He jams the ute into gear and they drive into the dusty, windblown main street. They climb from the ute. Walter strikes a pose in front of the town's only pub.

WALTER: Welcome to Walkabout Creek.

A few old sheds and red dirt make up the outlook.

SUE: Hmm.

WALTER: Oh, I took the liberty of booking you into our hotel. I trust that's in order?

SUE: Sounds just fine.

WALTER: There's just one other thing. Uh ... You did say that you were prepared to pay the $2500?

SUE: Absolutely. (*Walter looks relieved.*) And I will see where he was attacked and how he survived?

WALTER: Miss, I assure you, you're gonna spend a few wonderful days here.

$$16$$

Let's Make a Movie

Walkabout Creek was, for a while, one of the best-known destinations in Australia. But, of course, it doesn't exist. Well, not really. For Walkabout Creek we used McKinlay, a township with a stable population of nearly two hundred, in the dusty plains of north-west Queensland. It sits somewhere between bustling Cloncurry, with its 2500-or-so residents and the metropolis of Winton, which might have nine hundred or so people calling it home.

Not a lot happened in McKinlay at the time, and as the film crew moved in the locals were a little bemused. Even more so as we started to strip away the town's slight charm and rough up its already hard edges. We needed 'Walkabout Creek' to look as inhospitable as possible for the arrival of New York photographer and journalist Sue Charlton.

McKinlay was a town full of hard-working, hard-living people, and the late-night activities in the local pub, with its fighting and drinking, were probably not a mile away from the opening scenes we'd written for our film. The town's Federal Hotel underwent a make-under from the film's designer, Graham 'Grace' Walker, and became what we now know as the Walkabout Creek Hotel.

Seeing everyone arrive on day one of the shoot reminded me that a year or two earlier I'd been in the United States and happened to wander past a movie set on what was clearly the first morning of shooting. I saw the director stand up on a chair and tell the assembled mass of 150 people how it was going to be 'an incredible shoot'. They were 'going to work hard, make the best movie ever made', and so on and so on. There was then lots of whooping and hugging and high-fiving.

So now I thought, *I'm going to do that*. I climbed up on a chair with our crew of a hundred or so looking on, plus Corney and various others. I asked them all to hold hands. I said I wouldn't continue until everyone was doing this with the person beside them. Not a lot of the crew knew me well at this stage, so they dutifully followed the orders of 'the star'. Weather-beaten sixty-year-old men with names like The Rat and Slugger took the hands of the blokes next to them, and if they weren't uncomfortable when they saw me get up on the chair, they certainly were now!

I then said, 'Men, ladies, fellow workers. I need to point out that on this shoot, there will be no wanking. If anyone's going to be wanking on this production, it's going to be me because,

202

as many of you probably know, I'm the biggest wanker in the business. The rest of you just carry on like normal humans. Thank you very much.'

I then got off the chair and walked away. For a few seconds those who didn't know me were stunned, but then they started to laugh. Later they told me how many times they'd had to endure serious versions of this type of thing on US productions, during which the director would talk about the importance of the 'art' they were making. This let them know our production was going to be a little different.

• • •

It was only just before we started shooting that I first met my 'love interest', Linda Kozlowski. She seemed pleasant enough. She wasn't too sure about me though. She thought I was a little bit aloof, or perhaps a little bit closed off, either shy or reserved. She couldn't quite crack who I was. There was no real connection or common ground, and there certainly wasn't anything like a sudden, fatal attraction. We were opposites in every way, and now had the challenge of making it convincing when we fell for each other on screen.

She soon found out about me never rehearsing. She came from theatre, where they go through every line in fine detail for weeks on end before they even step on the stage. Now she'd arrived in a new country and had to work with a 'star' who'd never made a movie before, yet still thought he didn't need to rehearse. But I didn't see any reason to change my approach now.

I'm sure there were some frantic calls from Linda to her agent in the United States and even poor Dustin probably got an earful. But in the end she came to terms with it. She knew I'd written the script and so I'd at least know what my lines were. And even if I got them wrong, that's the way they would stay. Also, I would often change my mind halfway through a scene and do something new. After a while, Linda started to roll with it and was great.

Linda's a much better actor than I could ever be. I can do minor variations, but you're never going to see me as King Lear or Richard III. And I never write myself difficult parts. There's never a big emotional scene with the tears running down my face or anything like that. Some people were kind enough to say, 'You're a natural.'

'No,' I'd reply, 'it's just luck. That's all.'

With Linda, though, it wasn't luck. She went to Juilliard, the most famous theatrical school in America, the holy grail for budding actors, and on a scholarship. It was an opera scholarship, believe it or not. She's a singer, but she didn't bother pursuing it and switched to acting when she got to Juilliard. She's a seriously good actor too, the real deal, and yet, at this stage, the poor thing was hanging out with us clowns in the outback. At least she didn't need to do much acting to play the fish-out-of-water, big-city journalist in the sticks.

• • •

The shooting went smooth as you like. Australian crews are second to none. Whenever international producers come to Australia, they are always amazed by the quality of our movie production people. And it's not just that they're good at their jobs; it's that they have fun doing them, and that makes the whole exercise so much easier. We had the best camera and lighting team there is: Russell Boyd, or 'Russ Bob' as we called him, was our cinematographer; the legendary Ray Brown, or 'Mr Brown', was our key grip; and Brian Bansgrove, or 'Banza', did the lighting. They were like a bikie gang.

Mr Brown used to wear track pants and a sleeveless T-shirt like Hoges wore, and he always – and I mean always – had a tie on. It was a hell of a look but somehow it worked. And Banza would always wear those reflective sunglasses, so looking at him was like looking in a mirror. When he took them off, I noticed he had reflective eyes too. They were pale blue.

With Russ Bob at the helm, these guys had a real thirst for work and they grafted incredibly hard. They also had an equal thirst for drink, and partied incredibly hard too, every night. Next morning, though, they'd be first to set, full of energy and ideas, and wouldn't let up until wrap was called. Then the partying would start all over again.

· · ·

Crocodile Dundee

The Hotel Scene

Inside the Walkabout Creek Hotel. Donk rests a beer on top of his head.

NUGGET: Come on, fellas. Five bucks, anyone who can make Donk spill it.

SUE (*watching from the corner*): So tell me, what's the sideshow all about?

WALTER: Oh, that's just the boys having fun and games. You see, Donk's never spilled a drop. We're a pretty tough breed up here.

A *bloke punches Donk in the guts. He hardly flinches.*

SUE: And your Mr Dundee, does he …?

WALTER: No, no, no. He's very reserved. He's a legend up here. I mean, there he was out there doing a quiet spot of fishing, when all of a sudden … *Bang!* This giant crocodile came up, turned him over, bit half his leg off, dragged him down under. Killed it, of course. I mean, any normal man would have just turned up his toes and died. But not our Mick. No. Hundreds of miles … Snake-infested swamps … On his hands and knees … he crawled, right into Katherine.

IDA (*the publican, laughing*): Straight past the hospital and into the first pub for a beer. That story's getting better every time you tell it, Wally.

WALTER (*embarrassed*): No, we handle ourselves pretty well up here in the bush, Miss. But if you're talking legend …

From nowhere, a large knife pierces the bar.

SUE: Oh, my God!

Crocodile Dundee is flung into the pub. He wrestles a large crocodile. It is putting up one hell of a fight. Sue watches nervously,

Walter knowingly. Eventually, the crocodile is subdued and the man leans over the bar with the crocodile under his arm.

MICK: Two beers, Ida. One for me, one for me mate.

IDA: 'One for your mate', you mad bugger.

MICK (*spotting Sue*): Oh, hang on.

WALTER: I'm sorry if that frightened you, Miss. You see, it's stuffed.

MICK (*approaches*): Him and me both, Wal. (*He puts out his hand.*) Michael J. 'Crocodile' Dundee.

SUE: Never Never Safaris?

MICK: Yeah. Um, never go out with us; if you do, you'll never come back. Right, Wal?

Walter laughs nervously.

SUE: Sue Charlton, *Newsday*.

MICK: Yeah, I thought you might be.

The film took us to many incredible outback locations, such as the Yellow Water (Ngurrungurrudjba) wetlands in Kakadu National Park and various reserves in Arnhem Land, and there's no better way to appreciate the uniqueness of what we have in Australia than to have a New York actress in tow.

At one stage we had some others from the United States visiting the set and we took them out into the bush one night

On the set of *Crocodile Dundee*. The wonderful Mr Brown can be seen on the left, complete with shirt and tie.

and away from all the lights. We made them sit in the car in the dark till their eyes had adjusted, then we got them out and looked at the stars. It's something that many of us in Australia take for granted, but the visitors were absolutely gobsmacked! For most New Yorkers, a starry night is forty or fifty stars. Few have ever seen the full-on southern-hemisphere night sky.

'It's a pity it's a bit cloudy,' someone said.

'That's not cloud or mist,' I told them, and when their eyes adjusted further they saw it was billions of stars looking like cloud. Even Linda gasped and threw her arms out in amazement – hitting John Cornell in the mouth and splitting his lip in the process.

One thing it would probably be safe to say is that the accommodation throughout the Northern Territory and parts of Queensland was never of the Hilton, five-star variety. At Kakadu we stayed in a closed-down uranium mine. It was deserted and the old huts became our accommodation. They were fine, but many of the crew preferred to sleep out under the stars. Some of the most memorable nights were when we were in the middle of nowhere with the whole crew sitting around campfires, telling jokes and yarns. Linda was quick to take all the incredible changes in her stride and within days the crew had labelled her an honorary Aussie.

John provided the beer and food and, on one occasion in the middle of the Northern Territory, even served top-shelf Champagne. That made Corney both the most popular and resourceful producer in the country.

We loved every minute of our eight weeks in the bush together. We loved the solitude and the absolute quiet, but it was then time to move on. It was time to go to New York.

Opposites attract. (*Alamy*)

. . .

The International Brotherhood of Teamsters is a massive union covering transport and some other related industries, and it sort of ran the movie industry in New York. It was once famously controlled by the gangster-connected Jimmy Hoffa, who disappeared, presumed murdered, in 1975.

The guys running the union a decade later had strict rules. You would go to the Teamsters and they would tell you where you could shoot and how many trucks you had to have. They told you what you could do and how much, and who, you had to pay. These guys were notoriously tough, but they'd never encountered Australians before. Particularly Australians like Mr Brown, Banza and Russ Bob.

The Teamsters quickly saw that we were all great mates, and this struck them as weird. They then came out for a drink with us and Russ Bob's crew, in particular, drank them under the table. Word went rapidly through the Teamsters everywhere that these guys were different from other film people – the crew and producers and stars all hung out together and had a drink and a laugh. They loved this and were fascinated that we worked this way.

Because the big tough Teamsters thought we were all right, suddenly we were allowed much more flexibility as to, for example, how many trucks we could have and how many drivers, where we could park, and what we could shut down and where we could shoot.

The Teamsters broke all the rules for us. At times they would even climb down from their trucks and give us a hand. This stunned the New Yorkers who were working with us.

They'd never seen this before. Everyone noted how quickly and efficiently the Australian crews worked. One night we even had other cinematographers come to the set in the middle of New York just to watch Russ Bob light. The Teamsters became close allies and, in the end, they didn't want us to leave.

Anyway, with such a great mob around us, we finished our very first movie. And now we were ready to see how it'd go.

17

That's Not a Knife ...

Crocodile Dundee opened in Australia in April 1986. It didn't start super spectacularly, but it did make number one at the box office. The next week it was also number one. We allowed ourselves to start getting excited. And then I had a cerebral haemorrhage.

It was my own stupid fault. A friend of mine ran the Nautilus Gym in North Sydney. I'd hop in there occasionally in the mornings before too many people arrived. Some footballers and I shared a record there for chinning the bar. I was pretty strong, sure, but I also had the huge advantage of not weighing much. Then Terry Randall, the Manly-Warringah Sea Eagles rugby league player, broke the record and did it with a fifty-pound weight hanging around his waist. He was also talking and joking while he was doing it!

So, changing tack, I thought, *I wonder how much I can bench press*. I got on the machine and put twice my own weight on it. I had to strain like a bastard, but I lifted the bloody thing. I would have congratulated myself too, but before I could do that, this excruciating pain shot through me, like I'd pinched a nerve in the back of my neck. I tried not to make a scene in front of the boys, but I knew something wasn't right. By the time I staggered down to my car, my head was shaking uncontrollably. Doing my best to stay upright through the pain, I decided, *Whoa, I better go and see a doctor or something*.

I climbed into my car and tried to drive to my GP's practice at Mosman, but I started to black out a little. *I know what I'll do*, I thought, *I'll stick my head out the window*. So I was driving through the busy part of North Sydney, in a daze, with my head hanging out the side of the car while blowing the horn and swearing at anyone I thought was driving irresponsibly. It was just luck that I never ran over anybody.

Somehow I got there. My doctor, a great bloke and a friend, was amazed. 'You're probably the first man to drive a car while having a cerebral haemorrhage.'

'What?'

'You have bleeding in the brain. It's probably all right, as it's most likely in the sub-retinoid area. You should be okay.'

Should be okay? Bleeding in the brain didn't sound okay.

All I can remember of the drive to the hospital with my doctor is the pain. It was like a giant eagle had come down out of the sky and grabbed my head, got its claws right in there. We arrived in Emergency and, through the agony, I vaguely heard a conversation along the lines of, 'Oh, if this doesn't stop soon, he's in big trouble.'

I'm done for, I thought. 'It's okay,' I blurted out. 'As long as I don't have this pain any more!'

I was later told that Noelene sat with me for three days while I was completely out of it. John also came to the hospital. 'This is terrible timing, mate,' he said. 'You're missing all the parties!'

'Eh, it's going to be a long party, mate,' I replied, apparently. And you know, John never came to the hospital again. He didn't want to see me in there, all doped up and vulnerable. I've never known anyone to live for the moment more than John, and seeing me like that brought out that underlying fear that's in all of us.

What was really funny was that while I was in the hospital 'dying', the press were wonderfully kind to me. They said what a fabulous human being and wonderful Australian son I was. Then, a week or so later when I walked out of the hospital still very much alive, they turned on me. How dare I have the nerve to survive and walk out in good health?

Anyway, sure enough, my cerebral haemorrhage was in the sub-retinoid area. Apparently, I'd been born with a weak blood vessel and it had burst under the strain of me bench-pressing twice my own weight. I was assured it would heal and scar up and be stronger than it had ever been. 'The best thing you can do is pretend it never happened,' I was told. 'No walking around with your head in cotton wool. Just forget about it.'

So I did. But it was certainly a painful experience. Anything like that does make you think, and being someone not prone to doing a lot of thinking, maybe it changed me. Or maybe, at the very least, it reinforced the perspective I'd got on life when my dad had suddenly died at only fifty. You have to live for the day. Or, as the old saying goes, live every day as though it's your last and one day you'll be right.

• • •

Dundee continued to play and play in Australian cinemas. First it became the highest grossing Australian film ever at the Aussie box office and then the highest grossing film ever, from anywhere in the world, at our box office. I'd hoped it would do well but had never dared dream quite so big.

Even Mum liked it. She'd bought a new dress for the premiere. She was blown away and said she couldn't believe it was me up there on the big screen. She did add, though, that Dundee could have dressed 'a little nicer'.

Although my hospital visit meant I missed some of the fun in Australia, I was determined I wasn't going to miss any of it in the rest of the world. In the United States, Paramount had become very excited by the film's dazzling success in Australia. They said, 'Look, we love this movie, and because of the way it's gone down there, we're going to release it here in the States like it's a proper American movie.' Which meant it was going out on about 1500 screens. That, I have to admit, made me a little nervous.

But the first thing Paramount wanted to do was to dub my voice with a 'clearly speaking American one'. I told them, 'Forget it! We can't have an Aussie wandering the outback with an American accent, ya clowns.' Up until that point, Australian movies like the original *Mad Max* had been released in the

United States with dubbed American accents. Otherwise they were classified as 'foreign films' and released only in a handful of art cinemas on the coasts. Although I didn't anticipate we'd have much success in the United States, whether dubbed or not, I held firm. Truth be told, the only person who thought *Dundee* could be a mainstream success was John Cornell. Once again ol' Strop was showing us he was more of an entrepreneur and businessman than anyone. I still wasn't convinced. Why would anyone over there take the slightest bit of interest in it?

In the end my voice and accent remained intact, and the deal with Paramount was finalised. One of the many culture shocks was just how much signing that involved. The Yanks always arrive with a pile of contracts and I must have scratched out my name or initials five hundred times. Yet in all my years dealing with John and Kerry, we'd never needed more than a handshake.

Anyway, almost right away the craziness of promoting a film in America began, with a whirlwind of photoshoots and TV appearances. Then, within what felt like only a few months, we found ourselves back in Los Angeles – for the opening night.

Ours being a low-budget movie with a virtually unknown cast, there was no premiere and no opening-night party; instead John and I drove around Los Angeles, with the aim of sneaking into a cinema or two to see how our film played. We ended up in Westwood, I think, and we saw there was a queue stretching out of the theatre and around the block. I thought, *What the hell are they all going to see?*

John and I jumped out of the car and ran up to a guy at the end of the queue. 'Sorry, mate,' we asked, 'but what are you lining up for?'

Mick Dundee goes sightseeing in New York. *(Alamy)*

We were absolutely stoked by his answer! We were just
thrilled that anyone at all had turned up because, despite all
Paramount's promotion and the big number of cinemas it was
opening in and all that, it was still the sort of movie the Yanks
would normally treat as a low-budget foreign film filled with
wacky accents.

Back in Australia the line 'That's not a knife ... *That's* a
knife' had always got a good laugh. It came as a nice surprise
and people seemed to enjoy it. Months later, when gearing up
for the US release, the American studio had presented us with
the cut of their new *Dundee* trailer, which featured the '*That's* a
knife' scene, famous line and all.

I was furious. I didn't want it in the trailer. I argued that if
people saw it in the trailer they'd never want to see it again.
They'd know the gag. The surprise would be gone. It wouldn't
be funny a second time. This argument went on for weeks,
but, unlike the dispute about accents, this time I lost. I couldn't
believe the stupidity of these people. The trailer, including the
knife line, went into high circulation across the United States
and I was sure it was going to poison things.

But now, on opening night, the ever-increasing queue told
us something was working, so John and I bypassed the crowd
and, like teenagers, snuck into the screening and stood at the
back. The film seemed to play well. There was lots of laughter
and no one was leaving, so I started to relax. Everyone else in
the cinema was pretty relaxed too.

Then the mood started to shift and there was this new
energy in the room. A real ripple of excitement that both John
and I could feel. On the screen was the scene where Dundee
is walking from a New York restaurant, arm in arm with Sue

and suddenly he's approached by muggers. It was as though the packed cinema audience was now holding its collective breath. They'd been waiting for this moment. You could hear a pin drop. John and I were most intrigued.

As the knife line was delivered, the cinema absolutely erupted. People jumped to their feet, clapping and cheering, whooping and hollering. John and I looked at each other, thinking, *We just might be onto something*. And, though I hate to say it, we were also admitting to ourselves, *Paramount must know a bit about making trailers*.

We got the box office numbers at the end of week one. They weren't spectacular because *Dundee* had been released in the low season, but we were actually number one right across the United States. And we stayed there, and stayed there, and stayed there, and the take kept going up.

I love the movie *Dances with Wolves*, a Kevin Costner western that came out a few years after *Dundee*. What our movies had in common was that they were the only ones that ever opened at the top of the charts in October and just kept on going and going. October is a bit of a graveyard for movies. Smaller films are generally released then so that they have a short moment in the sun before the big Christmas blockbusters arrive and sweep them away.

Yet for nine weeks we were number one at the US box office and we actually took more on some subsequent weekends than on the opening one. Clearly, word of mouth worked gangbusters. This blew me and Paramount away. And even John!

I remember Paramount calling me just after our opening. They were feeling bullish. 'We've run the numbers and think we're going to do 20 million!' Then they called back the next week. 'No, more like 40 million!'

The third week they rang again. 'Look, it's lightning in a bottle, we've got no idea what it will do.' The box office takings went right on past the $100 million mark and just kept growing. When the film finally ran its last reel, it had taken around $170 million in the United States alone. And this was in the 1980s.

This success was so unlikely. Making a low-budget Australian movie that becomes a hit in the United States was just not something that happened. It was like turning up at the Olympics in your jeans and bare feet and saying, 'Can I have a run in the hundred metres?' And then winning the gold medal! It was that unlikely.

We were actually lockstep with *Top Gun* as the most successful movie that year in the States. Tom Cruise! I thought, *That's pretty good*.

Then the film opened around the world. I'd originally guessed that if it was to be big anywhere outside Australia it might be in the UK, since the TV specials and Foster's ads had worked so well over there. After all, we inherited our early sense of humour from the UK, and then dried it out a bit. But I didn't suspect they'd also be laughing at it in Germany and Israel and Lebanon and Chile and Japan and Nicaragua.

And while *Crocodile Dundee* was never officially released in Russia because of the Iron Curtain, or in China because of the Bamboo Curtain, I started getting fan mail from those countries, as the film was doing a roaring trade on the black market.

Often when something really works well, nobody knows why, but I think the character was readily identifiable. I think in countries where they didn't even speak English, they could still see Mick Dundee was a regular guy, an ordinary bloke who wasn't Superman and was just a little bit over-awed by the big city. This struck a chord, even with, say, a farmer in Vietnam.

Mick was a good role model, I believed. I think it was very important that he didn't rely on violence and didn't kill anybody. Yet he wasn't a wimp or a sissy just because he didn't shoot seventy-six people, like one of those commandos or terminators in so many other movies. Instead, he slayed 'em with humour.

Crocodile Dundee became the most successful Australian movie ever (a position it still holds) and the most successful independent movie of all time. It finished up reaching number one in something like twenty-seven countries.

What I don't think any of us understood at the time was that *Dundee* would be the first exposure many people around the world would have to Australian culture. Most people on the planet didn't know anything about us. And that's not strange. I mean, what did you know about the culture of Finland, Nicaragua or Chile in the late eighties? If you're anything like me, probably not much. So, Mick Dundee went out around the world and people believed he was typical of our culture. Suddenly *Dundee* was the image everyone associated with Australia.

Now, a lot of people, particularly sophisticated international Australian travellers, were not happy about this. 'It makes us look like a bunch of cowboys or hillbillies,' they said. 'We're not like that. We're a sophisticated, contemporary nation.' And that's the attitude they had until they went overseas and attended a function, particularly in America, where someone, often a charming American woman who seemed to love our accent, would say, 'Oh, you come from Australia. Gee, that's a wild, dangerous country. Your rivers are full of crocodiles, and there are poisonous snakes all over the place. Shark-infested waters. Don't you get scared living there?'

At this point, the sophisticated lawyer from Melbourne, whose idea of a day in the bush was a picnic at the botanic gardens, would slowly undergo a personality change. His chest would puff up and his arms would go out as though he was suddenly carrying a watermelon under each one.

'Yep, it's a pretty wild country all right,' he'd go, 'but you get used to it, you know. The odd snake, ya just break its neck. And sure, our rivers are full of crocodiles and the oceans are full of sharks, but there's an old Aussie rule and we just stick to that. When you're going to swim in shark-infested waters, always swim between fat people.'

• • •

People often ask me if I sensed that the line 'That's not a knife ... *That's* a knife' was going to become famous, one of the most quoted lines of all time. The answer is, of course, no. It was a line just like any other in the script. We smiled when we wrote it and moved on to the next gag. If at the end of putting the script together someone had asked me to write a list of the top five lines I thought people would like from the movie, I'm not sure if it would have made the cut. But sometimes something happens in the world of movies. Simple moments take on a magic that no one could possibly have predicted.

For me, '*That's* a knife' was simply a way of saying that instead of stabbing somebody, you could repel an attack with humour. But at the same time, of course, there was also the implication of 'Don't mess around with me or I'll carve you up, son.' Basically, letting people know that, even without using violence, you are still able to handle yourself.

Now, decades later, I can go into a restaurant in Japan or Mexico, or in a small country town in the outback, and inevitably the chef or cook will come out with their biggest knife. 'That's not a knife,' they'll say in their best Australian accent, '*That's* a knife.'

They always look pleased with themselves, as though they're the first people who have ever thought of doing it. I've literally heard it thousands of times, in every far-flung part of the world. So, does it annoy me? Not one bit. To be honest, I'll never get sick of it. I just enjoy the fact that two of my sayings went into the language and are still there. One of them is 'Slip an extra shrimp on the barbie.' The other's '*That's* not a knife.'

Actually, there may be a third one. I was on an Australian daytime television show in the early 1990s when power walking had just become a big thing. The presenter jokingly asked me if I was into power walking. I said, 'No, no, I'm more into power napping.'

He laughed, but it was true. I have always loved my short afternoon sleep. Countries like Spain have the right idea, and work it into their day. Even up on the very top of the Bridge, I'd link my arm around a cable for safety and grab a quick forty winks when I could, and on movie sets they always know to schedule me a bit of shut-eye after lunch. Anyway, after that television appearance I started hearing people refer to a 'power nap' instead of a 'nanna nap', as it had always been known up until then.

This made me wonder if I'd actually invented the expression. Recently one of my kids consulted Wikipedia, like you do. It says 'power nap' was coined in some highfalutin book by an American social psychologist named James Maas in 1998. Interestingly there was not a single mention of Paul Hogan, *The Midday Show with Ray Martin*, 1992.

Might be time to update the history books.

• • •

Crocodile Dundee

The Knife Scene

Mick and Sue walk from a New York eatery. They are approached by three young men. Sue is immediately wary.

MAN: You got a light, buddy?

MICK: Yeah. Sure, kid. There you go.

The man suddenly produces a knife.

MAN: And your wallet.

Mick doesn't move.

SUE: Mick, give him your wallet.

MICK: What for?

SUE: He's got a knife.

Mick chuckles.

MICK: That's not a knife … (Mick produces his large hunting knife.) *That's* a knife.

MAN: Shit!

The thugs run off into the night.

_18_

Under the Desk
with Johnny Carson

One thing I wasn't prepared for after _Crocodile Dundee_ went ballistic was the loss of privacy and freedom. I'd been known in Australia for quite some time, which made walking the streets tricky, but I'd been able to go to America and England and nearly every other place in the world and not be recognised at all. But things quickly changed.

I was in New York and asked Linda about walking around the streets there. She said, 'Oh look, this is New York. Woody Allen lives here. Jackie Onassis lives here. No one cares about Paul Hogan.' Happy to hear that, I went off down the street

Feeling a long way from the Bridge. (*Newspix*)

to do a bit of shopping and about half an hour later I went running back to the hotel, with two film crews and about ninety people chasing me. They couldn't have cared less about Paul Hogan, but they were very excited by *Crocodile Dundee*! I think most of them thought I was the real thing.

New York had a reputation for being cold and rude, but *Dundee* showed New Yorkers in a good light as wonderful, friendly, charming people. I could walk around Los Angeles and not be spotted, but in New York, for a short time, I was treated like the mayor.

So, yes, I lost my privacy. But celebrity has never really annoyed or bothered me, because people are always positive and friendly. They weren't throwing bricks at me or anything. They were saying, 'Hey, I loved your movie,' or 'Where's your knife?' or even, 'Welcome to New York.' That was good. And there's an old saying: if you don't want to be in the spotlight, stay off the stage. It's as simple as that. You can't complain about attention after doing things to draw attention to yourself. You just cop it.

And success allows you to fulfil a few dreams. In my case, I could do talk shows with people I had watched for years and greatly admired. The ultimate one, of course, was Johnny Carson. Amazingly, back before *Dundee* when I'd first started doing the tourism ads, I'd had the opportunity to appear with Johnny when the producer of *The Tonight Show* had got in touch and asked if I'd come on.

'Oh, yeah, I'd love to,' I'd said.

But then, in what suspiciously felt like a rehearsal, they went through a string of questions that Johnny Carson was likely to ask me and they wanted to know how exactly would

I answer them. 'I don't know how I would answer that,' I said to each question.

'Well,' the producer replied, 'we usually like to know what everyone's going to say or do or what area they'd like to talk about, so we need you to tell us how you would answer that or …'

I explained my aversion to rehearsing. 'I've done plenty of interviews before and I usually just sort of handle them however they come up, whatever the questions are. There's no point in giving you an answer right now, as I might even change my mind when I do the show.'

'Well, I'm sorry, but that's not the way we work here,' the producer said. 'We need to know how you will answer, so if you're not prepared to do that …'

'No, I'm not.'

'Well, we're very sorry, Mr Hogan, but you won't be doing the show.'

A year or two later, *Crocodile Dundee* came out and the Carson people were back on the phone. 'Would you like to come on the show? And if so, what will you and Johnny talk about?'

'Oh, whatever he wants to talk about,' I said. 'Johnny's the boss.'

This time there was no suggestion of a rehearsal, and it was great. Johnny had fun too, because he didn't know what I was going to say or do either. At one stage, we went to a commercial break and he dropped down behind his desk and lit a cigarette. I immediately dropped down and got one out too. The studio audience were all laughing at the clouds of smoke coming out of nowhere. Of course, that didn't go to air. But still, I had the distinct honour of hiding under the desk with Johnny Carson.

I also did David Letterman once or twice. Dave had the studio turned down to about fifty degrees (ten degrees Celsius). The guests and audience were freezing cold, but that was what Dave wanted, so that was how they did it. David is brilliant and hilarious but very intense. Appearing on the show was a pretty good experience and Dave made us both look good, but he was always a little contained and aloof. The people around him were a bit on edge too.

The opposite was Jay Leno. Jay was a lovely guy from the off. He would come back to the dressing room beforehand and have a chat, and he was as easy-going a bloke as you could find. He didn't care what you wanted to talk about. At one stage he even called me up at the last minute to say some guest had cancelled and would I come and have a chat. So I did. He always made it a laugh.

The reaction to *Crocodile Dundee* wasn't all bouquets though. I remember we had a particularly aggravated critic in London. He talked about how the movie was 'cruel and hateful'. He really took umbrage to a scene where we had a drag queen hooker in the bar. She and Dundee are chatting when someone calls Dundee over and tells him that 'she' isn't a girl, but a guy. Dundee goes back to her and puts his hand on her crotch. She screams and he's amazed: 'That was a guy, a guy dressed up like a sheila.'

Dundee didn't bash the person, he didn't do anything nasty. He wasn't being malicious. It was Dundee being naïve. I mean, the guy lived in the outback. If there were any gay people there, they were in the closet. No one even talked

On *The Tonight Show with Jay Leno*. Jay made it feel like chatting with an old mate. (*Getty Images*)

about someone being transgender in those days, certainly not in Walkabout Creek! It was done with no ill will and yet this critic considered it vicious. Before going to New York, Mick'd never even seen an escalator, let alone a man in a dress. He was shocked and what he did was inappropriate, but that doesn't make him cruel and hateful.

Another thing I heard at the time was people saying the tourism ads were what made *Dundee* work. While things have now changed a little in this era of streaming and digital television, back in the 1980s you didn't go from television into the world of movies, especially in the United States. And you most definitely didn't go from TV commercials to movies. No, as I've said, I was just extremely lucky. I stumbled from one thing to the next in this caper and, for whatever reason, my first film worked better than it had any right to.

When all was said and done, *Crocodile Dundee* grossed about US$328 million. This was around half a billion Australian dollars and that revenue didn't include takings in Russia or China. Seasonally adjusted, I'm told our little movie took around a billion dollars. Even now, so many years later, I still find it hard to believe. And I think the success of the movie overseas was partly because us actors were effectively first-timers. I don't think it would have worked if it had starred Robert Redford and Jane Fonda. I think it worked because we were unknowns and therefore the characters were credible.

Many parts of the world actually thought it was a documentary. I used to go into hotels in South America and, especially, the Orient, and they'd say, 'Welcome to the hotel, Mr Dundee.' They'd want to discuss crocodiles and wildlife and would have been devastated if they'd known I was just some actor pretending to be a bushie from the outback. As far as they were concerned, I *was* Mr Dundee and, believe me, that bloke's a lot more famous and popular than I am.

As for my stockbroker mate DJ and our investors, every one of them got their money back tenfold. And Kerry Packer grumbled every time we explained to him how much he had missed out on.

• • •

Homesick and somewhat overwhelmed by the success of *Dundee*, I actually thought it might be time to retire, but other people had other ideas. I was now flavour of the month. Actually the flavour of several months. I think I got offered every script Steven Seagal, Jean-Claude Van Damme and Sylvester Stallone turned down. It frustrated the studios and my agents when I said I didn't want to do any of it, but there was nothing among those scripts that excited me. I wasn't interested in how many people I could shoot. I only wanted to do comedy.

For a while the seemingly endless procession of scripts arriving at the door continued, some of them for films that were eventually made, some of them for films that weren't. I didn't think of myself as an actor for hire. In fact I've never thought of myself as much of an actor at all. I only do stuff that's in my wheelhouse and if it's not funny, it's not in my wheelhouse.

My friend Gary Oldman, now he's an actor! I personally consider him to be the best actor in the world. Gary can do anything, he's ridiculous. He starts out as Sid Vicious, then he goes to Dracula then Beethoven, and ends up winning an Academy Award as Winston Churchill. He's in a class of his own. At the other end of the scale is me. I can play one character. Two if I'm allowed to put a hat on.

Mentally too, I think, I retired after *Dundee*, knowing I could never top it. For your first shot at a movie, made with your mates, who were also first-timers, and unknown stars, to have achieved what it did, how could I follow that up? Whatever I did next was doomed to run second. It wouldn't matter how good it was either. It would be a step down. People often say I'm a one-hit wonder, but it was a helluva hit.

19

Oscar and Me

It was the fifty-ninth Academy Awards, in Hollywood, and I was there. And, amazingly, I wasn't in the stalls with my Maltesers. I was up on stage, all the while thinking someone's going to come and tap me on the shoulder and say, 'Oi, what are you doing here with these people? Off you go!'

The call had come in March 1987. It was six months after *Dundee* had come out in the States, and the film was still running in a lot of cinemas across the country. When the Oscar people came to see me, I assumed it was about presenting one of the awards, you know: 'And the nominees for Best Outdoor Lighting in a Foreign Documentary Short are …'

'No,' they said, 'we want you to co-host with Goldie Hawn and Chevy Chase, but you're to do the opening monologue. You welcome everyone to the Oscars, welcome the billion or so watching at home, do a funny five-minute monologue and officially get the ceremony underway.'

I thought, *Gee, no Australian's ever done that.* 'Yeah, okay.'

So, I turned up in the middle of the afternoon when they were setting up. It was bedlam, lighting being finalised, sets being painted. The orchestra and performers were trying to rehearse and everyone was doing their best not to trip over one another. Now, if you've seen any of the awards shows from back then, the presenter's dialogue was all up on giant autocue screens behind the audience. When someone like Warren Beatty said, 'Hi, I'm Warren Beatty …' even his own name was projected on the back wall, just in case he forgot it.

With live television, especially the Oscars, they're really nervous about any possible stuff-ups. Everything is by the book. So the stage manager gave me a script. I looked it over, and said, 'Yeah, that's amusing. But I'd prefer to do my own material. Give that to someone else, if you like.'

He was a bit taken aback. 'Umm, okay. Can we see your script?'

'Well, I didn't write it down,' I said.

'What? But everything goes on the autocue!'

The stage manager started to panic. And I said, 'There'll be nothing for you to put up on your autocue, mate. It's all in my head.'

Now he was *really* panicking. 'Everyone has to know exactly what you're going to say, where you're going to move, what you're doing …'

The poor fellow had nearly collapsed in tears by the time the director finally came over. The director was clearly better than the stage manager at being calm in a crisis. 'Don't panic everyone,' he said. 'We'll just tape his rehearsal and take notes from that.'

'Umm. You can't. I don't rehearse.'

Now the director was starting to panic too! He sang out for the producer. That year, it was Samuel Goldwyn Jr, the son of the legendary Hollywood mogul. Samuel Goldwyn Jr came on down and called me 'Hogess!' He must have seen the name 'Hoges' written down somewhere and decided it was pronounced 'Hogess'.

'I used to see your show on Channel 30 in New York, Hogess,' he said. 'You're a funny guy. What's the problem down here?'

The others were in a flap: 'This Australian guy doesn't have a script. He doesn't want to rehearse … We don't know what the hell he's going to say, what he's going to get up to.'

Samuel Goldwyn Jr looked at me. 'So you know this program goes out live to a billion people?'

'Yeah.'

'And,' he said, 'you're planning on walking out there and doing the opening five minutes with no one knowing exactly what you're going to say?'

'Yeah.'

'And you're not going to say anything that would be bleeped or anything?'

'No, no,' I assured him. 'I don't work that way.'

So Samuel Goldwyn Jr thought about it for a bit, then announced, 'I'm with Hogess! Let him on! It'll be fun for all of us if we don't know what he's going to say or do.'

And they did! They let me on. I loved that guy, because if it hadn't been for him, they would have dropped me. The whole organisation is terrified of anything they don't have complete control over. I still can't believe I got away with it.

• • •

Hoges at ...

The Oscars

Fifty-ninth Academy Awards, Dorothy Chandler Pavilion, Los Angeles, 30 March 1987

G'day, viewers. This is my first time at the Academy Awards. I usually watch it on television, and for that reason I've been asked to come out here and speak to my peers on behalf of the television audience.

G'day, peers.

This is of course the big event of show business and the atmosphere here is pure electricity. But as a television show, it does tend to go slightly off the boil, particularly as we drift into the third and fourth hour. What can we do about it?

Firstly, winners, when you make your speech, it's a good tip to remember the three Gs: be Gracious, be Grateful, Get off.

Secondly, don't be too humble tonight because we have up here a second envelope.

And don't get up onstage and say, 'I don't deserve this award.' If you really feel you don't deserve an Academy Award, just give us a wave from your seat.

Most importantly, tonight, in most categories, nominees will be on camera when they announce the winner. Please, nominees, let's not have the spectacle of all four lose— eh, non-winners giving us this one: (*smiles fake smile and claps*).

This is the I'm-so-glad-he-won-instead-of-me smile.

Think of the television audience. Give us a bit of variety. You know, maybe one or two of you could burst into tears. Storming out of the building in a huff'd be nice. Well, what's wrong with a bit of good old-fashioned booing?

Now, I'm nominated tonight and I realise I'm not exactly the odds-on favourite, but I travelled 13,000 miles to be here for this. I've come from the other side of the planet. And if they read out someone else's name instead of mine, it's not going to be pretty.

Anyway, listen. Most important, the producer of this program, Sam Goldwyn, said to me, 'Everyone's really tense out there. Go out and see if you can get them to relax.' Why? You didn't come here to relax. You want to relax, stay at home and watch it on television. That'll relax you.

No, no, fellow workers, brothers,
workmates, you're here to sweat. This
program is live. There's about one
thousand million people watching *you*. So
you remember: one wrong word, one foolish
gesture — your whole career could go down
in flames.

Hold that thought and have a nice night,
you hear?

Some people asked if I was nervous. Maybe a little bit, but I never took award ceremonies seriously. They're harmless fun, just a bit of overblown palaver. It's really just people getting up there hyperventilating and sobbing their way through thanking everyone they've ever met. I had nothing to lose. In my mind I was going to retire anyway. So I could just have fun.

As I mentioned in the speech, I was actually up for an Oscar myself that year. It was for Best Screenplay Written Directly for the Screen. Also nominated were Hanif Kureishi for *My Beautiful Laundrette*, Oliver Stone for *Platoon*, Woody Allen for *Hannah and Her Sisters*, and Oliver Stone and Rick Boyle for *Salvador*. It was nice to be among that lineup because only other writers vote for the nominations, so it's got nothing to do with whether you're popular or anything.

I didn't win though. Woody Allen did, but I didn't care. Oliver Stone got four Oscars for *Platoon* and I sat glaring at him every time he was nominated. It was all part of the fun. Awards are just an indication that some of your fellow entertainers or,

The all-singing, all-dancing, great actor that is Hugh Jackman. I taught
him everything he knows ... apart from the singing and, um, dancing ...
oh, and the acting ... *(Alamy)*

perhaps, the public or some pollies, think you are pretty good. But they are nothing to get terribly worked up about. When I won an Australian television Logie in the 1970s, I thanked 'Vincent Ribinzo, the cab driver who brought me here'. And, since for some reason I was wearing a big white tuxedo, I also gave a shout-out to 'Mr Whippy for the lend of the coat'.

In 1985, I was named Australian of the Year. A year later I was appointed a Member of the Order of Australia (AM) 'for service to tourism and entertainment'. When I was doing the tourism ads they had a Paul Hogan Day in Los Angeles, which was cool. Got a little plaque from the mayor.

The funniest thing of all, though, was in 1987 when I won a Golden Globe Award for 'Best Performance by an Actor in a Motion Picture – Musical or Comedy' for *Crocodile Dundee*. I reckon after the foreign press met me, they must have thought about taking the award back. 'He's just the same as Dundee, except Dundee wears a hat!'

True, there wasn't much acting in it. I actually bumped into Hugh Jackman, who is a lovely man and can sing and dance as well as act, in a year in which he was up for a Golden Globe. 'Mate,' I said, 'try not to take it too seriously. They gave me one, for God's sake.' Hugh, almost too quickly, agreed. I think if people remember I have one it will help them keep awards well and truly in perspective.

Anyway, back at the Oscars, I didn't spend a huge amount of time preparing my opening monologue. I was thinking, *If I make a fool of myself, so what?* Luckily, in the end the speech went over pretty damn well. I did notice though that a lot of people throughout kept looking at me, and then looking at the back wall. And of course, there was nothing up there.

When I finished, Dustin Hoffman and Dom DeLuise cornered me and said, 'So funny … And you didn't have a script, nothing on the autocue? We love that, we love that!' And Dustin escorted me around for the rest of the night, introducing me to people, saying, 'He never had a script up there, you know that!'

The whole thing was an unforgettable experience. And, for better or worse, the speech is still up there on YouTube today. These things never leave you.

• • •

I briefly met Liz Taylor at the Oscars, and soon afterwards she asked me to a fund-raising ball for breast cancer. I thought, *Yeah, I'll go to that. It'll be an A-list celebrity turn-out, and I'll get to see some big stars.*

I fronted up and they took me to my seat, and bugger me, it was at the number-one table. I was sitting next to Liz herself! *What*, I thought, *am I her date?* I started looking around. Harrison Ford was over there, Sylvester Stallone was at the table next to me. And then I spotted a tall, pretty familiar guy, and thought, *Ohh, that's Clint Eastwood!* I was thinking, *This is just so good!* And I was having this long squizz at one of the coolest guys in movies when suddenly he turned around, saw me and waved. *What? Clint Eastwood knows who I am!*

Then, about five minutes later I felt this big hand on my shoulder, I looked around, and it was Clint. He leant over, picked up my table knife and held it up in front of me. *Don't tell me he's going to say it!*

'So,' he began, 'how many times have you heard it?'

'Oh, a couple of thousand.'

'Welcome to the club,' he said.

I knew exactly what he meant. Imagine how many times Clint Eastwood's gone to go through a door or get into an elevator, and someone has said, 'Go ahead, make my day.' Anyway, he made to leave but then added, 'You wrote that movie, didn't you?'

I said, 'Yeah.'

'Did you write that line?'

'Yeah.'

'Oh well,' he deadpanned, 'serves you right.' And with that he wandered off.

Ten minutes or so later, Michael Jackson, who was co-sponsoring the dinner, turned up. As I said, it was an A-list room; I was probably the least known person in it. Yet Michael came in with four big lumping bodyguards. Why? Did he think Burt Reynolds was going to try to kiss him or something? Ridiculous. Stars everywhere, and he was surrounded by bodyguards.

Anyway, little Michael circulated – 'Hi, hi' – and stopped at the table next to me. One of the bodyguards backed up, presumably to keep people away, and in doing so he bumped right into Liz Taylor's head, thrusting her forward in her seat. So I leant over and shoved my finger in his lower back, 'Hey, get your big arse out of here,' I said. 'You're bumping the lady.'

He very politely went, 'Uh, uh.' And moved away.

The young Liz Taylor was considered by many to be the most beautiful woman in the world. She was in her mid-fifties back in 1987 and still glowed like a superstar with her pearly opalescent skin and stunning violet eyes. I'd never seen eyes like them. After I pushed the big arse away, she turned to me, grabbed my arm and, with those violet eyes flashing, said, 'Thank you, Paul.'

'Uughh, ohhh,' I said, and melted to the floor. Oh dear. I was so uncool. Still, we did talk a bit that night, though to be honest I wasn't really taking it in. All I could think about were those violet eyes.

• • •

The expectations raised by *Crocodile Dundee* have come back to bite me at times. Like when I took up skiing soon afterwards. It was something I'd never thought of in Australia. There were very, very few snowfields around Granville, or even Greater Sydney. But now I was around and about the world, and when I went to Aspen, Colorado, I got the opportunity and discovered I loved it. So much so, I quickly became a fanatic. I'd try to ski as often as possible and for as long as I could each day.

I quickly discovered I was under some pressure, because the ski instructors would say, 'Oh, we've had some Australians here before. They're really weird. When we get British people here it takes us a week just to get them standing up. But we get you Aussies here and you say, "How much are the lessons?" We say, "It's fifty bucks an hour." And you say, "Well, give us an hour! She'll be right."

'In one hour, you barely learn to put your skis on!' they explained, 'But then we don't see these Australians for the rest of the day. And three or four days later we'll notice them on the ski lift, covered in snow and blood and they're going up to the Wall of Death or Hell's Hollow or somewhere, and they'll give us a big wave!'

Now, they were telling me this, and I was someone famous for being an Aussie, so I didn't have a choice, I naturally had to follow suit. By my fourth day, I was covered in blood, going over the Wall of Death, sideways, backwards, tumbling or whatever. No doubt instructors saw me and said, 'Oh yeah, typical Aussie.'

All Australians now have that pressure. We have to live up to these standards that Mick bloody Dundee and all those other yobbos have set around the world.

Dundee, Take Two

After the phenomenal success of *Dundee,* John and I were determined to quit while we were ahead and not make any more movies. We'd had one hit, we thought, so why not just retire from the film world with our Bradman-like batting average intact?

And for a while, we sort of did. Paramount in the United States weren't happy with that, though. They'd picked the movie up for next to nothing and made a fortune out of it. They desperately wanted another. 'You have to make another one,' they said. 'You've got to make two!'

The studio started calling John all the time at his farm near Byron Bay, the beautiful little surf town in coastal New South

Wales where he and Delvene had moved in late 1980. It'd be the president of Paramount and John's kids would have fun saying, 'Sorry, Dad can't come to the phone right now, he's down the paddock helping a cow calve,' or 'Sorry, Dad's just gone to shoot a rabbit for dinner. What studio did you say you were from again?' This must have driven these powerful Hollywood executives crazy.

Then my oldest son, Brett, dropped in one day. 'I've got some ideas for *Croc II*,' he said.

'Sorry, mate,' I replied. 'I don't know if doing another one interests me.' Brett had a couple of ideas that were good and some that weren't. But then he said to me, 'Dad, you've got to make another one because we can't leave Mick Dundee in New York. He's got to come home.'

He was thinking of Mick as a real person and I started doing that too. 'Yeah, you're right,' I said, 'he's got to come home. Okay, we'll make another one!'

I rang John, who, unlike me, was still busy with a dozen different business ventures. 'Great,' he said. 'You do the script, I'll work on the deal.' Peter Faiman had moved on to new things, so I asked John if he'd direct it. He said, 'Why not!'

So Brett and I sat down and started writing. He started at the beginning, me at the end and we sort of met in the middle. After about four weeks we had the script for *Crocodile Dundee II*. I think we intended to do a second draft but never got around to it. Anyway, we had Mick living happily with Sue in Manhattan, having just the occasional mishap, like when he goes blast-fishing with dynamite from his dinghy, just off Ellis Island. When he innocently crosses a Colombian drug cartel, everything changes. With the bad guys after them, he and Sue flee back to Australia so Mick can battle them in the bush, where he'll have the advantage.

As always, I wanted to work with my mates, and luckily we were able to put most of the old team back together, including fabulous cinematographer Russell Boyd, lighting guru Brian Bansgrove and key grip Ray Brown. In terms of actors, my friend Johnny Meillon was returning as Wally, and Linda Kozlowski was booked again as Sue.

Another mate of mine from the first one, Stevie Rackman, had fought pretty hard to steal every scene he was in as Donk. After he read the new script, he complained about Donk's workload, or lack thereof.

'Mate,' he said, 'I've only got one word in this whole bloody scene. How do I work myself up for that? One word!'

'Mate, just trust me,' I replied. 'You've only got the one word, but you will own the scene.'

'Okay,' he grumbled.

And when it hit the screen, he was the star of his scene, completely. No one could play Donk like Stevie.

• • •

Crocodile Dundee II

The Donk Scene

NUGGET (*sitting on a cooler of beer in the bush*): G'day! Want a cold one?

DENNING (*approaching with a gun*): Who are you?

```
NUGGET: Call me Nugget. I've been looking
    for Walter Reilly. Haven't seen him
    around, have you?

DENNING (cocking his rifle): You shoulda
    bought a gun instead of a beer, mate.

NUGGET: Nah. I don't need a gun. I've got
    a Donk.

DENNING (laughing): You got a what?

Donk springs up behind him, takes the gun
from his hands and —

DONK: Donk!

— knocks him out.
```

A new addition to our *Dundee II* cast was the fabulous African-American actor Charles S. Dutton, who played Leroy Brown. One time we were shooting in Manhattan and Leroy, Mick's new friend in the film, had just saved his arse. The scene was taking place in Alphabet City. If you don't already know, Alphabet City, despite sounding as though it might share a postcode with Sesame Street, is a very tough neighbourhood. Well, it certainly was back then.

As is often the case with film crews, we weren't exactly loved by the locals. We were just another nuisance, closing down streets and restricting access as we set up for our shots.

A couple of louts decided they'd had enough. They didn't like these poncy film people and actors strutting around the place and taking up their territory. They forced their way past security and into the area where we were filming and decided

Crocodile Dundee II. Just waiting for the camera to roll before I gelignite some fish in New York Harbor. *(Alamy)*

to stir things up. You know: 'We're the ones who fucking live here, we can do what we want.'

They walked towards the makeup trailer where, inside, Charlie was being prepared. He had tissues tucked inside his collar so the makeup artists wouldn't get cosmetics on his gaudy outfit – leather flat cap, bright red shirt, blue suit with handkerchief in top pocket. He wore this outfit because, although his character was a stationery salesman, his name was Leroy Brown, and he wanted to live up to the reputation of that name, as in the Jim Croce song 'Bad, Bad Leroy Brown'. So he had the bad clobber to go with the name, but in the script he was a gentle soul.

Anyway, Charlie happened to walk out of the makeup trailer, with his tissues nicely tucked in, eating pizza, right at the moment these two guys arrived. One of them sized up this poncy actor and shirt-fronted him. All this took Charlie completely by surprise. They laughed at him; this was their turf, they said, and they were going to show everyone who was boss.

It wasn't the wisest decision they'd ever made, because Charlie wasn't the poncy actor they took him for. In his teens he'd been an amateur boxer known as 'the Roc' and in 1967, aged sixteen, he'd been jailed for five years for manslaughter after getting in a knife fight. A subsequent arrest for armed robbery saw him incarcerated for three more years, and a fight with a guard extended his sentence by another eight years.

So Charlie wasn't scared of these guys. He started to tell them off for their pathetic behaviour and that's when one of them foolishly shoved the pizza right into Charlie's made-up face.

Charlie knocked him out cold.

The great Charlie Dutton appearing with me in *Dundee II*. *(Getty Images)*

He hit him so hard he flew right over the front of a car. Charlie couldn't get to the other guy, unfortunately, as he ran away squealing, leaving his mate snoozing on the ground.

Charlie's life story is quite amazing. Once in jail, he quickly learnt the error of his ways. He started to visit the prison library and among the reading materials on offer were several of Shakespeare's plays. Charlie quickly became a fan and started to stage these plays. He had murderers and serial killers and what have you auditioning for and performing in his shows. That in turn led him into show business and he's now one of the world's great actors. Talk about someone they need to make a movie about!

• • •

When we made *Crocodile Dundee II*, CGI and green-screen effects weren't what they are today. If you had a scene forty storeys up on the ledge of a building, it looked best if you went up forty storeys and stood on the ledge of a building. Being an old rigger stood me in good stead for one particular scene I wrote, set right up there in the clouds. At the time I thought it would simply be a funny bit. But it wasn't until some years later that I wondered whether I wrote the scene because for once I wanted to be able to control the outcome of a situation reminiscent of so many we had dealt with on the Bridge.

I've mentioned how the Bridge was a popular spot for jumping off and ending it all. While it's always easy to remember the people we were able to talk out of taking such a drastic step, the others are more painful to bring to mind. Even half a century and more later, I can tell you it's like nothing you can imagine when you see someone go.

One day there was a guy on the very top of one of the Bridge pylons. We were walking around the edge trying to talk to him when, without warning, he simply leapt. I was standing on the ledge outside the railing and, as he dropped, in my mind the whole ledge started to warp. I suddenly stumbled and had to grab the railing. It was a devastating end for the poor man and was perhaps the first time I really became conscious of the height we worked at. Up until then I'd figured, *If I can walk across a plank four foot off the ground, I can walk across one four hundred feet in the air.* If you weren't like that, you shouldn't have been up there.

Anyway, as for the scene in *Crocodile Dundee II*, comedy ensues and Dundee saves the day. Not only does the character live but I actually bumped into the actor who played him at LAX not too long before the big coronavirus shutdown of 2020. I so wish all the real encounters like that could have played out as simply and happily.

• • •

Crocodile Dundee II

The Ledge Scene

```
A suicidal man stands with his back
against a wall on a narrow ledge, forty
storeys up. Crocodile Dundee strolls
around the corner of the ledge and stops.

SUICIDAL MAN: Don't try to stop me.
```

MICK: I don't want to stop you, I just want to get past.

SUICIDAL MAN: What?

MICK: I walk around here every day. Get away from all the noise and the traffic. Get up here and get the fresh air.

SUICIDAL MAN: I'm about to throw myself off this building.

MICK: You could kill yourself.

SUICIDAL MAN: That's the whole idea.

MICK: Oh. Oh, right. I'll just wait till you're finished. Would you mind getting a move on? I'm on my lunch break.

SUICIDAL MAN: I can't do it with you watching.

High drama. (*Alamy*)

Generally, the *Crocodile Dundee II* production was without serious incident. Looking back, though, I'm surprised the studio didn't pressure us to use an established director. When we said John was not only going to produce but would also direct this time, they didn't blink an eye. I think they were just so thrilled they were getting another film.

Even though he was a first-timer, John handled directing superbly. No problems at all. I was on the floor, standing alongside the actors, and, as I'd done for our television programs, I offered a few suggestions or pointed stuff out. But I never wanted to direct. That's too hard, too much work. A lot of actors and writers dream of being a director. Not this one. I like to write a story and then hand it over.

But I had John at the helm and it was terrific. He was a natural and the crew loved him, and they loved that he didn't have any airs and graces, like 'I'm the director and you'll do as you're told.' It was all a fun and collaborative effort.

After the second *Dundee*, Russ Bob (Russell Boyd) continued his amazing work on films such as *Forever Young*, *Master and Commander,* and *Ghost Rider*. Recently, he filmed me again for the Tourism Australia commercial that appeared in America during the 2018 Super Bowl telecast (more on that later). Mr Brown (Ray Brown) worked on movies such as *The Matrix* trilogy, while Banza (Brian Bansgrove) did the lighting for *The Lord of the Rings* trilogy, as well as *Avatar*. Tragedy struck in 2001 when Banza died in Thailand in very mysterious circumstances. He is greatly missed and certainly left a lasting impression on anyone lucky enough to have known him.

• • •

The original *Crocodile Dundee* had become the second most successful movie of all time in the UK, behind *The Sound of Music*. So, when we had *Dundee II* ready, the Palace got in touch and asked, 'Would you like to donate the opening night proceeds to one of Prince Charles's charitable funds?'

'Of course,' I said, and they explained that the Prince and Princess Diana would therefore attend the June 1988 premiere. So it was that, about twelve months after we wrapped shooting *Dundee II*, I found myself sitting at the premiere in London with Prince Charles on one side of me and Princess Diana on the other. It was a bit overwhelming, even though I'd lunched with one and danced with the other, but a hell of a buzz. I was thinking to myself, *Don't they know I'm just a rigger off the Harbour Bridge?*

Charles is a great audience. He loves to laugh, and he laughs like a drain. And of course when he laughed on this occasion, everyone nearby had to laugh too. He's the Prince of Wales after all.

So there I was, sitting there in the cinema, and we're all watching *Dundee II*, and I'm starting to get real comfortable. Feeling good about watching my movie with Chaz and Di, me old mates. And the longer I sat there, the more comfortable I got. Charles was chuckling away, giving me a little nudge every now and again, and Princess Diana was really casual. She sort of slid down in the seat and put her knees up on the seat in front, like some people do. Long legs.

Something happened on the screen that appealed to her, and she gave me a little dig in the ribs with her elbow. Something else happened a minute later. She gave me a dig again. About the fifth time she did this, I was feeling so relaxed I reached my hand out to place it on her thigh. Fortunately, common sense prevailed and, about an inch away from my hand landing, I thought, *Oh, what am I doing? You can't grope a princess, for God's sake.*

They could cut your hand off for that. Or, even worse, you could end up in a cell with Rolf Harris. Imagine that? That'd be ugly, wouldn't it? He'd be going, 'I'm Jake the peg diddle-iddle-iddle-um, with my extra leg …' and I'd be going, 'Get away from me with your extra leg, or I'll …'

Needless to say, it was a memorable night.

Soon after, the film opened in cinemas all around the world. Right away I read in the Australian papers that it was 'a huge disappointment'. One of the critics said, 'Unlike the first *Crocodile Dundee*, which was an original masterpiece, the second one is a limp copy, a let-down.' A masterpiece? I thought, *What are you talking about? When it came out, I remember you wrote it was a piece of crap.*

Dundee II might have been 'a huge disappointment', but it still managed to go to number one all over the world. In its first week it out-earned *Rambo III*, and it ended up as the fourth most successful film at the US box office that year, finishing ahead of that *Rambo* sequel, *A Fish Called Wanda*, *Die Hard* and several other very well known films. It did almost $350 million worldwide. Not as much as the first one, so it *was* a let-down in that sense.

Still, you learn to live with these disappointments. Fingers crossed I'll have another disappointment like that one day.

21

Stepping Out with Linda

As I mentioned, Linda Kozlowski and I were opposites, so no surprise we both found each other a bit hard to work out. She was a New Yorker, through and through. I was a working-class Westie, througher and througher.

She'd been classically trained at a prestigious US institution. I'd left a Sydney high school at barely fifteen. We shouldn't have been drawn together, but for some reason it just happened. On the first *Dundee*, we maybe flirted a little bit, but had different commitments in our lives. So, after the words 'It's a wrap' were uttered, we both went our separate ways.

Then, during the second movie, our feelings started to grow. It was a slow burn and I couldn't tell you when our friendship turned into something more, but I know the feelings were intensifying and all of the differences between us suddenly became intriguing. Linda also made me laugh. A lot. She liked to mock the craft of acting. She had a funny turn of phrase. I made her laugh too, and laughter is the greatest of equalisers. It washes over everything else and can't help but bring people closer together.

It was just after *Dundee II* finished shooting that we knew this was real and slowly began to let the world know that we were together. And did anyone care? Yes, the media went absolutely nuts.

A few years earlier, in the early 1980s, I'd said to a journalist, 'The nicest thing about my success is that, generally speaking, people haven't wanted to chop me down.' It had been largely true up until then, but now that sure as hell changed, and fast! Suddenly we were the most hated people in the land. Headlines were calling Linda a homewrecker and she was getting slagged off in all sections of the media and by people on the street, many of whom had failed marriages themselves but somehow thought it was okay to be judge and jury with her.

I was an evil villain for leaving my five children, and the press painted this picture of our little kids standing at the gate wailing, 'When's Daddy coming home?' The truth is that three of them weren't even living at home. Todd was in England playing rugby union, Brett was in Perth making videos for rock groups, and Clay, the musician of the family, was off playing in bands and as a session muso.

My daughter, Loren, was still in the house, but she had a guest cottage out the back and was preparing to move in with friends. So it was really just Scotty at home and he was fourteen.

They were all practically grown-ups, but that didn't stop the press telling stories and lies to make it look as nasty as possible.

The other small detail that the media failed to mention was that Noelene had already divorced me once, and then we'd got back together for the sake of the kids, who at that point were a little younger. As I said earlier, I just couldn't bring myself to leave the house, to leave my tribe. Now, several years later, Noelene and I divorced for the second and final time, as clearly our relationship hadn't been trouble-free for quite a while.

It's so stupid of anybody to pass judgement on other people's relationships. It was sort of like, *Well, I'd better not get a divorce because they'll have a bad thing about me in* TV Week. *So I'll stay unhappily married.*

Anyway, I was now the tall poppy everyone seemed determined to cut down. The real problem was that the press had turned me into a saint and I didn't want to be one. I was a larrikin, a stirrer, a tap-dancing knife thrower, for goodness sake. And I resented the picture the media painted of Linda wrecking a perfect picket-fence family.

The magazines in Australia made it seem grubby and sordid. But I was not much of an Errol Flynn really. One wife in thirty years and now one lover. My friends and family knew the truth, so it was only those flicking pages in the queue at the supermarket who thought they had inside knowledge of a very different situation.

The press reaction in the UK was pretty hostile too. I don't remember much about it, but there was a story about me going into a restaurant with Linda and saying, 'I want that table over there by the window. Move those people right now.' When I read this we were at a hideaway on a deer farm in Wales,

'No, you're the one who's overdressed.'

which a friend had organised for us. Yet I kept reading in the papers about my appalling conduct in London. I'd go, 'What? We haven't even been there!' It was just too silly, total bullshit, so there was no point in worrying about it.

There's a funny postscript to all that. Not that long after the launch of *Dundee II* in London, a story was published saying something like 'Hogan never goes anywhere without his bodyguards' or his 'minders', as they called them. There was a picture of me with three 'hoods'. Turned out they were three of my sons. You know, the tiny tots I'd left crying at the gate. Now only twelve months later, they were my fearsome minders. Gotta love it!

• • •

Linda and I decided it'd be nice to get away from everything – including the media – so we followed John and Delvene to Byron Bay, the town they had 'discovered' a few years earlier. It had great beaches and lovely people, and you could buy a big chunk of property that was pristine and not over-developed. Possum Creek, a few kilometres inland from Byron, was the perfect place for us to hide out and leave all the madness behind. Well, that was our hope anyway. Being romantics, Linda and I also decided it was time to get married, and where better than in our new hometown?

The wedding took place on a sparkling winter day in 1990 and the guests included Sylvester Stallone and Arnold Schwarzenegger. Even Madonna and Sean Penn made the long journey to Australia. And Cher, God bless her, sang our bridal waltz. Actually, the last few sentences are bullshit. There were no celebrities there. Not one, unless you count my old mate, former *60 Minutes* journalist George Fungus, sorry, Negus, and his partner. That didn't stop the Byron Bay locals having a helluva lot of fun winding up the media circus that arrived in town.

I watched some of this playing out on TV and the locals gave some wonderful performances. The butcher said that Barbra Streisand had requested kosher steak and he was feeling stressed because he didn't know where in country New South Wales he'd be able to find a Jewish cow. Another, who ran the fish and chip shop, claimed Madonna had asked if she could hire a bicycle from him. He said he'd panicked, taken $5 from her and handed over a bike he saw leaning against a wall.

There was even some old biddy taking a camera crew through her house and explaining how she'd gone out and bought new sheets and a duvet because Burt Reynolds and a very fussy Loni Anderson were staying with her. She said she'd originally had Jack Nicholson and Clint Eastwood booked, but they hadn't been keen on sharing a bed. Especially when it was just a standard double.

Everyone in the town went onstage. When a journalist asked a local taxi driver if he'd seen any celebrities, the driver said, 'Yeah, last night I think I ran over Lassie.' I'd never been prouder of my neighbours.

We had paparazzi and media running around like lunatics looking for all these imaginary stars. It drove them nuts. At the same time, another myth started. It was said I had bred two-metre-long brown snakes at my property to put in the grass to keep the press away. I may not have put them there, but there were certainly some large snakes living on the place. One photographer came sneaking down the back hill one night and was confronted by a seven-foot brown and took off. After that, all media reports described our place as 'snake-infested'.

Our 'snake-infested' property was about three hundred acres and, in the end, the paparazzi and the media couldn't get close enough to experience the wedding, so thank goodness the locals gave them something fun to report.

Unfortunately, in the months following the wedding the media continued their obsession with Linda and we'd still find desperate paparazzi hiding up the hill with their telephoto lenses or waiting for her at the beach. This invasion of privacy made Linda feel incredibly uncomfortable. No one likes to be slagged off and abused by anyone – let alone people you've never met, who base their opinions on tabloid newspaper and trashy magazine reports – or be stalked by strangers with cameras.

Around this time we learnt that sadly Linda's mum had been diagnosed with cancer, so we went to be with her in Fairfield, Connecticut. Unfortunately, Linda's mum died shortly after.

With Linda obviously devastated and having felt somewhat displaced in Australia, we decided to stay in the United States for a while. It was great to get away from the Australian mags and tabloids, which were full of my so-called bitter custody battle with Noelene, which of course had never happened.

The following scene is more typical of what was actually going on in our family. Right in the middle of one particular media storm, I was in LA and there was a knock on the door. It was my son Brett, who was about twenty at the time. 'Congratulations, Dad,' he said, rubbing his feet on the mat. 'You got custody! Where's the fridge?'

22

Starstruck

Linda and I ended up staying in LA for quite a few years. After that we moved back and forth between the United States and Australia. We lived in Byron and Sydney again for about three or four years in the early 2000s, then went and spent more time near Linda's family again. Since then, I have spent time in both countries every year. But because I don't call a press conference every time I book a plane ticket, some media decided I'd left Australia and never come back.

I've got to say, being a boy from the Western Suburbs, I do find LA extremely entertaining. There are lots of galahs there and lots of people with very distorted opinions of themselves, so that's good fun. And it's a fascinating town because effectively it's an industry town, but the industry is Hollywood. And unlike most, say, mining towns, 90 percent of the populace is unemployed and hangs around those who are working, asking, 'So what's it like?' This adds to the feeling that you're in a bad, somewhat desperate, soap opera.

When it came to dealing with the studios, John usually stepped in. LA is full of sharks and the studios are famous for ripping off arms and legs, as anyone in the business will tell you. Corney, however, loved all that. He loved the studios trying it on, and, I can tell you, no one ever, ever ripped off John. But the main attraction of being in LA back then was that Linda and I were left alone there. We were small fish in a very big pond and no one gave a damn. There were many more-exciting people and things to be reporting on than us two!

It turned out that Linda, like me, is a bit of a gypsy. (Maybe it was growing up in that small house in Granville that made me so restless.) I think we moved something like eighteen times, to various parts of California. Linda had an incredible eye for interior design and did amazing things to every place we lived in, before moving on.

A fun thing that never failed to surprise us was suddenly finding out who our new neighbours were. One time it was Michael Douglas, who's a nice fella. Me and Michael shared a terrible trait, though: we were both closet smokers. If I went to a show-business function and Michael was there, he'd see me and he'd give me the nod and a flick of the eyes and we'd find a place where we could sneak outside and have a smoke.

At Serra Retreat, a gated community in Malibu, James Cameron was a neighbour and friend. Dick van Dyke too. He and James used to have a competition to see who had the best

Halloween display. Dick always won. Mel Gibson lived there too, and Martin Sheen – lots of show-business people. Kelsey Grammer was another neighbour, and another top bloke. A very funny, down-to-earth man. He wore leather jackets and rode motorbikes and was nothing like the pompous Frasier character he played so brilliantly.

Pierce Brosnan was one neighbour I had issues with. No one should be that handsome. He made everyone around him look ugly. So I tried to never stand next to him. Despite that, I have to admit he was a good Irishman with a great sense of humour.

For quite a while we lived in Santa Barbara, and I used to point out the nearby mountain to our house guests. 'You need to be careful if you go over that hill,' I'd warn them. 'It's pretty scary.'

'What, are there bears?' they'd ask.

'No, Michael Jackson lives there.'

· · ·

Another place we lived in in the nineties was Montecito in California. It's a beautiful little town that quite a few prominent show-business types call home. Among them then was that legend Kirk Douglas.

One time the grand old actor was throwing a party to celebrate his wife's eightieth birthday or something like that. Linda and I were invited, I suppose because of all those cigarettes I'd smoked with Kirk's son Michael. So we obviously went along.

I was standing around when a person came up behind me, grabbed me by both shoulders and said, 'Don't look around.' It was Kirk. He'd had a stroke then, so one side of his face sort of didn't work, and he spoke out the side of his mouth in a strange distorted voice. Anyway, he grabbed me in this firm grip from behind and said, 'There was movement at the station, for the word had passed around that the colt from Old Regret had got away.'

What? I thought. *Banjo Paterson ... from this American legend?* Then I remembered that Kirk had been in the movie version of *The Man From Snowy River* and spent quite some time in Australia when shooting it in the 1980s. He spun me around: 'All right, what's next?'

'And had joined the wild bush horses,' I recited, 'he was worth a thousand pound, so all the cracks had gathered to the fray.'

'Yeah, yeah,' he went, with a glint in his eye. I knew the poem. It was one of those national poems we'd all learnt at school, and, like many Australians, I'd never forgotten it. Kirk and I had a little conversation about how much he'd enjoyed his time doing that film and being with some of the people who were in it, and then he headed up on the stage.

There was a band, and Kirk went to the microphone. 'I'm going to do a little song for you all. It's my wife's favourite. It's her birthday, so I'm going to sing it.' And he sang this song, which, to be honest, was pretty hard to listen to, partly because he could only really growl out the side of his mouth. But it was what he said afterwards that won me over. 'As you can see,' Kirk pointed out, 'I've got a band up here tonight, so if any of you have got a favourite song, let me know what it is, and I'll be only too happy to get back up here and murder it for you.'

Yes, he knew how terrible he sounded, and that really endeared me to him. We recently lost him. At 103.

• • •

According to Hoges ...

'Waltzing Matilda'

I think if you want to look at the psyche of a nation, you look no further than that internationally recognised symbol, the national anthem. Every country in the world has one. But in Australia we sorta have three.

For the old diehards, it will always be 'God Save the Queen'. Which doesn't really work any more because the bulk of our population today no longer comes from Britain. Then we've got our official and proper national anthem, 'Advance Australia Fair'. That's the one we all know and love. That's the one that goes 'Australians all let us rejoice, for we are young and free ... umm, dum da dum da dum da dum, our home is girt by sea.' I've actually always wondered who this 'girt-by-sea' was. Sounds like some scrubber who hung around the waterfront a lot. And then of course, there's our unofficial anthem, 'Waltzing Matilda'. That's the one that always brings a tear to my eye, but probably not for the usual reasons.

You see, I recently had the pleasure of explaining and translating our unofficial anthem to some Americans. Have you ever tried to translate the story of that song? 'Once a jolly swagman camped by a billabong ...' They don't have swagmen in America, but they have bagmen. So they could understand that. Swagman equals bagman. Easy translation.

And of course, our bagman is 'jolly'. Which I assume means he walked around giggling a lot. And he camped by a billabong. Billabong, I explained to my friends, could be translated as 'swamp'. Now anyone who camps next to a swamp in Australia, particularly up north, is obviously not too bright. Something's going to come out of the swamp and get you in the night – at very least the mozzies.

So it's established in the opening line of this 'anthem' that our giggling bagman is probably not the sharpest knife in the cutlery drawer. Okay, and what does he do around this swamp? 'Waltzing Matilda, waltzing Matilda, you'll come a-waltzing Matilda with me.' He dances, but with what? I had to explain to the Yanks that Matilda's not a woman, but, as we learnt at school, Matilda is actually the swag. All the bagman's worldly goods are rolled into a bundle called his Matilda.

Translation: Matilda equals shopping trolley.

So, this guy dances around the edge of the swamp with a shopping trolley. What does he have in the shopping trolley? A jolly jumbuck. A sheep. Once again there's the adjective 'jolly'. Now, to the best of my knowledge and my observations, sheep don't giggle. They do however grin. So, this guy's got a grinning sheep in his shopping trolley. And he's dancing with it.

'Up come the troopers, one, two, three.' Basically, the cops arrive. They call, 'Oi, what are you doing with that grinning sheep in your shopping trolley?' Now here, just in case there's any shadow of a doubt about the sanity of this giggling bagman, he removes it by shouting back to the cops, 'You'll never take me alive!'

He then grabs hold of his poor grinning sheep, jumps into the swamp and necks himself and the sheep! And that, in a nutshell, without poetic licence or distortion, is the story of 'Waltzing Matilda'.

You should have seen the looks on the Americans' faces! Now tell me that wouldn't be the weirdest national anthem of any country on this bloody planet!

I think because I didn't get into show business until I was over thirty, and was reluctant to do so, I still get a real buzz out of meeting big stars. I'm not talking about the second idiot voted off *Big Brother*, or one of *The Real Housewives of Rooty Hill*. I'm talking real, genuinely famous people – people who got there through talent and persistence.

Some kids today go on *The Voice* at sixteen or something, and they have a hit record by seventeen or eighteen and they believe they're stars themselves, so they don't get a buzz out of meeting others. But I still do, because deep inside I'm still a blue-collar Westie. I still think like that bloke off the Bridge.

Nothing would quite match up to the time I met The Duke, but there have been some other spectacular brushes with fame. When I was doing the talk-show circuit promoting *Croc Dundee* in the United States, one of the shows played an old clip of me impersonating Charles Bronson on a *Paul Hogan Show*. The very next night I was at some social function and the real Charlie turned up. He spotted me and came straight over and said, 'Hey Mick' – he thought my name was Mick – and then just stared at me for a while. Finally, with absolutely no expression, he said, 'I saw you on *The Johnny Carson Show* last night. You did a sketch of me?'

'Yeah,' I said. 'It was an old one.'

He looked at me blankly and said, after a very long pause, 'That was funny.' And that was it. Nothing else was uttered. A man of few words, Charlie.

Another big shock was in 1988, when I was staying at the Bel-Air Hotel in Los Angeles. I'd just left the hotel and climbed into my car. I was about to drive off and I saw this guy rushing across the parking lot, trying to catch my eye. He was waving this sheet of paper at me. I looked at him, thinking his face was familiar. Having decided I might know him, I wound the window down, and he rushed up.

'Hi Paul,' he said, 'I'm George Harrison.' And he was. *The* George Harrison. 'Look, I don't want to be a pest, but I've got this script. We started a little production company, and we were looking through the script and we all thought this would be great for you … if you wanted to do it.'

'All right, I'll have a look at it,' I said.

'I'm staying here too,' he mentioned. 'I saw you by the pool yesterday. But I was a bit nervous about coming up and waving a script at you.'

'No, no, it's cool.'

'Have a read of it, and if you like it, give me a call and maybe we'll do something.'

'Yeah, George, yeah, no worries,' I said, and off he went. I wound the window up in the car, sat there, took a deep breath and thought to myself, *That was George Harrison. He was nervous about approaching me. He didn't want to be a pest … He was a friggin' Beatle! How modest is that?!*

Even from that short meeting, I could tell he was a lovely guy. And the 'little production company' he'd mentioned was the one that had made the fabulous *Monty Python's Life of Brian*!

The new script was a good one too. It was about the IRA, and they wanted me to play an Irishman. However, as always, I only wanted to make people laugh, so I passed on it. Mind you, if I had tried to play an Irishman, it probably would have made people fall about.

Another guy I met once was Shaquille O'Neal, one of the greatest NBA basketballers ever. He was an utter giant, at 216 centimetres, which is over seven feet tall, but he was also ridiculously nice. The most giant giant that I ever met, though, was another basketball legend, Wilt the Stilt Chamberlain. I ran into him back in the 1980s when I was doing *Dundee* and I went to Nicky Blair's on Sunset Strip, an Italian restaurant and bar a lot of movie industry people went to.

I was looking around and I thought, *Look at the guy over there standing on a chair or a platform or something, preaching.* Then he moved and I thought, *There's nobody on a bloody chair at all. He's standing.* He looked over and saw me and came bounding over. 'Crocodile Dundee!' he said. 'Yeah, I'm your biggest fan.' He put his hand out to shake and the bottom half of my arm disappeared – his hand was like a shovel. 'I'm your biggest fan,' he repeated.

I looked up at him and said, 'Yeah, you sure are.'

I still can't forget that hand. And I still remember reading a claim that he'd slept with twenty thousand women. He certainly was pretty charming … and big!

Not everyone I met was someone I necessarily wanted to meet. Back in Australia, I remember having a dinner in Beechworth, a former mining town in north-east Victoria. It is one of the most charming places in the country and has a rich history stemming from the gold rush and the exploits of Ned Kelly. It also has a large prison with cobblestone walls, which sits about two hundred metres from the town centre.

Most people who are sentenced to enjoy Beechworth's hospitality for an exact number of months or years leave town the day they're released, but not all. I was with friends in one of the town's many pubs when a bloke who'd make Mark 'Chopper' Read look like ya kids' babysitter excitedly announced from the bar that he was my biggest fan.

Before I could thank him, he'd pulled up a chair and sat down at the table with us, putting the married couple I was with a touch on edge. This man told me that he'd only just been released and that he'd been a bad, bad boy. The crude prison tattoos squiggling up and down his arms and neck helped paint that picture. He continued telling me how big a fan he was, and was quoting sketches and bits of *Dundee*. I said thanks and tried to wave him off, but he said, 'No, I don't think you understand. I *really* love you.' And he pulled up his top lip to reveal the name 'Hoges' tattooed right along the top of his gum.

Forget the two friends I was with, I was now the one shitting myself. I was about to become someone's bitch. And right in front of Sunday night's dinner crowd as they're quietly trying to enjoy their counter meals. By the time our garlic bread arrived, we were already on our feet, saying how lovely it had been to meet him but that we hadn't realised it had got so late. My parting words to him were, 'Keep your nose clean. I don't wanna hear you're back inside.'

'You won't, Hoges, I promise,' he said. I certainly hope he kept that promise because, boy, this guy could do some damage. Luckily, it wasn't to me that night.

23

Big in Toongabbie

Hollywood loves a hit and it loves back-to-back hits even more. So after *Croc I* and *II*, the world, as they say, was my oyster. Paramount suggested, quite strongly, that I do a new movie of theirs called *Ghost*. One of the Zuckers – Jerry – was directing it. The Zuckers were famous for doing *Airplane!*, or *Flying High!* as we call it in Australia. It's an amazing film, full of mad visual jokes and hilarious lines that people still quote today ('Looks like I picked the wrong week to quit sniffing glue.'). I loved it and expected *Ghost* to be the same string of laughs. And Paramount did tell me it was a comedy.

Although it turned out *Ghost* was nothing like I expected, I really enjoyed reading the script. It was the best of all the ones

I'd been offered, and certainly better than all those shoot-'em-up action flicks that kept landing on my doorstep. I thought *Ghost* would make a good film – but probably not for me.

I had the craziness of *Airplane!* in mind when reading it, and said, 'It's not funny enough, I'm passing on it.' The real reason may have been that again, mentally, I had retired. This time I really thought I was done. I didn't know what exactly I'd do to fill my days, but figured it wouldn't be making movies. But then I got bored …

Needing something to do, I sat down and wrote a script based on an idea that had been bouncing around in my head for a while, called *Almost an Angel*. Again I asked Corney to direct it and he agreed. The story was about a criminal who thought he'd had a miraculous escape from death and believed he was now an angel on Earth doing good deeds. I got onto Patrick Swayze because I wanted him to play the part of Steve Garner, a guy who's in a wheelchair with spinal cancer, and a vital part of the movie. Most actors love being in a wheelchair and all that actorly stuff they can sink their teeth into.

'Oh, yeah!' he said immediately. 'That sounds great. Let me know when you're ready to go.'

With casting soon underway, I told Paramount that we had Patrick Swayze for Steve. But a day or two later I received a call from Patrick saying, 'Sorry, Paul, I'm afraid I won't be able to do it. I just had an offer from Paramount I really can't refuse.'

'Fantastic,' I said, 'what's that for?'

'Oh, a film called *Ghost*.'

I chuckled to myself and said, 'Go for it. Good on you, son.'

I never told him I'd passed on *Ghost*. You don't do that. I should add, though, that he was great in it, much better than I would have been. So I intend no disrespect when saying Patrick Swayze wasn't the first choice. He was the best choice.

Meanwhile I was the guy who had passed on *Ghost* to write and star in his own 'afterlife' movie. One of the two films was a massive hit.

Actually, *Almost an Angel* was popular in Peoria and Toongabbie, if I remember right. Yeah, okay, it flopped. I think if we'd made it as a Christmas Eve special for CBS, it would have rated the house down, but it was too little a movie and a bit too sappy, and we couldn't make a good trailer out of it. My mum, who was well past eighty at the time, summed it up best. 'I think people had trouble seeing you as an angel. Even when you were a little kid, they always said, "Oh, he's a little devil."'

Also, I think punters thought *Almost an Angel* was going to be a religious movie, even though, as it happens, I'm a devout atheist. So that turned a few away at the start. But no regrets at this end. I made my own thing, and I loved doing that. For example, I had Charlton Heston playing God, and I was sitting in my trailer with Charlton dressed up like, well, God. A biblical God.

He was running his lines for me, and saying, 'Is it all right if I say it like this …' I mean what a giant ego trip. At that time Charlton Heston was huge, an absolute megastar. And there he was asking me about his acting! This gave me the same kick as the television shows: the satisfaction of hearing someone saying a funny line and thinking, *Yeah, I wrote that*. And as nice as it would have been to have had the success of *Ghost*, which made 600 million bucks and delivered Whoopi Goldberg an Oscar, I wouldn't have changed doing my film for anything.

Almost an angel? Not quite. More a little devil. With John Cornell on set.
(*Alamy*)

As for the role I'd originally wanted Patrick for, I got Elias Koteas, who was later on television in *The Sopranos*, *House* and *Chicago P.D.* He was really great. Also, I forget exactly how it came about, but we got to work with one of the most legendary film composers of all time, Maurice Jarre. A lovely man. There was no detailed brief about the music I wanted. We let him decide, as that was his gift. He worked from the completed film with no temporary music guide. He simply composed from what he saw and heard on the screen. And he delivered, big time. In another coincidence, Jarre also did the score for *Ghost* that same year.

• • •

It can be said that studios are a predictable lot. They are always so desperate to work with anyone who's had success that if, in the early nineties, I'd wanted to play Hamlet on screen, like Mel Gibson did, they'd have said, 'Okay!' They let you do anything. But I wasn't interested in doing other people's stuff, and there ended up being other movies I passed on that turned out to be huge successes. For example, *Three Men and a Baby* was the biggest film of 1987. The offer to be in that came straight after the original *Dundee*. I won't name any more of those films, though, because it means saying publicly that someone else was the second or third choice. It's okay with *Three Men and a Baby* because I could have played any of three roles.

Missing out on other people's big films didn't matter at all. I never set out to be a movie star, or a great actor, or anything like that. The joy for me was making my own material. That was my thrill. Sure, I was still a little disappointed in the public's response to *Almost an Angel*, but that's all. I don't know how to cry. My life's too good. I have too much luck.

• • •

Living in Los Angeles always brings the possibility of drama. One time we were broken into. We were living in Beverly Hills. There'd been robberies, or at least prowlers, in a couple of places near ours earlier in the week. The neighbours had warned us to be on our guard. Anyway, we were in bed, about to go to sleep, and could hear someone scratching around at the back of the house. We lay there as quiet as we could, hoping it would stop but, no, it became pretty obvious someone was trying to jemmy open the door.

I grabbed a cricket bat. Not sure why I had a cricket bat in LA – it might have been a gift from one of the kids – and it wasn't supposed to be used as a weapon, but I grabbed it anyway and snuck across the landing and started creeping down the stairs. I wasn't going to kill anybody, but the combination of surprise and a Gray-Nicolls bat can often be pretty effective. I'd just about got to the bottom of the stairs, ready to have a red-hot swing at anyone coming through the door, when all the lights suddenly came on and Linda yelled out from the landing at the top of her voice, 'You die now, motherfucker!'

And I was standing there like an idiot, with the lights on me in my jocks and my pathetic cricket bat. Who knows what the other guy had – maybe a sub-machine gun? – but fortunately with the sudden brightness and yelling, he bolted. As we heard him scurrying away, I said, 'What the hell, Linda?'

'That's how we do it in New York,' she said, 'when someone's trying to break into your house.'

That was me and Linda: me with my sneak-up, cautious approach, and her with her take-it-head-on, tell 'em to fuck-up-and-die onslaught. Linda was very New York. She always said if you're walking home on your own and see anybody lurking around, act like you're absolutely nuts. 'They'll be more scared of you than you are of them, and they'll always leave you alone.'

In 1992 there were the LA Riots. A horrible business. The place went crazy for about six days and sixty-three people were killed and more than two thousand injured. My lawyer was carjacked, another friend was assaulted. I had a gun in the car, just in case. Fortunately we escaped any real drama, but it was a wild time and I felt a long way away from Granville.

In 1994 we were living on top of Coldwater Canyon when the Northridge Earthquake struck. Measuring 6.7 on the Richter scale, it was one of the biggest ever in a modern city, collapsing those double-decker Los Angeles freeways, flattening buildings and tearing craters in roads. It literally threw us out of bed and busted a whole lot of windows in the house.

We raced outside in case the roof caved in. I was limping because I'd hurt my foot during our escape, but we made it out and sat in the car. It certainly woke us up quickly, but if you get out of an earthquake with just one sore foot between you, you've dodged a pretty big bullet.

• • •

By the early 1990s, I had another film project brewing, but for the first time John Cornell wasn't going to be part of it. Soon after *Angel* wrapped, Corney started having some struggles, health-wise. Then, around 2000, he was diagnosed with Parkinson's disease. True to their nature, he and Dele faced up to this challenge together and never took a backwards step thereafter.

I would take a bullet for John, and he'd take one for me. Corney's my blood brother, still the best friend a bloke could ever hope for, the one who's been with me through everything. He's sick, but he still has a good time. There's nothing wrong upstairs, the brain's still there, it's just that he has a little trouble communicating. But he gets on with it.

'Okay, I've got Parkinson's, so what?' That's John's nature and he and Dele are an unbreakable force.

24

Playing Cowboys

I went to the John Wayne and Clint Eastwood Academy of Drama. Neither of them were great actors but what they did, they did well. I'm not saying for a minute I'm in their class. It's just that, like those guys, I play a few small variations on myself. If you went to see a movie and John Wayne or Clint Eastwood was playing the part of a compassionate psychiatrist, you'd hate it. But if it was a western …

Being a huge fan of both those guys, I decided that I too wanted to make a western. I think most kids, when they're little, play cowboys in the backyard and certainly every boy I knew growing up wanted to be John Wayne. So I started to write *Lightning Jack*.

Dinking the fabulous Cuba Gooding Jr, in *Lightning Jack*. (*Alamy*)

Even though it was to be a western, I wanted it to be funny and I wanted the hero, Lightning Jack, to be a guy whose main obsession is publicity. Lightning Jack didn't really care whether he was a successful robber or not, he just wanted his name in the paper and was basically jealous of Jesse James and Billy the Kid. He was a dopey bastard who wanted to be famous, rather than rich.

I set the film in Monument Valley, the Valley of the Gods and all those other places where the good old-fashioned westerns took place. Just imagine this for a Westie who expected to spend the rest of his life hauling cables up the Sydney Harbour Bridge: I got to get up in the morning, dress up as a cowboy, and ride my horse through Monument Valley. Whether the movie worked or not, this was an absolute childhood fantasy coming true.

I've now been to almost every famous museum and art gallery in the world, and have seen the Sistine Chapel and the like, but nothing can match the thrill and magic of riding on horseback through Monument Valley as the sun peeks over the horizon.

It was on this film that I met Cuba Gooding Jr, who is famous to many now as the 'Show me the money!' footballer from his Academy Award–winning performance in *Jerry Maguire*. Originally, I had written the part of Lightning Jack's mute sidekick for Johnny Depp. I'd met him at some party and liked him and thought, 'Yeah, he'd be a good sidekick.'

When I learnt Johnny was off in Europe doing something else, I auditioned a couple of other guys and was pretty close to choosing one of them. Then I saw Cuba on a talk show. I think it was on Arsenio Hall. He'd just appeared in *Boyz n the Hood*, and he was just so expressive and full of life that I thought, 'No, that's my sidekick.'

With this character not having any words, it was all about personality and Cuba was bursting with that and charisma. I cast him purely from that talk-show appearance and it worked out terrifically! We had great fun, as he too loved playing cowboys. Together we got to spend half of that movie on horseback in the wild, wild west. Fabulous.

I then had some people say *Lightning Jack* was racist because Cuba didn't have dialogue. But I originally wrote it for Johnny Depp, and I never changed a word in it. How's that racist?

Lightning Jack never set the world on fire, but it was mine. It wasn't a big hit, but it did make a little money. People thought, *No, it's not* Crocodile Dundee, *therefore it's a flop*. But it did okay. In fact, *Lightning Jack* was more successful in the United States than some of the Aussie movies like *Strictly Ballroom* and *The Adventures of Priscilla, Queen of the Desert*, which, I read in the Australian press, were 'taking the US by storm'. I guess it's all about expectations.

I loved the experience of making that film and working with those good people. But then I retired once again. This time for real.

Well, for a few months, until Subaru decided to release a high-riding, all-wheel-drive station wagon. They chose the name Outback and then immediately came to me. It looked like a fun project and offered a chance to spend some time in Mexico. Yes, Mexico. The ads were to be shown only in the States, so they thought they could get away with having Mexico play the part of Australia (where, naturally, everyone drives a car called an Outback).

Then I went to the Bahamas in late 1995 and did the first movie that wasn't my own project. It was the kid's film *Flipper*. I did it for two reasons. It was for a friend of mine, Lance Hool, who was the executive producer, and because it meant spending ten weeks in the Bahamas. I don't care who you are, that's an almost impossible thing to turn down. My co-star, apart from the grumpy dolphin, was a boy by the name of Elijah Wood. He was only fourteen at the time, but he went on to play the lead role, Frodo, in *The Lord of the Rings* trilogy.

Flipper was fun to make and the location outstanding, but it didn't do much at the box office. Some of the reviews were a little harsh about the film's pacing and writing, though a few critics (including one in *Variety*!) were kind enough to praise my efforts as Uncle Porter. To be honest, I haven't given *Flipper* much thought since the day the director said, 'Wrap!' When asked about it on a US talk show, I apparently said, 'It's about a dolphin and it's not going to change your life.' Can't say I pitched it too hard.

Two years later I starred in a little TV movie called *Floating Away*, alongside Judge Reinhold of *Beverly Hills Cop* fame, Rosanna Arquette and Brendan Fletcher. John Badham had approached me directly about making it. He was a highly regarded director and a good guy and it was a sweet little story. It was also going to be shot over six weeks in beautiful Vancouver and its surrounds in the summer, so it didn't take him too much work to talk me into it. Generally it was a pleasant experience, and Rosie Arquette was wonderful. Working with Judge Reinhold? Let's just say he was great in *Beverly Hills Cop*.

The highlight of 1998, though, was when Linda and I had a beautiful little boy. I couldn't have been happier! We called

'Listen, kid, a movie about hobbits and magic lands is never gonna
work!' Shooting *Flipper* with future *Lord of the Rings* star Elijah Wood.
(*Alamy*)

him Chance. Most people assumed it was Linda who chose his name because all my other kids had pretty conventional names, but no: Linda wanted Madison, and I was the one who came up with Chance. It was John Wayne's nickname in *Rio Bravo*. And Chance just sounded right to me. Linda and I didn't fight over it, which turned out to be a good thing. Madison is also a girl's name and later one of Chance's girlfriends was a Madison. So that could have been a tad confusing.

I loved being a dad again! Because there'd been such a long gap between Chance and my older children, I enjoyed everything about fatherhood once more. I've adored it each and every time I've had a child in the house. You have them and you just love them, and you do the best you can. I kind of like too that for the first few years the kid thinks I'm really smart and know everything. Pity you can't give them back for a few years, though, when they're about fifteen and get pimples and grow bigger than you.

I've been a father for longer than I was ever a son. I've been a dad since I was a teenager, more than sixty years ago. I've been the youngest dad at the PTA meeting and the oldest. Not many people could say that. Actually, not many people would want to say that. But I've loved it.

I'm sure Chance is my last child, but one of the advantages of being an older dad for me was that by the time we had him my life was set up. When I was younger, I was working like a dog to make ends meet and feed the family. This last time around I could be at home with him much more during the day, and I loved that.

25

One Too Many

It may come as a surprise to many, but there was a *Croc III*. It had been twelve or thirteen years since *Dundee II* yet I stupidly let myself be talked into doing another one. I had Lance Hool to blame. He's a good mate and produced *Flipper*, and I guess he and my agent at the time were sick of me saying no to everything. They were desperate for me to do something. Anything!

A couple of American galahs wrote the screenplay, and I had to rewrite it within the constraints of the set and the budget. It came out in 2001 and was officially known as *Crocodile Dundee in Los Angeles*. The basic idea was that Mick and Sue were still in Australia, where he'd been reduced to wrestling crocs for tourists. Then they move across the Pacific with their son, Mikey, who impresses his classmates with his outback survival skills, and Mick gets involved in a murder investigation and, then there's an art heist and … whatever. It never really worked.

It also wasn't the same fun to make, as many of the crew who had made the first two shoots so memorable had retired or were on other jobs. The wonderful Johnny Meillon had passed away by then too. I should have seen the warning signs …

Anyway, early in the process I realised I needed another Aussie sidekick. So I invented a character, Jacko Jackson, who's Mick Dundee's rival. The two of them are always arguing about which of them is the best croc hunter in the Northern Territory. There was never any doubt in my mind who should play Jacko Jackson: Alec Wilson, my horse-wrangling mate from the mini-series *Anzacs*.

Alec had also played the small part of Denning in *Croc II* – he was the guy who was knocked out by Donk. Now in *Croc III* he was back as Jacko, making his first trip to LA to visit Dundee. Alec's a real dry, outback bushie. The real deal. And he gave me a reminder of just how big our country is. Hardly anyone in the world, including most Australians, truly understands this.

Australia is roughly the size of the United States but has half the population of California. When I was a kid there were fewer than 8 million Aussies. Now it's about 25-and-a-bit million and, of that total, about 20 million of us live on the coast and are suburbanites, like me. Another half a million live adjacent to the coast, inland a couple of hundred miles or less. The rest of the country? Very few people live there and those that do are widely scattered. South Australia, Western Australia,

There are Aussies and then there's my mate Alec Wilson: a true Australian cattleman, actor and low-flying bush pilot.

Northern Territory: they have their capitals on the coast and a few inland towns, but otherwise there's mostly nothing there. Yeah, a few places have populations that run into the hundreds, but not many have thousands of people. So, aside from a fair proportion of the continent's Indigenous inhabitants, most of us Australians, who like to think of ourselves as outback people, really aren't.

That said, there are obviously a few people who do live in the outback, and one of them is Alec. He was born and raised on Frome Downs, which is a cattle station or, as they call them in America, a ranch. Frome Downs is 607,899 hectares, or just over 1.5 million acres, and sits nearly six hundred kilometres from the nearest decent-sized city, Adelaide. Growing up on a property like that gives you a different sense of distance and area. I was once filming a tourism commercial in a place called Wilpena Pound, which is set amid the beautiful, rugged Flinders Ranges in South Australia. A couple of days after I'd left there, I had a call from Alec.

'You were filming in Wilpena Pound,' he said. 'Why didn't you come up and see me?'

I asked him how far Frome Downs was from Wilpena Pound. 'No more than ninety miles,' he said. Ninety miles was just like next door as far as he was concerned.

'That's to the front gate,' I said, 'but how far from the front gate to the front door of the house?'

'Only about another ninety,' he replied.

So that's Frome Downs, where it's about ninety miles – more than 140 bloody kilometres – from the front gate to the house. There are whole countries that would fit inside that property.

Funny, when we were filming *Croc II* we had three or four actors come over from America to keep the storyline going. They'd never visited Australia before and they were playing Colombians. Anyway, we were sitting around the catering tent, eating and talking about the place and one of the guys said to Alec, 'You're a cattleman, are you?'

'Yeah,' Alec said.

'How many head of cattle do you run?' asked the American.

'About nine thousand at the moment.'

'Wow, that's … How big's the property?'

'Oh,' said Alec, 'it's a bit over two thousand.'

The American said, 'You run nine thousand head of cattle on two thousand acres? How's that possible?'

Alec looked at him like he was stupid. 'No, two thousand *square miles*, you dopey bastard.' Where Alec comes from, they talk in square miles. Nobody has a couple of hundred, or even a couple of thousand, acres.

When Alec said I should come up, I said, 'I wouldn't want to drive all that way.'

He said, 'I can fly down and get you. I've got a plane to herd the cattle.'

'Oh, I didn't know you had a licence.'

'Oh, I don't have a licence,' he said.

'You fly a plane without a licence?'

'Yeah,' he said, 'But I don't fly very high.'

There was an eight-year drought around Frome Downs back in the 1980s and into the early 1990s. The bank eventually seized the property, which is a shame because it had belonged to Alec's family since the 1940s or something. Then the bank sold it to some other guy who owned a huge sheep station.

Must be hard to be born and raised on your own country, virtually, and then have to sell it.

I thought there was at least a small upside, though. He'd been living like a hermit – you live on a property that big, you never see anyone else. I thought it would do him good to get off there and get out into the world. But he hasn't been happy about it. He missed it. We tried to find a part for him in my last movie but couldn't make it work. When he gets the chance, he's a bloody good actor.

· · ·

Crocodile Dundee in Los Angeles

The Jacko Jackson Scene

Mick pulls into a drive-through burger bar.

MICK: Now, you pick out what you want on that menu there. Then you yell it out into that box. Then in two minutes, you're scoffing it down, without even getting out of the car.

JACKO: So, you can eat like a pig … and nobody can see you. (*Winks.*) Clever buggers, these Yanks.

It's hard to imagine a bigger contrast to this authentic cattleman and great Australian character than another bloke

Scared not to laugh. In the embrace of Mike Tyson on the set of *Croc III*.

I worked with on *Croc III*: Mike Tyson. 'Iron' Mike grew up in crowded Brooklyn, New York, and became the world's youngest heavyweight boxing champion in 1986, at just twenty years old. I'd met him in the 1980s on the *Late Show with David Letterman,* when he'd just become world champ. Yet he still said, 'Can I get your photo, Mr Hogan?'

He called me 'Mr Hogan'.

So we got together to take the photo and he reached around and draped his arm over my shoulder, and it was like someone had dropped a bag of concrete off the back of a truck. My knees nearly buckled. He was so dense, muscle-wise; so heavy, so strong. No wonder he knocked everyone out. But he was still like a kid, that first time I met him.

I didn't tell him about my own career as a boxer, just in case he thought I might have been interested in challenging him. But he knew I knew a bit about the game. He became a friend in a way, but then his life obviously took a bad turn. There has always been much conjecture about what happened in Mike's life, but whichever way you look at it he had to deal with some demons.

What happened on *Dundee III* was that we were searching for the least likely person we could find to be doing yoga and meditation in a park. I thought of Mike and approached him. He remembered me, and was keen to take part. I think we were the first people to hire him after he'd served his jail time. He then went on and did all the *Hangover* movies and a Broadway show and I even saw him in the opening number of the Tony Awards one year.

Mike clearly had a dark side, which had no doubt been aggravated by being brought up like a tiger. Trainers put young boxers in a cage when they're kids and effectively poke them with a stick and turn them into fighting machines. But Mike behaved like a real gentleman, and displayed a really soft nature, like when he was playing with our son. I have a photo somewhere of Chance up on Iron Mike's back, punching him in the nose. Chance was only about three.

During the filming of *Dundee III* they were calling us on set and Mike came over and said, 'Come on, we're wanted.' He grabbed my hand to pull me up because I was sitting on the grass. Then we walked over towards the set, with Mike still holding my hand. The whole way. And I thought, *This is a little strange, but it's Mike Tyson, what am I going to say?*

Mike's hand was like a sledgehammer. But he was just so happy to be filming and playing. It was a cameo appearance and he refused to charge me anything. 'No, I've got time, I'll be in it,' he'd said. All I had to do was fly him and some of his entourage, who turned out to be his relatives, into town. We shot for a couple of days and that was it. He was great.

For all that, the audiences stayed away from *Crocodile Dundee in Los Angeles* in droves, and it was given a good kicking by the critics. It ended up grossing only a tiny fraction of the earlier *Croc* films, and I thought, *Yeah, I shouldn't have done that.*

While I don't watch *Dundee* films any more, I still understand some of the reasons the early ones worked. I guess what's been more surprising is that they have stood the test of time the way they have. But two was the right number. My favourite movie of all time is *Rocky*, and *Rocky II* is also great, but we both should have stopped there. There shouldn't have been a III for us, and when Rocky then went to IV, I was really like, *Come on. No, that's enough!*

26

A New Beginning

You know when you're in a helicopter and you're flying over your own theme park? Actually, unless you're Walt Disney, you probably don't know what that's like. But, bizarrely, I do. It's up there with various other surreal things that have happened in my life.

It was in 2004 when Paramount flew me out to Santa Clara, California, to open the new 'Crocodile Dundee's Boomerang Bay' water park. It was the full catastrophe, with water slides with names like 'Screamin' Wombat', 'Downunder Thunder' and 'Didgeridoo Falls', and then there was the inevitable Australian-themed restaurant. Never did work out if they served crocodile, but it's amazing how many restaurants and cafés around the world do have *Dundee*-themed burgers, steaks and drinks.

I even went into a Chinese restaurant at Southbank in Melbourne and they had 'Crocodile Dundee Black Bean Beef' and 'Walkabout Creek Chilli Prawns'. Talk about a stretch. The owners watched a little nervously from the bar as we went through the menu, probably worried I might sue.

These things prove that I'm never going to get away from *Dundee*, but so what? Never begrudge a hit. And look at it another way: you know when you hear a funny joke and you can't wait to get home and say, 'I heard this gag today.' You want to spread it around. If you can create a joke and share it through a film, by the time it appears in cinemas then on DVD and television and everything else, millions or billions of people might have enjoyed it. So, with something like *Dundee*, I got to do the ultimate share.

But by 2004 I was in my sixties. I'd worked on the Coat Hanger for a decade, had six kids, made countless television shows, specials and commercials, done concerts, three *Dundee* films, *Almost an Angel*, *Lightning Jack* and a couple of others, and hosted the Oscars. And I'd opened an American theme park with a billabong-shaped swimming pool and met Elizabeth Taylor and Clint Eastwood. So surely, now, I could finally retire.

It wasn't to be. As I was being choppered over 'Crocodile Dundee's Boomerang Bay', I was getting ready to launch a new film. It had all started, out of the blue, when a bloke named Dean Murphy had managed to get a script called *Strange Bedfellows* under my nose. Dean knew someone in LA, who dropped a print-out of the script into the office of my agent, Douglas Urbanski. Douglas skimmed the first couple of pages while waiting for a phone call. He ended up staying back and reading the whole thing, and was so impressed that he detoured on the drive home to drop it into my place.

I also decided to skim the first couple of pages – I don't know why, because the last thing on my mind was making another film – and then ended up reading the whole bloody thing. I read it again the next morning too and dialled the writer's mobile number, which was printed on the front. Within about a week I was in Sydney spending the day with Dean, who turned out to be a straight-up bloke, so low-key and easy-going that I thought, *Yeah, I wanna work with this guy*.

The script was about two old-fashioned country blokes in Yackandandah, in north-east Victoria, called Ralph and Vince, who've never met a gay person, as far as they know, in their whole lives. Yet, after making some bad decisions, they find themselves involved in a scheme that forces them to pretend to be a same-sex couple. At first, they are clueless and quite wary of anyone thinking they are gay, but by the story's end they have been enlightened.

It was charming and it was funny. At no point did I think I'd need to write anything or change anything or try to add more jokes. As far as I was concerned, Dean had nailed that dry, subtle Australian humour like no one else. Dean's humour lingers long after he's left. Even today I'll hang up the phone from him and think, *Did he really just say that to me?!*

The location for *Strange Bedfellows* seemed authentic on the page. I quickly found out why. Dean is the son of a Yackandandah dairy farmer. Well, actually, he's off a farm in nearby Kergunyah. How Australian can you get?

So much for my retirement, but with *Strange Bedfellows* being shot in the Victorian countryside I knew and loved, I thought, *It'll be just like a nice holiday.* With no ambition to do anything but enjoy myself and work with nice people, I embarked on another movie. Glad I did too, because I had a wonderful time in Yackandandah. It's a charming little former mining town that still has some lovely architecture and a dairy industry in the surrounding valleys. There are about nine hundred residents and almost every one of them's a delight: 'Want to shoot in our house? Sure!' 'Want us to knock the shed down to give you more room? I'll get onto it tomorrow!'

I also got to work with great Aussie actors such as Roy Billing and Michael Caton. Michael was so good as the dad in *The Castle,* and on screen he epitomises the working-class Aussie man. There's a real warmth and decency to many of the characters Michael plays.

Northern English actor and Academy Award nominee Pete Postlethwaite, who'd been so great in films such as *The Usual Suspects, Brassed Off* and *In the Name of the Father,* was also joining the cast. We were all excited and the very day Pete arrived in Yackandandah, Steven Spielberg, in Hollywood, gave his opinion in an interview that Pete was the world's greatest living actor. But Pete couldn't have been more humble and, in that brilliant tradition of ageing English thespians, was wonderful fun.

One day Pete wasn't required but decided to come and hang out on the set all the same. Not wanting to be a distraction, he didn't let the rest of us know. Eventually the first assistant director came up to me. 'Have you noticed we've got a new extra?' he said.

Playing dress-ups once more, on the set of *Strange Bedfellows* alongside director Dean Murphy.

A real actor is on set. The fabulous Pete Postlethwaite.

I hadn't, but I looked around at the couples dancing in the ball scene and noticed an extremely unattractive – traffic-stoppingly unattractive! – woman. Yep, that was Pete. On the other days he'd been in a suit, but this day the hair and makeup team, along with the costume department, had squeezed him into a big blonde wig, a red sequinned ball gown and high heels.

Pete thought he looked fabulous! One of the local farmers was happily waltzing with him and it took quite some time before he got an inkling that maybe not all was as it seemed. Pete just did it for a laugh, and it was typical of the fun we had shooting *Strange Bedfellows*.

Perhaps my favourite weird moment was when I was sitting on a chair in a street in Yackandandah waiting for the cameras to be set up. A little old lady, easily in her mid-eighties, was making her way up the street with a walking stick in hand. She was about to pass me when she suddenly stopped and pointed right in my face and declared, 'There's Paul Hogan!'

I looked around. 'Where?'

She started whacking my legs with her walking stick then stared right into my eyes and said, 'That's him, right there in the chair!'

By now somewhat unsettled, I feebly agreed with her, and she turned and continued on up the street. To this day I'm not sure what was going on in her head.

And I wasn't quite sure what was going on in my head on another day when I turned up at the Yackandandah Community Hall. Like all community halls, it's the hub of the town. There'll be civic meetings, cards, parties, wakes, knees-ups and scouts, sometimes all on the same day. It doubles for a

'We've gotta do what?!' *Strange Bedfellows* with Michael Caton.

childcare centre and an emergency centre at times, and when we were in town it became a screening room where we would show the rushes – as in what we'd filmed the previous day – for ourselves and the crew.

I was going to the rushes one night and for absolutely no good reason decided to dress up as a punch-drunk fighter. I put on a black beanie and used sticky tape to flatten my nose, then paced around the hall on edge, as though looking for the next bloke that might try and hit me. It was funny because no one recognised me. The crew wouldn't come anywhere near me and others diverted their eyes. But one of the locals, a guy probably in his mid-seventies, who was using another part of the hall for line dancing, wandered up to me and asked, 'So what are you guys doing here?'

I explained we were screening some of what had been filmed yesterday.

'Will that Hogan be coming?' he asked.

'I doubt it,' I replied. 'He probably thinks he's too good for a place like this.'

'Yeah, that doesn't surprise me. I've never cared for him much. And he's certainly not funny.'

'Yeah,' I agreed, 'and from what I've heard he's a real prick too.'

The man nodded, added a quick 'Yep', and wandered off and started line dancing again.

When *Strange Bedfellows* came out in 2004, it divided opinion, and often not along the lines you might think. In some cases we had openly gay critics praising the film for having two straight Aussie blokes telling people to get over their fears of gay men; yet we also had some straight critics attacking us for making fun of the gay lifestyle. Luckily the vast majority of viewers, both straight and gay, understood there was no malice, and appreciated the film's quiet message of tolerance – and that, above all, it was just a silly caper film.

I have to say, today I can see how stupid this sort of prejudice is, but I probably had it when I worked on the Bridge all those years ago. Now I realise that nobody wakes up one day and thinks, *I'll be gay because my life's too simple. I want it to be more complicated, so I'll tear up my poster of Madonna and I'll put that picture of Elton John on the wall.* Eventually, unless you're particularly daft, you realise that who other people love has nothing to do with you.

Early on in *Strange Bedfellows*, my character, Vince, sits with Michael Caton's equally unenlightened character, Ralph, attempting to fill out a tax return falsely claiming same-sex status. They are greatly relieved that the tax form is labelled 'Private and Confidential', but of course everyone in their small town finds out their little secret. By sheer coincidence, I too was about to find out that when the tax office labels something 'Private and Confidential' it's utter bollocks.

Strange Bedfellows was a small film with a small budget, but it was the top-grossing Australian film at the Aussie box office in 2004. And three years after we made it, a remarkably similar plotline turned up in the Hollywood film *I Now Pronounce you Chuck & Larry*, via Universal and Adam Sandler's crowd. I guess that's the most sincere form of flattery.

Whatever the case, my work was done. I thought, *Now I can leave showbiz all behind. I'm getting too old.*

• • •

Strange Bedfellows

The Tax Form Scene

Inside Ralph's garage, daytime. Ralph and Vince sit at an old desk in Ralph's country garage. They pore over official-looking government forms. Vince has a pen poised.

VINCE: Okay, I go in this box and you go there.

RALPH: Hey, hang on a moment. (*He double-checks.*) 'Spouse'? Why do I have to be the spouse?

VINCE: It's not important.

RALPH: It is to me. I don't want to be the spouse. It sounds kind of … wussy.

VINCE: Of course it sounds wussy. That's the whole point.

RALPH: Why can't you be the spouse?

VINCE: All right, if it's such a big issue, I'll be the spouse and you can be 'Head Of Household'. Will that make you happy?

RALPH: Well, happier than being a spouse.

VINCE (*muttering as he starts to fill in the form*): For these small mercies, thank you, oh Lord. (*He moves to the next line.*) Okay. Period of co-habitation?

RALPH: What?

VINCE: How long we've been living together. Well, we want the full five years back benefits, so let's say six.

RALPH: Hang on. When did your missus shoot through?

VINCE (*thinking*): Ah … about six years ago. It's perfect.

RALPH: So, what, she leaves and almost straight away we move in together?

VINCE: What's wrong with that?

RALPH: I don't want to look easy.

Vince rolls his eyes.

RALPH: Well, it'll look like I got you on the rebound.

VINCE: Okay, so we started seeing each other on the sly about a year before that. All right?

RALPH: Sounds reasonable. Means neither of us rushed into anything.

VINCE (*writing*): Sometimes I seriously worry about you, Ralphie. (*He checks the next column.*) Address of shared residence?

RALPH: My place.

Vince looks at him questioningly.

RALPH: I'm not going down as living in a projection booth.

VINCE (*writing*): Picky … Occupations?

RALPH: Just put down mechanic.

VINCE: No, you work in the travel
industry. And I … am in theatre. Trust
me. Orientation?

RALPH: Jeez, I think the backyard's north-
east, but all I know is that morning
sun plays buggery with the carpets.

VINCE: Nah, sexual orientation (*writing*).
'A couple of old uphill gardeners'
should cover it.

RALPH: Bloody hell, what if my old mum
ever saw that? She'd be spinning in her
grave.

VINCE: Look, will you get it through your
head? This is just a form. It will go
to Canberra and that's the last we'll
ever hear of it. So who cares if some
government pen-pusher thinks we're gay?
No one else is going to be any the
wiser.

RALPH: You're sure?

VINCE (*indicating the return envelope*):
Mate, look … 'Private and Confidential'.
It's privileged information, between us
and them. How would anyone around here
ever find out?

27

Taxing Times

At the age of sixty-five, I was thinking about taking it a bit easier. But suddenly things got real busy. I've had lots of bad reviews, gossip and lies written about me over the years, but none of that prepared me for the craziness that was about to ensue.

Project Wickenby was the name of a taskforce the ATO launched in 2006, 'to protect the integrity of Australia's financial and regulatory systems'. There was a lot of politics behind it and great fanfare about finally nailing those rich bastards who don't pay tax. And they did get some in the end: almost fifty people went down, though Wickenby went after many more than that.

I was first investigated by the Australian Crime Commission, at the request of the ATO. The Crime Commission people were quite reasonable, but were so ignorant of the film industry it was embarrassing. They told me, 'Your movie made $300 million at the box office, so you owe $150 million in tax.'

'Oh, come on,' I said. 'The first 55 percent or so goes to the people who own the cinemas. Then Paramount, the distributor, takes its chunk, then there's dozens and dozens of investors and this mob and that mob all taking a share and on and on it goes. Oh, and you've got to pay to make the film in the first place, then publicise it. That costs a lot – millions. But it's not my job to have to teach you what happens with money at the movies.'

I think a lot of people, in the media and elsewhere couldn't quite work me out. They didn't understand that I've never really cared about the folding stuff. I got money automatically. I loved doing my job and making people laugh, and money just arrived. I was never driven by the dollar and some can't relate to that. They think, *What are you hiding? You must be hiding something*.

The only decision I ever made about tax, and this is true, was taken soon after I moved to America. Financial advisors all said to me, 'We'll need to get your Green Card quickly, cos tax in America is cheaper.' The top rate there was about 32 percent, and in Australia it was about 48 percent.

'Nah,' I said. 'I wanna pay me tax in Australia. I got rich in the movie world cos I played on my Australianness, or the image that people have of Australia, and so my countrymen and women should share in it. Plus my kids and grandkids live there, use the hospitals, go to the schools. I once lived in a Housing Commission house, where I got cheap rent. I appreciated that.

And if I pay it in Australia, as opposed to the US, not all the money will go to propping up some huge military.'

My financial advisors said, 'You're an idiot!' I heard that from them quite a lot. And in a sense they were right, because to pay my tax in Australia I had to make sure I was never in the United States for longer than six months. Had to go down to Mexico every so often to get out the country, and I couldn't buy a house or car, and couldn't get a driver's licence, or I'd be classified as a US resident for tax purposes.

I paid my 48 percent, or whatever it was, all through that period when the money was coming in from *Dundee* and *Dundee II*. My old employer, Kerry Packer, would spin in his grave if he found that out. He wasn't that keen on paying a cent more than he had to. 'They're not doing that good a job,' he'd say.

I'm not making out I'm a holy person or anything. Just grateful. I'm so lucky I was born an Australian. I'm an Australian by nature, and I really love the things we do. We're terrific, with our *have-a-go* attitude, with our *fair go*. But after about seven years the Yanks changed the visa laws and I had to get a Green Card. After that, I paid tax in America. Still do.

I'm probably the only person who's made his money all around the world and brought it back into Australia just for the pleasure of paying tax on it.

• • •

Meanwhile, Dean turned up again with another script. This one was called *Charlie & Boots*, about a son who tries to reconnect with his grieving father by taking a fishing trip to

Cape York, the northernmost part of Australia. Again, it showed Dean's mastery of that laid-back Australian humour – humour that doesn't always travel internationally, or even to the inner city, but who cares?

I'd be paid, not much, because Dean keeps a tight grip on the wallet, but I'd be playing a character I liked and travelling all over regional Australia and having fun with great people. I said, 'Okay, *Charlie & Boots* can drag me out of retirement one last time. But that's it. Then I'm really done.'

Another incentive to do the film was that Dean had the same rules that John and I had when we made movies: no arseholes. Quite simply, if someone's being a bit precious or a bit of a prima donna, or nasty to those below them, just get rid of 'em on the first day. As I've mentioned, I don't believe that you need to have drama and tension and aggravation to end up with a good product. All that stuff about, 'Oh, you've got to suffer in the movie or it'll turn out to be a failure,' that's rubbish, and Dean agreed completely. You're making a comedy, you should have fun doing it and be surrounded by fun people.

I was Charlie, the father, and Shane Jacobson was the son, Boots. Three years earlier, Shane and his director brother, Clay, had made *Kenny*, an ultra-low-budget feature film about a man who works for a portable dunny company. It was very funny and became an enormous hit and won lots of awards. *Kenny* made Shane look like an overnight, come-from-nowhere star, a bit like me all those years earlier. But Shane had been quietly working away as an actor for years and years, and really knew his stuff. He also turned out to be a really terrific guy, one of the funniest I've ever met, and we became great mates immediately.

Enjoying all the big things Australia has to offer, including Shane Jacobson, while filming *Charlie & Boots*.

Starting in Warrnambool, a small city at the very south of the Australian mainland, we began shooting *Charlie & Boots* with just the best group of people that you could ever run into. I remember, part of the way along, in between shooting scenes in the Victorian country town of Echuca, Shane and I pulled up at a set of lights in the old banger we were using for the movie, a Holden Kingswood. This woman looked at us and scanned our faces in a sort of disbelief then yelled to her husband, 'Darl, Kenny and Crocodile Dundee are in the car next to us.' As we drove away we could hear the husband saying, 'Oh, don't be silly …'

I must say, Shane and I, on camera, were in one of the funniest scenes I've ever been in. It involved Charlie and Boots in their broken-down Kingswood being towed at a higher speed than it could ever achieve on its own. I love the scene, but am still really annoyed, because Dean wrote it, not me.

Charlie & Boots was the second highest grossing Australian film of 2009. It really struck a chord among Australians with fond memories of road trips with their families – you know, the simplicity of service station meals, and motels with flaps in the wall to put your breakfast through. It sold surprisingly well around the world too. In Germany the film was renamed *Crocodile Daddy*. Inexplicably, there's a crocodile on the poster, and another lead actor is credited alongside Shane and me. No one had ever heard of him.

• • •

Gone fishing ... three thousand kilometres away.

Charlie & Boots

The Towing Scene

Charlie and Boots's broken-down car is being towed at high speed along a country road by a couple of shearers with a fast ute and a short rope. Boots clings on nervously behind the wheel. Suddenly a siren can be heard. Boots looks around. A motorbike cop pulls alongside.

MOTORBIKE COP (*signalling*): I want you to pull over!

BOOTS (*confused*): You want us to what?

MOTORBIKE COP: I want you to PULL OVER!

BOOTS: Pull over??!

CHARLIE: This should be interesting.

BOOTS (*to cop*): You probably should talk to the guys in the other car.

MOTORBIKE COP: Don't worry about them. I'll deal with them in a minute.

BOOTS (*laughing*): He's a bright bugger.

The cop suddenly works out what's going on.

MOTORBIKE COP: You know you're being towed?!

BOOTS: Oh really?! And here I was just about to try and overtake the bastards!

MOTORBIKE COP: Stay here.

The cop rides up to the ute doing the towing and signals to the driver to pull over.

28

Two Losses and a Win

I got angry about Wickenby, but I never lost sleep. Under what was probably the greatest pressure I ever had to deal with, the traits I'd inherited from my mother, of being cool, calm and collected, generally held me in good stead.

Mum had become a widow at fifty and never married again. She was in her late nineties by the time I was under attack, still living by herself, on the third floor up. I'd ring her and she'd say, 'I have to get me hearing aid, I can't hear you! Just a minute!' She'd put the phone down and never come back, having forgotten all about her son on the other end of the line.

Eventually she accepted she was no longer totally in control. 'Okay,' she said, 'I better go into one of those places now.' And she did, moving into a retirement home at ninety-eight. I think it was her attitude that made her live so long. She didn't cling to life, just sort of took it in her stride. Funny old bird, eighty pounds wringing wet, but ate like three truck drivers. Living through a Depression will do that to you. 'Aren't you gonna finish that? Don't leave that chop on your plate, give it here.'

Mum got a telegram from the Queen on her hundredth birthday. She was totally thrilled, but, aside from that, boredom had set in and she was ready to go. We'd visit and she'd ask, 'Why have they forgotten me?' *They* being whoever was meant to take you away from this life at that age.

'I don't know why they're keeping me here,' she'd say. 'All me friends are dead. I've got no one to play Scrabble with.'

She was a lovely lady. 'It costs nothing to be nice,' she used to say. I think I've taken that from her. If offering a simple kind word or gesture can make someone's day that little bit better, why wouldn't you do it?

In August 2010, my dear old mum, Flo, passed away, at 101.

• • •

Meanwhile, out of the blue, I got a call to be in the promotional film for Australia's bid for the soccer World Cup of 2022. It was all at the highest level. The new prime minister, Julia Gillard, was involved. So we had this weird thing going on where the top politicians wanted me to be the face of Australia for the World Cup commercial, while at the same time some in the media seemed to want to portray me in a very different light.

The World Cup video was directed by Phillip Noyce, the great Australian director who made *Dead Calm*, *Clear and*

Flying out of Sydney airport 'incognito' in 2010. I was having a
little too much fun as an 'International Tax Fugitive'. (*Getty Images*)

Present Danger, Rabbit-Proof Fence and so many other wonderful movies. It was a big production, with Cathy Freeman and Ian Thorpe and several Socceroos in it. I shot it, free of charge, and was set to go overseas with Julia to make our pitch.

As it turned out, we never went. We got word that it was pointless because the decision had already been made, even though no one had yet cast a vote. In Noyce's film I rode a motorbike into a football stadium to chase a kangaroo that had bounced away with the World Cup trophy in its pouch. Now we know it was more likely Sepp Blatter and the pelicans at FIFA who had stolen the cup. They'd given it to Qatar, which didn't have any stadiums or a track record of hosting major events, and where it was going to be about forty-five degrees each day at the time of year the Cup is meant to be played. If the contest had been legitimate, we'd have had a good chance, me and Julia, of persuading them.

• • •

And as if there wasn't enough going on, there was the small matter of my marriage …

I'm probably not a great husband. I'm good early, but then I retreat a little. Twenty years or so and they get sick of me. The novelty wears off. Reality is, I'm a little bit of a hermit, I do enjoy my own company. You know, I'll sit around doing crosswords, or go for walks by myself, that sort of thing.

Linda and I eventually drifted apart, but it had been a great marriage for many, many years. I still see her regularly, we're good friends and we have a son to share. But we were always, and we still are, such opposites. For example, Linda doesn't mind

Chance and Linda brave a red carpet with me. (*Alamy*)

a bit of shopping, to put it mildly. I hate it. If I need clothes I'll just as likely go into a Kmart. And if I find something that does the job – say a white T-shirt – I'll literally buy twenty of them so I don't have to go back.

Linda gets a great deal of pleasure from upmarket, adventurous food. Not me. I've had to talk fancy restaurants into serving a sausage on white bread because that's exactly what I felt like. I've seen a poor sous-chef sneak out to find a supermarket because he didn't keep that sort of stuff on the premises. At fancy hotels I've phoned room service and pretended to have kids with me so I could order the nuggets and chips, and maybe even a milkshake off the children's menu, rather than have to eat any of the elaborate rubbish they dish up for us grown-ups. Would it kill them, for example, to use iceberg lettuce in a salad instead of that grass they try to pass off as 'salad mix' instead?

Linda also likes to have a bottle of water within reach at all times. I tried water once, back in the 1970s. Didn't go for it much.

While these may be trivial examples, for many years the opposites in Linda and me did attract like crazy, but one day we woke up and were just opposites. With such different tastes in everything, we had drifted apart over a long period of time. We're still close, but we're not in love.

When the end came in 2014, it was the most civilised divorce you could imagine. There were never raised voices, bitterness or battling. The tabloids would later say I was devastated by Linda's remarriage. Not at all. I'm pleased she found someone afterwards. I'm also pleased that that someone, Hafid, is a lovely bloke. We all catch up every so often. He even drives me to the airport, and picks me up again, if I'm flying somewhere.

I feel the same for Noelene. She remarried, to a fellow I knew, Reg. He was a really good bloke as well, but sadly he passed away too soon.

Anyhow, I got custody of Chance, which I wanted, and there was no bitterness about that either. That may be hard to believe, because it rarely happens, but it did.

I've been blessed. I was married to two really great women for something like fifty years. With each of them I had many years of happiness, and we have amazing kids and grandkids. That's all that I could hope for out of life. Everything else is a bonus. Or an entertaining distraction.

• • •

The Australian Crime Commission investigation went on for several long and unnecessary years until they came to the conclusion that there was no evidence against me, because I hadn't done anything wrong. The Crime Commission dropped their investigation in late 2010, and took the unusual step of issuing a press release – something that the super-secret organisation almost never does. That was reported in the press briefly, but the stories about me owing millions, and being on the run, and hiding money on tropical islands, got a lot more ink.

Initially, it was kind of flattering, hearing stories from all around the world about how I was so smart that I had bamboozled the Australian Tax Office, as well as Eliot Ness and his mob at the IRS. But then it became tiresome.

In 2012 we agreed to sign a 'ceasefire'. Because of the confidentiality clause I cannot discuss the terms of the settlement, but when I offered to provide copies of documents to the Senate Estimates Committee, the ATO objected and threatened court proceedings.

In the end, apart from learning through the investigation that there are so-called tax havens in exotic locations I'd never heard of (whose names I couldn't spell if you paid me), as well as acquiring some wonderful expressions associated with that seedy world, like 'Dutch Sandwiches', it was otherwise just a ridiculous period of my life.

29

Matters of the Heart

I should mention my heart attack, if only because, once again, I stupidly drove myself to the hospital when all logic said I should've stayed where I was and called the ambos. It was 2013. I had just dropped Chance at school in LA. As I was driving back, I could feel my heart slowing down. I wasn't in pain, not like with the cerebral haemorrhage, but I felt dozy and weak. Everything was starting to happen in slow motion.

I thought, *Now, that's strange. There's clearly something wrong here.* I should have stopped the car and phoned 911. But I listened to the Wombat part of my brain again and turned towards the hospital and kept going. When I got there I had one doctor come out, and he went and called out another one, and then another one. It was like, 'Come here, have a look at this poor bastard.' It was because my heart rate was down to twenty. *Boom ... boom ... boom ... boom.*

Luckily it wasn't clogged arteries, all that usual stuff you expect from a smoker and person with my takeaway diet. It was just an electrical thing. So they stuck a pacemaker in me and sent me home, just in time for Dean Murphy and Shane Jacobson to turn up to make a long-planned doco with me. I'd only been out of hospital a couple of days, but I didn't want to let them down.

When I insisted we go ahead, they cut out most of the walking scenes and filmed me being driven around LA in this huge chrome-laden 1950s Cadillac de Ville – you know the type with mile-high tail fins, the sort of small, inconspicuous car you use to sneak around Hollywood in without being noticed.

The doco was called *Hanging with Hoges* and it was made for the ABC, the Australian channel, not the US one. Shane was at the wheel and we visited the iconic spots but I was feeling like a bit of an idiot, attracting attention in that massive convertible car, and I was feeling pretty ordinary too, which didn't help. People kept pulling up next to us and saying to me, 'Oh, cool car. Cool car.' I'm going, 'Oh, yeah. It's not mine. I don't want to be in it. I need a sleep.'

I felt even sillier when we descended Mulholland Drive behind the camera car and ran out of brakes and nearly punted our poor camera crew, driving ahead of us, into someone's mansion. Shane had to do everything to pull the hefty bugger up, and then the bloody thing broke down and we were all standing around with the bonnet up in peak-hour Los Angeles and holding up traffic.

We were behind schedule and it was about to rain, but the demeanour of our director, Dean, didn't change. He was like, 'You get behind, you get behind.' The trick with Dean is he doesn't get agitated. A true country Australian. If we don't get a shot, he'll say, 'Oh, don't worry, we'll get something else tomorrow.' It's the same with the whole crew that he's put together for our films down there. Dean just goes with the flow, which is the way I've worked, so it's sort of like we're kin.

During the shooting of *Hanging with Hoges* in LA, I realised the heart attack had taken more of a toll than I'd realised. One night's shooting was meant to show Shane and me standing on top of Mulholland Drive looking down over the vast, never-ending lights of Los Angeles and chatting about my time there. However, while this was being shot I was actually at home in bed, trying to recover, and instead our driver was wearing my clothes and hat and being shot only from behind. The front-on shots of Shane and I looking over the city were actually filmed in a hotel room in Sydney some weeks later, with the two of us standing in front of a black curtain and using either the minibar or kettle as our eyeline. Once these scenes were edited together, no one was any the wiser. The show must go on.

Despite such dramas, the doco was fun. I long ago stopped thinking of anything as work. To me I was just chilling out with mates and having a chat. By the time we'd started *Hanging with Hoges*, Dean had already wrecked my retirement plans by getting me to agree to yet another project. The brilliant idea was a 'live tour' around Australia, where I'd tell audiences stories of my weird and lucky life.

I'd explained to him it was at least twenty-five years since I'd last walked on a stage and done anything other than deliver a short speech. Dean assured me it would work, that he'd do all the production and that we could use pre-recorded videos to show highlights of years gone past. The tickets had gone on sale just before I'd had the heart attack, and, again, I wasn't going to let anyone down.

So it was that a few days after we shot the LA segments for *Hanging with Hoges* I flew to Australia and took to the stage. I wondered if anyone was going to be interested. Fortunately, they were. They came for *An Evening with Hoges* and they listened and they laughed. And laughed and laughed. It was kind of shocking and exciting to find they hadn't forgotten me, and that I hadn't totally forgotten how to entertain people.

We went to Canberra, Sydney, Melbourne, Perth and the Gold Coast, and it was a ball to do, partly because it was all so different. When I'd done stand-up years before, I was telling people what I was going to do in my life. Now, forty years later, I'd done it. I was giving a report, really.

While we were doing the tour, we continued to film some Australian segments for *Hanging with Hoges*, which was due for release in 2014. This time we were driving in the Holden Kingswood from *Charlie & Boots*. Shane had fallen in love with it and bought it from the film production company. It felt kind of nice to be back in that car. Far more my kind of machine than the Caddie.

It was particularly pleasing to do the live show at the State Theatre in Sydney because some of my family, including some of the grandkids, got to see it. I heard one of my granddaughters afterwards saying to a friend, 'I didn't realise Grandad has had such an interesting life.' She then said, 'I've heard him and Dad

With my entourage, backstage at Sydney's State Theatre.

banging on about things over the years and never really listened, but some of the stuff he did is actually pretty cool.'

A few years earlier I'd observed that Chance, like a lot of little kids, had no great interest in what his parents had once done. When he was about seven or eight, Linda and I sat him down in front of the TV to finally watch *Crocodile Dundee*. After about five minutes he asked, 'Where's Paddy?' Paddy was our beloved golden retriever. He saw Dad and he saw Mum but couldn't see the family dog. I explained that Paddy wasn't in the film and he said 'Oh' and got up and went outside and played. I still don't know if he's ever seen the full movie.

A few years later, at the Melbourne show on the 2013 tour, Chance tentatively came along with a couple of his mates. He was in his mid-teens and obviously a bit nervous about whether the old man would embarrass him. But he came backstage after the show and his friends said how cool they thought Leo Wanker was, and how hot the girls were, and he said how excited he and his mates were by the whole shebang. Dean asked Chance if it was weird to see people stand up and cheer when his dad walked out onstage. I think Chance had never heard a bigger understatement in his life. 'Yeah, a bit!' he replied.

A few weeks later we were back home and I went up to Chance's room and he and his mates were watching some old *Paul Hogan Show* clips on YouTube. You're obviously proud if you make a successful movie or win an award or whatever, but to see your son and his mates cracking up at stuff you did forty years ago, now that takes the cake!

During our big-city tour we learnt that smaller cities and country towns were trying to book the show. We couldn't fit them into the schedule, and I was frankly out of energy anyway.

Turned out the pacemaker, which was otherwise working well and doing its job of keeping me alive, needed some adjustment, as it was keeping me constantly drained and unable to eat. At the second Melbourne opening of *An Evening with Hoges*, it was so bad I was struggling to stay on my feet. A day after the tour ended, though, the medics fine-tuned things and I was instantly back to my old self. Healthy again and full of enthusiasm, I did a regional tour in 2014, this time visiting some of the exotic outback places that someone like Mick Dundee would have frequented: Townsville, Toowoomba, Port Pirie, Alice Springs ...

My only condition for doing the country tour was that I didn't want to fly from town to town. I wanted to be a tourist, in a car, and stop and read every plaque and pose with every statue. With our tour manager Chris Veerhuis and wonderful publicist Katherine Marmion generally asleep in the back seat, that's exactly what Dean and I did. We never ate in any of the bigger towns. We'd try and find some little nursery just outside a little country town with a café attached, and have world-class scones with jam made from local ingredients. We'd wander through a little bric-a-brac shop, learn what was happening by reading a community notice board, and wander on to the next little place. On the nights we had a show, I'd go and do it, and afterwards meet a few locals, then be ready to jump in the car early next morning to go off exploring again.

We did a show at Mount Isa, a mining town in north-west Queensland, far from the coast and pretty well everything else. It's about as old-fashioned an Australian town as you can find. 'I don't know if we should go to Mount Isa,' I said to Dean during the planning stage. 'The audience will turn up and they'll all be miners, and they'll be in blue singlets with stubbies in their hands and be yelling out and maybe throwing things.'

'No, no,' Dean said, 'we're going to Mount Isa.'

So we did, and they had a beautiful, modern, sophisticated theatre, and all the miners turned up in their suits and ties with their wives and girlfriends all done up too. It was the same in Alice Springs, Darwin, Bundaberg and other remote places, where we had more sophisticated audiences than in the big cities.

The press was generally good too, except perhaps for the *Northern Territory News*, or *NT News*, as it is more often known. It is one of the more interesting newspapers on the planet. They give the daily news and all the important stuff, but only after they have reported all the latest happenings involving crocodiles. Yep. They're obsessed with crocodiles presumably because their readers are obsessed with crocodiles. And they apparently have the biggest online readership of any Australian newspaper because croc lovers the world over log on daily to see what's happening with their favourite reptile.

As you might imagine, Mick Dundee coming to town to do his one-man show got the paper into something of a lather. There were pages and pages about my arrival, to the point where it was impossible to tell whether or not they were completely taking the piss. My fears were further stoked after doing a radio interview at the entirely respectable ABC Darwin. I headed out the front door to find members of the newspaper's staff waiting for me. They demanded I go with them right away to wrestle a real, full-sized crocodile named Burt.

I was seventy-four at the time, and I wouldn't even have done it if I'd been twenty-four, for a couple of reasons. First, you'd have to be insane. And second, well, actually, I think the

An Evening with Hoges. A 'shovelist' once more.

first reason covers it. But they didn't want to take no for an answer. They followed me to the car, demanding to know why I wouldn't wrestle an eight-foot man-eating crocodile. And, as my car drove off, they took a photo. It appeared on the front page the next day, with the headline: 'Crocodile Dun-Flee!'

Some other papers came out with articles that said I was looking for love. No, I wasn't. I might've been looking for a bit of lust, just maybe, but I wasn't looking for love. Been there, done that. That's not to say that if a devastatingly attractive woman with poor eyesight had come along, I'd have rejected her out of hand. Mind you, she'd have to have been younger than me, cos every time I look in the mirror I'm shocked to see an old bloke staring back at me.

To be honest, I'm not sure how I'd handle it now if it did happen. Case in point, a couple of weeks after those articles declared me 'Looking for Love', we were doing the show at a stadium in north Queensland and two ladies went to great efforts to answer the call. They were in their late forties or early fifties and had made fake security passes. This enabled them to sneak past the real security and into the back of the theatre. To look like they were part of the show, they were carrying a box full of odd comedy props, including a plastic sword and a rubber chicken, and had earpieces in. Suddenly they saw me in my dressing room and ran and grabbed me and started trying to hug and kiss me. One lady kept declaring, 'I'm single, I'm single!' Dean was with me and watched with a huge grin on his face, ignoring my desperate looks.

'Do you want me to give you some time alone with the ladies?' he asked. I could have throttled him. He started to leave. 'Do you want me to close the door on the way out?'

Just as I was about to grab a chair and belt him with it, he turned back and explained to the women that I needed to be onstage soon, and that they needed to head out front and take their seats. It was a nice boost to an old man's ego, but why I work with that bastard Dean, I'll never know.

For all that, the stand-up tours were wonderful. I was so lucky to have the chance to go to all the major outback centres and legendary places in Australia to talk, make people laugh, have a good time and be reminded, yet again, what an amazing country we have! It wasn't about making money or satisfying my ego or anything. It was about having fun and issuing a bit of a summary of the extraordinarily lucky life I've had.

. . .

One of the things I talked about on that tour was accents. When I first went to the United States in the 1980s, no one there had ever heard an Australian accent. Except perhaps Bryan Brown's accent, as he was the only genuine Aussie who had appeared in the United States. But with so many of our countrymen and women in the United States now, they're going to have to start putting meat pies on the menu. Every time you see a new star or action hero or some really smart young woman in a film or premium television series, it's a good bet that it's an Aussie. Initially nobody in the United States knows they're Australian. Then they hear them on talk shows or at award ceremonies and are stunned. And now, more and more, we are starting to hear our stars keeping their accents in movies and TV series.

The version of *Crocodile Dundee* that was screened in the United States was about ten minutes shorter than the Australian release. The studios were okay with having an Australian talking to an American, but they cut parts where we had two Australians talking to each other because they said it was too hard to follow. They felt we were pretty much speaking a foreign language. While things have improved a lot, even many years later Shane Jacobson's *Kenny* was released in the United States with subtitles.

Anyway, the new breed of Australian actors, such as Chris Hemsworth, Toni Collette and Margot Robbie, now work mainly in the United States and can master whatever accent they like, so no one has trouble understanding them. And I'm so pleased that the anger and vitriol that I faced in the Australian press for daring to move to the United States has passed. We all now proudly watch these Aussie stars kicking goals around the world and happily call them 'ours'.

Funnily enough, I sold Chris Hemsworth my house at Point Dume in California in between our two *An Evening with Hoges* tours. The estate agent told me the person who had just bought the house was going to call in, and I opened the door to see Thor standing there. The whole doorway sort of went dark as this man-mountain stepped inside. But he was a really nice kid. And I gave him the Australian discount – I left the beer in the fridge.

It's interesting, whenever I meet up with young Aussie stars who have had to base themselves in the United States for work opportunities, the first thing we talk about is Australia. The United States may be where people are living and working, but Australia is home. I have always been the same. There's just an aura that the people at home have. And even when things are bad, the weather is good. Or, at least, it's the way I like it.

30

Facing Up

In Sydney in 2016, I got an AACTA Award from the Australian Academy of Cinema and Television Arts. They tell me it's the highest screen honour in Australia. Now, I don't normally take awards that seriously, but I paid more attention to this one because John and Delvene insisted on coming along.

Decades after I had organised their introduction, John and Delvene were still inseparable and mad about one another. They'd been absolute soul mates from day one, and remained a force to be reckoned with, even when John started to become unwell. They'd stayed in Byron Bay, raised their two gorgeous daughters there, and still called it home. And Delvene had hardly slowed down. By this time she was running Rimfire

Films, JP Productions, Hogan Enterprises and many other things. Sharp as a tack, as always.

At the AACTA ceremony, John kept a low profile, understandably. Delvene, though, took to the stage to present the award to me. Beforehand she kept saying, 'No one will know who I am. I haven't been on television for thirty years.'

She was shocked when everyone gave her a great, welcoming ovation. She kept looking around to see if someone else was behind her. John couldn't have been prouder. Simply wonderful people.

A year after this, John and Delvene, and many other people in my life, were played by actors in a two-part Channel 7 mini-series. It was called *Hoges: The Paul Hogan Story*. Sadly, it was boring and didn't work and, worse still, some people even blamed me for it. Yet I'd had nothing to do with it!

It's true the production company had sent me the script in advance. But my secretary had looked at it and said, 'It's pretty awful but harmless.' And I was told to forget about it, as we probably couldn't have stopped them from making it, even if we cared enough to take it to court.

After torturing everyone with promos for weeks, Channel 7 broadcast the first part on 12 February 2017. I started watching, but didn't recognise any of the characters or situations. They tried to replicate some sketches but changed them. I thought, *Whoever's in charge of this thing has no sense of humour, or doesn't know what they're doing, or both*. Look, I'm sure there were some lovely and talented people involved and assume their hearts were in the right place, but they missed the mark completely.

About twenty minutes in, I clicked the remote and found something more interesting. Some of my kids made it to the end, but they found it equally squirmy, and delighted in quoting things I'd apparently said or done with them. It seemed that pretty well everything was wrong, or made up, and certainly not funny. Ah well, I was flattered that they at least had tried.

There was another Hogan-related 'movie' a short time later. In very early 2018, a series of teasers started appearing online for *Dundee: The Son of a Legend Returns Home*. They set up the story of Mick Dundee's son Brian, played by US actor and comedian Danny McBride, flying out to Australia and trying to emulate the feats of his dad. Really badly. Unlike the mini-series, this looked very funny – and worth watching.

McBride was a very, very unlikely choice. The internet, as they say, went crazy. Some people were furious about such a cynical cash-grab of a movie, others excited. New teaser-trailers were released and new stars were revealed to be in the cast, including Chris Hemsworth, Russell Crowe, Margot Robbie, Hugh Jackman, Isla Fisher and many more. This, combined with some magnificent cinematography, sent the internet really wild. People were desperate to see this new incarnation of an old Aussie story. But all was not as it seemed.

In the States, Super Bowl Sunday is not only the biggest event of the American sporting calendar but is also famous for launching the year's greatest commercials during the breaks – and for the eye-watering amounts of money that are charged for the ads. It is the most expensive commercial airtime anywhere in the world.

It was here, with tens of millions of American eyes on their television sets, that the main, two-minute-long *Dundee: The Son of a Legend Returns Home* trailer was launched. All started as usual, but then, halfway through this version of the trailer, it slowly became obvious to the huge viewing audience that the purported movie wasn't to be a real film at all. Instead it was a novel way of advertising Australia as a tourist destination.

In some ways it was a successor to the tourism ads I'd made thirty-four years earlier, but featuring a character I'd created thirty-two years earlier! I even turned up in a little cameo. Again the internet went crazy, with some people saying it was brilliant and others feeling ripped off, as they'd been hoping for a real movie. Either way, people were talking about Australia.

The series of fake trailers was a brainwave from John O'Sullivan, who was then the head of Tourism Australia. He'd figured that the last time such a campaign had really made an impact was with our ads in the 1980s, and he'd got people playing around with different ideas. They did a survey in ten countries and asked people what they knew about Australia and whether they could name a famous Australian? Amazingly, Mick Dundee was the most popular choice. Not me, I didn't get a guernsey. It was Mick Dundee that hit the top spot in nearly every country. I think it was Nicole Kidman who came second in most places.

That stirred them on to do the teasers, which went viral, and then the Super Bowl ad. It worked. Bookings for tourism went up. And surveys showed that the viewers' recall of the ad was the highest of anything that premiered that year. So, as it turned out, it was a good idea.

When they'd first approached me though, I must admit I was a little bemused. The first two *Croc* movies had been so, so long ago. Then again, I was spending most of my time in Venice Beach in the United States and I'd often hear 'That's not a

Thirty-five years after we first teamed up on *Crocodile Dundee*, I was back on set with the brilliant cinematographer Russ Bob (aka Russell Boyd), shooting the *Dundee: Son of a Legend* ad. Remarkably, neither of us has aged a bit. (*Tourism Australia*)

knife,' or 'Throw a shrimp on the barbie,' even on things like the news. Mick Dundee, or versions of him, had also appeared in programs such as *The Simpsons*, *Beavis and Butt-Head* and *Modern Family*, and it was as though the movies were on a television loop. At one stage the original *Croc* was something like the second most re-licensed movie of all time behind, I think, *Indiana Jones*. So I guess Mick never really left the psyche.

• • •

I mentioned my heart attack. Another 'medical' issue I should discuss is the series of facelifts I've had since filming *Dundee*. That's the reason that even though I'm now in my eighties, I only look twenty-five. I've had facelifts, eyelifts, butt-lifts and pec implants and have bathed in virgin goat's milk. Seriously, I've read all that and more!

Unfortunately, I don't look twenty-five and the stories of plastic surgery and multiple facelifts in those glossy supermarket magazines are all, to put it plainly, bollocks. Half the time the proof those gooses offered for my latest facelift were photos that *they'd* had Photoshopped to remove the wrinkles.

The reality is that the only facial surgery I've had is to remove skin cancers, a throwback to my time on the Bridge. Sunscreen and hats just weren't done in those days. In the late 1990s there was a scar across the top of my left eye, where I had eleven stitches after getting skin cancers removed. The scar tissue came down over one eye, and I was getting a lot of eyelid droop, giving me limited vision and headaches. So I had the stuff taken off the top of that one eye so that I could open it properly.

When the bandage came off, maybe I looked a bit different, a bit better, around that one eye. But suddenly everyone decided I was ageing too well and various gossip columnists said, 'Hoges has had a facelift, and he should ask for his money back!' That was the running gag, along with, 'Hey, why don't you do your neck? Your neck's all saggy.' Now that's what you want to read.

In 2003 I was to be interviewed on Andrew Denton's television show *Enough Rope* after another skin-cancer procedure and it didn't heal in time, so I turned up with a bandage on my forehead. Andrew Denton, I should say, is as good as they come. I've been interviewed by most of the famous American television interviewers, but Denton, along with Pommy Michael Parkinson, are the ones I consider the best in the business. They are lovely men, they know what to ask, and they are experts on quietly peeling away layers without ever losing the comedy and entertainment side of it. Both are happy to explore things without knowing exactly where the conversation will go. Anyway, Andrew, and fair enough, asked the facelift question. I pointed to the bandage. 'Yes, I've had an extra eyebrow added,' I explained, 'so I can be more expressive as an actor.'

At the start, I was actually pleased people thought I'd had a facelift. I was almost chuffed. I thought, *I must be looking all right.* But, truth be told, while I've been seen by a plastic surgeon in Beverly Hills many times, it's never been for anything so Hollywood as a nip and tuck. Nah, as a consequence of not 'Slip-Slop-Slapping' I've had maybe a dozen skin cancers cut off, and about thirty frozen off. Not glamorous, but I'm alive.

The plastic surgeon always laughs cos most of his customers are getting their lips pumped and chins re-sculpted, and I'm in there to get cancers attended to. I had a large one cut off my lips recently and, as a result, I've got a bit of an Elvis thing happening with my snarling top lip. It's pretty cool.

Personally, I don't mind ageing. It's certainly better than the only alternative anyone is offering at the moment, which is death. Although that doesn't worry me too much either. Anyway, when people stop mentioning facelifts I'll probably be just a little disappointed, as it'll mean I'm starting to look my age. Might have to get some plastic surgery …

31

Lucky, That

I don't buy into the idea that the youth of today are lazy. I know some amazing young people, my youngest son being one of them. Chance is now in his early twenties. We live together near the beach in Los Angeles and I love having him with me. He sings and writes lyrics for his punk band and has a great group of mates, and it's so fantastic seeing him make his way in the world. Luckily, he can cook a little bit, because I'm hopeless. Actually, to be honest, neither of us is a hatted chef, or even a food connoisseur. We have takeaway, a lot.

Having a young son means it's impossible to disconnect from the world, which I think is important for everyone in their fourth quarter. He's always showing me new music or comedy clips on YouTube, and some nights I head out to dark and dingy clubs to listen to his band or we go riding along the beach.

People ask why I haven't moved back to Australia, and I ask myself the same question. I've had a dose of homesickness for many years and I've come back as often as possible. And when I return to the States I always curse and say, 'What am I doing here?'

It's mainly because I want to be with Chance. Of course, he's in his twenties and can take care of himself, so he doesn't need me here. But I *want* to be here. And for the moment, so does he. He has his band and girlfriend and mates here, so the timing's not right for him to move to Oz. But one day …

I had an advance screening of my most recent movie, *The Very Excellent Mr Dundee*, in Los Angeles in late 2019, when my eldest son, Brett, was visiting. I had Chance, who was twenty, on one side of me and Brett, who was sixty, on the other. Brett is old enough to be Chance's grandfather, but they're both my boys and I love it!

I still adore kids. Those early years are magic, the sweet innocence about them. Kids just tell it like they see it. But the reality is I'm too old to have any more. That's my only real regret about getting old. I love being a dad and that's why I'm still clinging to Chance, my last one. If Chance said to me, 'I want to get married,' I'd say, 'What? You're insane. You're a mere child.' But I had three kids at his age. Hard to imagine. But it was a different world then, you know.

Since I first appeared on television, I've tried hard to keep my children out of the spotlight and let them all grow up to be independent and shape their own lives without feeling like an attachment of mine. And they have. So, at my grand old age, surely now I'm allowed to say a few things about them as a proud parent.

My eldest, Brett, has had various jobs over the years, including working as a cameraman, shooting music videos, and helping me write *Dundee II*. Nowadays he's a landscape gardener. He has no formal qualifications but has a good eye and good ideas and is able to charm the pants off his clients. He doesn't do any physical work himself. The heaviest things he carries are coffees for the workers. I don't know where he learnt about landscaping, but he gets great results.

Clay's name was at least partly inspired by Cassius Clay, but it was also a popular name in western movies. I've always said Clay is the weird one. Now by that I mean he's one of those unusual people who can do everything. As a kid he could fix almost anything. If the old radio packed it in, we'd give it to Clay. The toaster didn't toast, we'd give it to Clay. Even though he was just a kid, he'd fix the bloody things, make them good as new. He then decided to take up the guitar. In a day he was better than his brother who'd been learning for months. He went on to become a brilliant musician – he can make a guitar talk – and for a while had a band called Beethogan. There hasn't been a day when that kid hasn't amazed me with what he can do.

Todd, I always say, is the absolute pick of the wider Hogan family. The rest of us are mere mortals. Todd is a saint. He has gone through more personal hardship than the rest of us put together but is the most caring, compassionate and loyal person there is. He's a brilliant parent too, as are all of the kids, thank goodness. Todd has managed bottle shops and other businesses most of his life and has always been involved in various levels of rugby, first league then union. He's about my height, five foot nine, but solid. He always wanted to be called 'Flash' on the field, but instead was known as 'Truck'. This frustrated him no end, but Todd played union in England for Wembley, and was picked for the England Under-23s to tour Spain, France and the United States. He wasn't fast, but his enthusiasm and vigour were outstanding. He was also incredibly tough. Hence the nickname.

Loren was the second youngest of the original five, so had four brothers growing up, and she now has four sons of her own. Yet Loren is tougher than any of them. She looked like a little princess as a girl but was as feisty as could be. She is a real stirrer too and ribs me for apparently now being a soft showbiz guy. Loren doesn't let me get away with a thing and she is easily the coolest person I know.

My second youngest son, Scott, has always been a bit of an entrepreneur. He's dabbled and often succeeded in a wide range of ventures. The one I am quietly proudest of is the surf school he opened in Fiji. With perhaps a nod to my old lifeguard days, he came up with this innovative proposal. What an idea! If I was forty years younger, I might have a rival set-up two doors down.

As for Chance, unfortunately it's been hard to keep him out of the media. He's copped more than his fair share of long lenses and pesky reporters sticking microphones under his nose – even when he was just a tiny kid. And of course every photo needs a story, which has led to so-called journalists making a lot of stuff up.

Still, he's doing well for a devil-worshipping, drug-addled, punk-rocker maniac. Actually, he's at least a little guilty of provoking some of those sensational headlines. He too has inherited my stirrer streak and when he knows there's some clown with a camera around he plays up to it in crazy ways and the photos then show up in bad Australian magazines. Loren used to send copies to him to take to school and show his mates. They thought it was hilarious.

I now have five sons and a daughter and ten grandchildren – with hopefully more grandchildren on the way, and great grandchildren too! It seemed like I started too early, yet all my children have turned out to be terrific and they're all healthy, so it turns out I was very lucky. I'd like to see more of them all, so coming back to live in Australia has always been the plan.

As for my siblings, my brother, Pat, ended up working at that Gold Coast movie theme park until he retired thirty-odd years later. He'd often come across and stay with me in the States, and we'd hang out together and get on famously. I was on a plane from the United States on my way to visit him in Queensland in 2019 when I got the news he had died. There were three hundred people at his wake, just friends he'd made along the way, every one of them saying what a lovely guy he was. Like Mum, he never seemed to worry about anything much, did Pat. I badly miss his dopey grin.

My sister, Wendy, and her husband, Johnny Devitt, are elderly now, but still going strong and living happily in Sydney.

What else motivates me these days? Staying alive. Family. I don't care about much else. That's why I owe a debt to Dean Murphy, who won't let me retire, because he keeps bowling up projects that sound like fun. Otherwise, I'd just sit around, scratching myself. I get lots of offers still for all sorts of things, but I've mainly worked with Dean for the past twenty or so years.

When I was younger I loved horse riding, cutting cattle and skiing, and I was still a big swimmer until fairly recently. Being too old for skiing is a bummer, particularly because if you're seventy-five or more in Aspen, you don't pay for the lift. But, you know, you can also damage yourself a bit.

Now my days are filled with catching up with friends and, if I can find a quiet moment, doing the *New York Times* crossword. I don't play golf. I don't take photographs or do any gardening. I don't have a Facebook page, or Tweet, though I'm still fascinated by physics. I've recently been dipping back into the book *Conceptual Physics* by Paul G. Hewitt and trying to figure out how to supply free electricity to the world. Seriously! I have a couple of theories …

One friend I did catch up with recently was Bob Hawke. I had him on the show in 1975, and he was hilarious, and I bumped into him and Brownie a lot during the Tourism Australia ads campaign – two really good Australian politicians who knew what needed to be done and got on with making it happen. Hawkie and I hit it off too because we had similar backgrounds. I was even the representative in the Ironworkers' Union when he was the head of the ACTU. I never ran into him then, but I knew of him, and so we'd been down the same road in a different sort of way. When he was prime minister, I went to his Sydney residence, Kirribilli House, a few times. What a fabulous place.

I visited Hawkie at his real home and had a drink with him just a few months before he died in 2019. It was great to see him again that last time. He was a wonderful, larger-than–life Aussie character and crammed a huge amount into his 89-and-a-bit years.

• • •

As much as I miss Australia, anonymity is the best thing about where I live, at Venice Beach. I wander down the Boardwalk, with all the ratbags in the world there and all the tourists, and no one knows who I am. I have my sunglasses on, and maybe a cap pulled down low, and it's nice. You don't have to be on any sort of special behaviour.

I'm not a nostalgic person. I'm dreadful at holding on to the past. I don't keep a diary or scrapbook. I've never put any old sketches on YouTube – they just miraculously turn up there. I never took photos when I was young. Almost nobody did. But, boy, how that's changed. I used to go to a function somewhere, and there'd be, you know, like a thousand people there and one or two photographers. Now if there's a thousand people there, then 990 of them are snapping away with the cameras on their phones.

I've had to start limiting selfies at these things. I'm terrible at saying no to anyone, so instead I just leave functions after half an hour or so. It's flattering that people like to have their photo taken with me, but it's hard to catch up and chat with friends in that environment.

The whole celebrity thing was a driving force behind my latest project with Dean, *The Very Excellent Mr Dundee*. It uses a real incident I had with a snake as its starting point. It was Dean's idea that I play myself, exaggerated of course, and we have fun with that and people's perception of me. Making it was a laugh from start to finish.

I've seen some awful Mick Dundee impersonators, but none more so than Shane Jacobson. On the set of *The Very Excellent Mr Dundee* with director Dean Murphy.

Spending the day with Nate Torrence (centre) and John Cleese is as much fun as you can have at work.

The movie – which would have been released in April 2020 if not for the coronavirus – could actually be called *No Good Deed Goes Unpunished*, because my character keeps trying to do the right thing, only to find it turning out wrong. And then the whole world turns against him. We have a range of stars commenting on how disgusting he is, including Olivia Newton-John (who I finally got to work with after all these years), and many other greats who pop in unannounced and sort of confirm that 'Paul Hogan' is an arsehole. I love it, even though I come out of it as a real grub!

Loyalty is important to me. I had my working relationship with John, and now I have a similarly loose partnership with Dean. These partnerships are a bit like my marriages. I've had two of them, each for a long time. When you're making a movie, you're sort of living together all day, so you need to get along.

I'm no longer trying to win awards or make massive amounts of money. It's more just, *This'll be fun to do, and these are great people.* For example, *The Very Excellent Mr Dundee* offered a chance to work with John Cleese, and what a thrill that was! I've been an adoring fan of Cleese's since *Fawlty Towers*. Yes, there was *Monty Python* before that, but *Fawlty Towers* for me was the cream of the crop, as good as comedy could get. And John Cleese is still clearly excited by life. After only a few minutes on set he knew the names of half the crew, where they came from and the origins of their surnames. Like me, he loves to laugh and is always keen to find the humour in any situation.

The timing for John being in Melbourne, where we shot most of the film, was perfect, as John heard that another Python, Michael Palin, also happened to be in town, doing his one-man show. John and Dean thought it'd be fun to surprise him, so after a full day of filming, we headed to the Athenaeum Theatre.

A quick chat to an immediately star-struck backstage attendant and John was let in. Michael was onstage, mid-show and John went and stood in the wings, waiting for his moment. When Michael was telling an anecdote that finished with something like 'Well, that's how I remember it anyway. I'm sure if John Cleese were here he would disagree,' John couldn't believe his luck. He burst onto the stage. 'I do disagree! That's rubbish!' Michael simply couldn't believe his eyes. He had no idea John was in town and was shocked into silence, completely forgetting where he was in the show. I loved that even though John, like me, is now in his eighties (I'm three weeks older), he still got a kick out of being mischievous and making his friend laugh.

Chevy Chase is another actor I worked with on that film. He has a reputation for being, let's say, tricky to work with. We had him playing an arsehole, and had no complaints whatsoever. Seriously, though, Chevy was just great and no trouble. He was lovely. A true pro. I'd first met Chevy when we were both guests on a US talk show in the 1980s. We then co-hosted the Academy Awards, though, hard as it might be to imagine, our paths didn't cross on the big night. So it was fun to have him come to Melbourne and spend time with us on *Mr Dundee*. We share a birthday, 8 October, though not a stature: Chevy is about six foot five. So is John Cleese and so is Dean Murphy. Michael Caton is about six foot three. So if any of you see me standing with those guys, keep in mind that it's not me that's short, I just work with a lot of freaks.

• • •

The Very Excellent Mr Dundee

The Restaurant Scene

A Hollywood restaurant, daytime. After having his reputation trashed, Paul Hogan has been ordered by his agent to sit down with Hollywood actor Chevy Chase and discuss his career issues. A waitress who has seen Paul's apparent antics is reluctant to take his order. Chevy attempts to help.

CHEVY: You do know who this is?

The waitress glances at Paul.

WAITRESS (*dismissive*): Yep.

She walks away.

CHEVY (*laughs*): Wow, you've really been through the wars, haven't you.

PAUL: Na, it's fi—

CHEVY: People ask me constantly, how is it that I'm so loved and adored. And, you know, it's actually quite easy.

PAUL: How?

Chevy beckons Paul in close.

CHEVY (*sotto voce*): Just win an Oscar.

PAUL (*doubtful*): What did you win an Oscar for?

CHEVY: *Caddyshack*. First one.

PAUL: Uh-huh.

CHEVY: Yeah, win one of those suckers and
you can do just about anything …

*Chevy sneakily slides the condiments to
the edge of the table. He looks up at
Paul, smiles like a naughty kid and lets
them smash to the floor. In an instant a
waiter darts over.*

WAITER: Are you okay, Mr Chase?

CHEVY: Yes, you need to have these fixed.
They slid right off the table.

*The waiter shoots Paul a disapproving
look.*

WAITER: Certainly. I'll talk to the owner
about … gluing them on.

*The waiter darts away with the mess. Chevy
smiles at Paul.*

PAUL: Now, listen, I was actually
nominated for an Academy Award.

CHEVY: Really? What for? (*Grimaces.*)
It couldn't have been acting.
No offence.

I mentioned that *The Very Excellent Mr Dundee* deals with snakes. Americans ask me a lot about the dangerous ones we have in Australia. On my property up at Possum Creek, near Byron Bay, we had lots of bush and scrub so it was totally crawling with them. We always had to kill the brown snakes because they're aggressive and highly venomous and if one of us or the kids or grandkids got bitten, it'd be touch and go whether we'd get to hospital in time. I've seen an angry brown attack a car! That's how ferocious they can be. But we also had carpet snakes, which are harmless, and we never killed red-bellied black snakes because they eat young browns and they're not overly aggressive.

To get rid of the browns, I'd have to shoot them, or hit them with a shovel, depending on where they were. If they were up in the bush I'd wish them a nice day, but I always killed them if they were anywhere near the house because you're also worried about them getting one of the dogs.

The funny thing is, though, I actually dealt with more snakes, specifically rattlesnakes, when I was living in Beverly Hills, at the top of Coldwater Canyon. We had a large allotment, an acre or so, and it backed onto Franklin Canyon, which was a reserve. We had the odd coyote wander into the yard and stay briefly, and I must have killed six or seven rattlesnakes hiding right next to our swimming pool! I could always tell by the way my dog barked that there were snakes around. One of the gardeners even got bitten one day by one of the smaller rattlers. Strangely, they are more venomous than the big ones, as they haven't learnt how to manage the load and pump all the poison out. We also had deer that used to wander into the backyard and eat all the rose bushes.

I was in the heart of Beverly Hills, yet had to deal with more wildlife than on my property in the Australian bush. But let's not tell any Americans that, or they might decide we're not as cool, or tough, as they think we are.

• • •

I'm at that stage of life when people ask me, if I could change one thing, what would it be? And the answer's simple. Nothing. Absolutely nothing, except maybe I would have somehow stopped smoking along the way, and maybe tried harder to meet Muhammad Ali.

Things have sort of worked out for me.

'What do you do?'

'Oh, I try to make people laugh and forget about their troubles.'

What a great job! And the celebrity part is nothing but humbling and a further reminder that I just got lucky, got all the breaks. I'm not special, not God's gift to anything. But I do think that when I got my chance I had a big advantage over a lot of people in this entertainment industry, in that I had lived in the real world until I was in my thirties. I had a proper working-class, blue-collar background before getting into this fame and fortune thing. Going to work on the bus, on the train, and having kids, and bills to pay, and all those sorts of woes, they're priceless.

I'd worked in construction and all sorts of shit jobs. God Almighty, I was scraping to pay the rent when I was thirty, so I really appreciate everything that happened after that, instead of thinking *I deserve it*, or, you know, *I'm fabulous*. I just fluked doing the right thing at just the right time, and it paid off. Suddenly people wanted me on television, making shows or flogging wares. I made my first movie at forty-six and, again, it was just what people wanted at that very moment.

I worry that when some kids get lucky too early and have never got their hands dirty – the Justin Biebers or whatever – they think that's how life is. They think that's the position they're entitled to be in, because of some great, God-given talent. No. Even if you have bags of God-given talent, it is luck and timing that are still going to be the main factors that decide whether or not you are going to take off. And if you've lived in the real world first, you realise just how lucky and rare it is to be given these opportunities.

It's also a matter of keeping everything in proportion. When you go into this business you very quickly learn that there are people who like what you do and are entertained by it. Then there are others who, for reasons best known to themselves, can't stand you and have it in for you, and want to see you fail. But the thing to remember is that the great majority, in the middle, don't even think about you. They see you onstage or on a screen and they might go 'Oh, that was good', but then they get on with their own lives. They never give you another thought.

My fame has been bloody ridiculous, but it was never what I was chasing, and fame has never brought me particular joy in itself. It has, however, brought me many other things, including the chance to write for television and films, which I never would have believed I could be good at. There's that saying about finding what you like doing, and if you do that, you'll never work a day in your life. By that measure, I haven't worked for nearly fifty years. Which is extraordinarily lucky.

I've had a great time and been paid to make people laugh, and it's all because other people made me laugh. They still do. And we all like to share something funny. When I'm walking along the Venice Beach Boardwalk, looking at the galahs that go down there, I sometimes think, 'I wish I was still doing my television show ... this guy would be terrific.'

Many of our current celebrities and pollies would provide material too. Donald Trump? The most entertaining politician since Caligula. That includes Idi Amin, Mussolini, all the greats. I was backing Trump in the 2020 election because he's the comic relief we all need in our newspapers. Look, I don't want him touching nuclear buttons or involved in anything where brains are required, but if I was still doing *The Paul Hogan Show*, it's easy to imagine he'd have a place in it.

I've certainly had a fortunate life, even though I've suffered a cerebral haemorrhage and a mild heart attack and had to go twelve rounds with the Australian Tax Office. I deserved all those things, probably, because everything else always worked out for me. I'm definitely not going to complain. If I do, something hairy and thunderous will come down from the sky and whack me on the back of the head and say, 'How much luck do you want in one life?'

Yeah, for a bloke who can't really tap-dance, or throw knives with any great accuracy, I've done all right.

Acknowledgements

I'd like to thank Tony Davis for his great input, words and expertise.

Also, Bec Asha, Russell B. McKenzie, Sandee Turner and the Smarts for your research and endless transcribing.

I'd also like to thank the Murphys for not letting me say no, along with Jude McGee and the fabulous team at HarperCollins for your great enthusiasm.

A special mention must go to John and Dele for always being amazing, along with all those viewers who laughed and stuck by me when I sucked.

But most importantly I'd like to thank the Hogan family. Those who came before, are here now or yet to come.

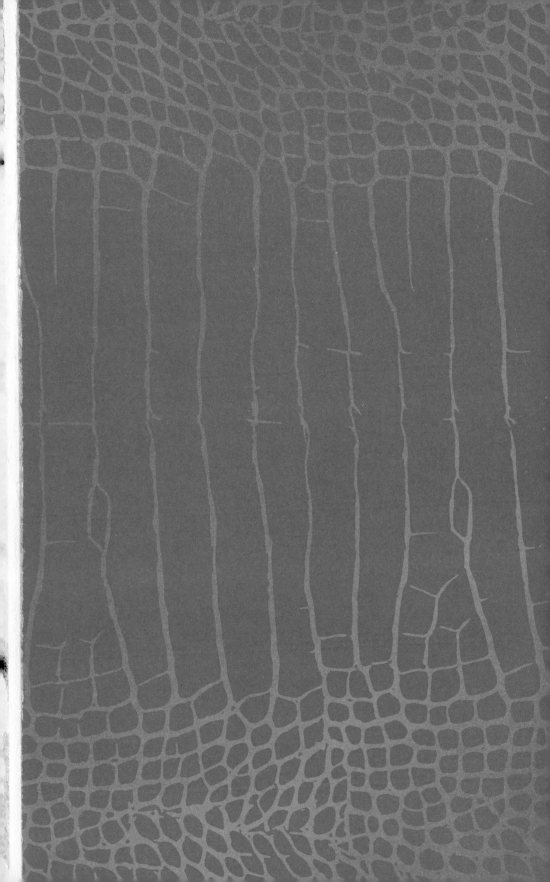

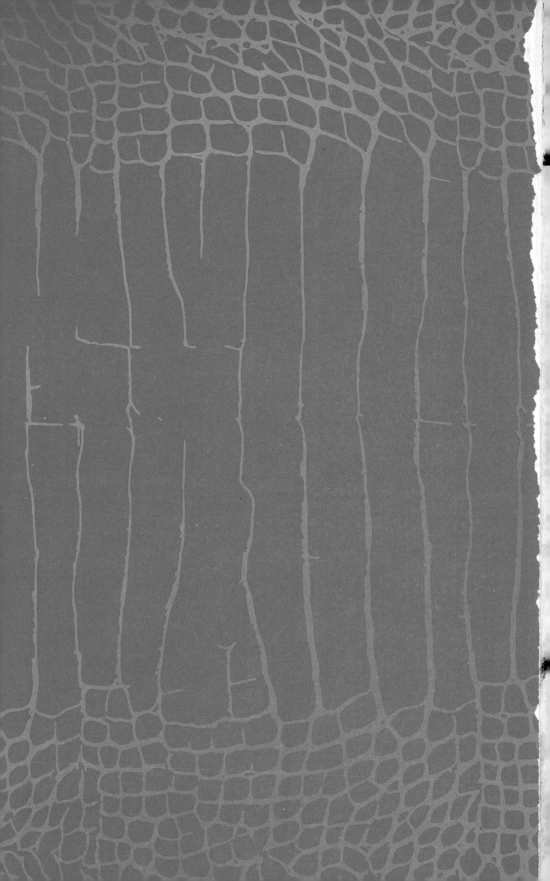